W9-AXO-251

Get It Together

ALSO BY JESSE WATTERS

How I Saved the World

Get It Together

Troubling Tales from
the Liberal Fringe

Jesse Watters

BROADSIDE BOOKS

Some names and identifying characteristics have been changed.

GET IT TOGETHER. Copyright © 2024 by Jesse Watters. All rights reserved. Printed in the United States of America. No part of this book may be used or reproduced in any manner whatsoever, without written permission except in the case of brief quotations embodied in critical articles and reviews. For information, address HarperCollins Publishers, 195 Broadway, New York, NY 10007.

HarperCollins books may be purchased for educational, business, or sales promotional use. For information, please email the Special Markets Department at SPsales@harpercollins.com.

Broadside Books™ and the Broadside logo are trademarks of HarperCollins Publishers.

FIRST EDITION

Library of Congress Cataloging-in-Publication Data has been applied for.

ISBN 978-0-06-325203-5

24 25 26 27 28 LBC 5 4 3 2 1

To Mom and Dad,
You raised me well. I love you.

"Get it together."

—*my mom*

Contents

Introduction

Humans amaze me. Especially radicals. I've always been drawn to crazy. Or what a college-educated conservative East Coast white guy thinks is crazy. Like a heat-seeking missile, I lock onto them and gaze in awe. Then I ask them questions and listen in a state of wonderment and bewilderment. Trying to reserve judgment. Trying and not always succeeding. The smirk gave it away.

The audience likes the smirk. They know what I'm thinking because it's exactly what they're thinking. Your issues aren't my issues; let's keep it that way. No disrespect. Much love.

This curious and semi-condescending attitude is what's made me a successful cable news personality. Obviously, my ability to deflect and ridicule has helped too. Bake in some fake modesty under the guise of self-depreciation, and you have yourself a winner. Nobody will ever know how insecure I really am.

But do insecure people ask for advice? I sure as hell asked for advice when Fox promoted me to the 7 p.m. hour. Before *Jesse Watters Primetime* launched January 2022, I called around to all the top talent. And listened. This is what they told me.

Bill O'Reilly's show, *The O'Reilly Factor*, always ended with the email segment. Viewers would email comments, and O'Reilly would read chosen ones on-air. They had to "keep it pithy." O'Reilly suggested I bring back that interaction with the audience, which I have.

Except now viewers text instead of email. "Keeping that connection with the audience is important," he told me. Also, he advised me to give viewers a window into how I felt each night. What I was thinking about, day-to-day stuff, open up about my personal life a little. Before we end each show with texts, the "Watters Window" segment is usually me venting for twenty seconds. Unscripted. It usually consists of me pontificating about why women don't like taking out the trash (is this only a man's job?), sharing a new diet fad (only eat meat on the bone), or bragging about how I beat my eleven-year-old daughter at Ping-Pong (she's really good).

Sean Hannity told me to "be myself." "You've succeeded by being who you are, don't change that," he said. Hannity explained that he LOVES politics. That's his bread and butter, and he sticks with it. He doesn't get outside his wheelhouse because he doesn't cover stories if they don't interest him. I've noticed that the audience can tell when you cover a story you don't care about, so I've taken Hannity's advice. Every story on *Jesse Watters Primetime* is something I personally am interested in. We covered the cover-up of Paul Pelosi's DUI arrest all summer because, you guessed it, I cared. The audience knew I was invested. So did Pauly P.

Tucker Carlson told me to hit the sauna. "If you're faced with getting your mental health right or preparing for the show, take care of your mental health." Tucker, who dedicated much of his day to reading, writing, and producing the show he hosted at the time, explained that I should "shut out the noise." "Don't read the comment section. Don't read your press clippings. Focus on you, your show, and your family and friends." Tucker revealed he doesn't watch TV. When he wasn't getting his show together, he spent time outside in nature as much as possible. This was a valuable lesson. Balance your body and mind. Looking back, I wish I'd listened more carefully to this.

Laura Ingraham revealed how challenging the job would be. "My show airs at ten p.m. ET," she said. "By that time, each hour, all afternoon and evening, has covered the same story. My challenge is, how do I attack a story from a different angle than everyone else?" Laura stressed how important it is to be an original thinker. "How are you going to be different?" She challenged me. How was I going to distinguish my analysis from the pack? Be creative and unique. This requires constant reflection.

Brit Hume told me not to sleep with my assistant. My assistant is a guy, so not an issue.

I cast a wide net inside and outside of Fox. Bob Costas, Bret Baier, Steve Doocy, Anthony Scaramucci, Mark Levin, Greg Gutfeld.

I listened to everyone closely. After we launched *Jesse Watters Primetime* we had great ratings, number three in all of cable news. Averaging over three million viewers a night. I was waking up at 5 a.m., working out, reading, and writing. Getting into the office at 1 p.m. Working, co-hosting *The Five*, hosting *Primetime* at 7 p.m. Coming home, eating dinner, reading, and going to bed. Like a machine.

Then my back went out.

I dropped to the ground in my bathroom. Somehow, I made it to the bedroom. I couldn't stand. I couldn't move. The pain crippled me. I screamed in agony. I was a fit guy in my early forties who ran, swam, and lifted. Now I couldn't walk. The pain was so excruciating my wife called 911. Paramedics rolled me onto a stretcher and wheeled me out of my apartment into an ambulance.

"You must see some crazy stuff here in New York," I say to the paramedic on the way to the ER. "What's the craziest thing you ever saw?"

"Well, probably the Jeffrey Epstein call," he answers.

He has my attention now. I forget about the pain for a minute.

"When we got to his cell, it was packed with people. Nobody should have been in there. It should have been empty. People had moved the body. They've moved things around in the cell. He was dead when we arrived, but they made us rush him out to the hospital like he was gonna make it."

"What do you mean?" I ask.

"Like, protocol wasn't followed. His cell was a mess; the scene was a mess. People were there who shouldn't have been there. Nobody is supposed to move the body, touch the body. Items in the cell were being messed with. It wasn't normal."

I'm taking mental notes. But before I can get this guy's contact information, I'm taken out of the ambulance and moved through the hospital doors. Almost booked an exclusive on the way to the emergency room.

They stick me in the middle of the ER behind a curtain. New Yorkers are in there with knife wounds, head injuries, and I'm lying on a stretcher with a bad back. They're pumping me full of narcotics to numb the pain, but it's not feeling great.

Suddenly, there's drama. A hostile homeless woman is making a scene. She's loud. And big. And naked. She apparently needs to use the bathroom. I peel my curtain back to catch the action. The naked homeless woman is crouched on the toilet with the bathroom door open. She refuses to close the door. When nurses suggest she close it, she screams. She has a list of demands. She's demanding a shower. Had she gotten herself taken to the emergency room as a ruse to take a shower? Unclear.

Then all hell breaks loose. The naked homeless woman falls off the toilet and hits her head. She's bleeding. There's a lot of commotion. Security arrives and a negotiation takes place involving her, her "partner," nurses, and hospital security. I need a private room. I'm getting pretty close to pulling a "don't you know who I am?" Not really, but when the next doctor comes over to ask me my name, I say, "I'm Watters, and this is my world." Doesn't work. The doctor doesn't watch Fox. He just thinks I'm as crazy as the naked homeless woman now.

Eventually I get an MRI, and hole up in the hospital for a few days. It's a severely herniated disc. I get an epidural shot. Doesn't help much. I go back to work. Can barely get in and out of a car. Have to lie down on a couch in my office while dictating scripts. I see a surgeon. I don't want to, but the pain is unbearable and not getting better.

"You need surgery right away," he tells me. "You've lost sensation in your Achilles. You've lost strength in your right leg. The nerve is screaming. We need to operate."

"Okay, doc, I have a speech in DC on Friday. Let's do the surgery Saturday." It was Wednesday.

"You can't risk riding a train to DC. If anything happens you could be paralyzed."

"Emergency surgery it is."

I was getting back surgery at forty-three years old. This was a wake-up call. For the first time in my life, I was scared.

"Sitting is the new smoking," the doctor explained. "Humans aren't designed to sit all day." He continued. "You're sitting all morning, all afternoon, for two hours each show, sitting in between shows . . . and you're sitting in a car driving on weekends. It's destroying your back."

I had been sitting a lot since Fox promoted me to the 7 p.m.

"What kind of chair are you sitting on at your office?"

I texted my assistant Johnny to send me a picture. I'd bought the chair myself. It was a black leather Chesterfield executive swivel desk chair. I bought it for my new office, and Johnny had put it together. I showed the doctor the picture.

"Look at this. The chair is crooked. It's leaning to the left. It's wrecking your back."

Johnny had assembled my chair cockeyed, and it had blown out my back. Another reason not to sleep with my assistant.

I had a microdiscectomy. Surgery went well, and I was out of work for two weeks. *Primetime* had launched in January, and by April I was recuperating from emergency back surgery. It took about five months to fully recover. My lifestyle completely changed. I walked all day. Stretched and planked. Avoided chairs, cars, and unnecessary sitting. Sitting and reading newsfeeds on my phone, sitting at a desk, sitting in front of a computer was going to put me back in the hospital. I had to establish new routines for working and living. I had to listen to my body.

Being aware of my own pain made me aware of other people's pain. When I limped down the street, I noticed others who limped. My eyes were drawn to addicts, foot shufflers, shoulder slumpers. Was I becoming more empathetic? No way. Couldn't be. I was only concerned with myself usually. But could Watters go deeper? This book tries to.

Interviewing wild characters on the street only gets you so deep. It's a ten-minute conversation condensed into a few sound bites for air. Cable TV interviews are even shorter. I wasn't getting close to the core: *Why* do people believe things? *How* did they end up with their worldviews? *What* gave them these radical ideas?

I set out looking to interview out-of-the-mainstream Americans. Not debate them, just listen to their life stories. I'd listen for two hours, three hours, sometimes four. What I found was that their maverick ideology was rooted in personal struggle. I'd always assumed someone's political belief system was based upon the books they'd read or the media they'd consumed. Not entirely. A big factor in a person's policy preference or political identity? Formative experiences in their youth.

Almost every individual I interviewed had a chaotic childhood. I found that people become dissidents for psychological reasons. Their ideology isn't logical, but the path toward that ideology was. During these interviews I found myself thinking, "Of course you believe this, you have daddy issues."

Sociopathic parents are creating a strange generation. Parents are drug addicts, sex addicts . . . never around. . . . Do you think that child is going to grow up to be a well-adjusted, patriotic voter? Not a chance. Children are being traumatized and then spit out into adulthood. Now they're society's problem. They're our problem. Then their problems become our problems.

No wonder people vote the way they do. No wonder they love anarchy. No wonder they hate. Trace a line directly back to their teenage years. Some were raped. Others were spoiled. A few got no attention at all. So much of their adult crusade is just a reaction to what they experienced growing up.

Many of the characters I interviewed for this project had experienced drugs and alcohol early on. Almost all of them had disastrous parents. Some of the most damaged people had wealthy parents. Money wasn't a major driver of ideology. Class played a larger role, but not in the way you'd think. I noticed much more class rebellion. The family dynamic was key. Sibling rivalries, horrible moms, and ghost dads were consistent features.

Whereas I used to smugly judge oddballs, I began feeling sorry for these people. Even the real nasty and dangerous ideologues I felt sympathetic toward. Because I began to understand them. I understood why they thought about life the way they did. Society would look like that to me too if I had their lives. If my mom was a Mötley Crüe roadie and I took my first hit of crack at fifteen.

People join movements not always because the movement makes logical sense. Oftentimes radicals just want attention. This book examines why. What makes people believe humans are going extinct this century, when the science doesn't say that? Maybe they have a savior complex they developed in college. Certain people join cults. Others are straight-up mentally ill. A few create injustices just to fight them because their life lacks meaning.

This book runs the gamut from true believers to larks. Attention whores to academic nihilists. Abuse runs through most of them, psychic and emotional. A lack of respect of others is often justified. Some don't respect themselves, and there's usually a clear reason why.

Not everyone I was able to crack. Some wouldn't let me, like the communist. The statue toppler spun my head around. Some of these people are generally harmless; they're just bizarre. But by listening I can at least say that I understand them. Understanding is impossible without listening. This format could very well have been a podcast. People really opened up to me. Raw stuff. They cried. Yelled. Laughed. We both got annoyed with each other. But I listened (which is very big of me).

What I discovered is that people have issues. And these issues are getting bigger . . . and crazier. And because the way society is now wired—the internet combined with a strain of political correctness—everything is fair game. All the pillars of Western civilization, social customs, behavioral and legal norms—it's open season. Much of the groundswell is projection. People projecting their problems onto the rest of society. Even though your problems aren't my problems, they are. Because you're making them my problems. We do not need a social revolution because somebody has personal problems. Your issues aren't our revolution. We're not going to turn everything upside down because somebody needs to act out a revenge fantasy on the father they never had. Get your life under control because you're making the rest of our lives harder. I love you but just chill. We're not on the same journey. We can't pay the price for your problems. Don't pay me back for your suffering. I had nothing to do with it. How to fix it? Here's a start: just be better than your parents. For most of you, that's easy.

Get It Together

The Open Borders Professor

When you think "open borders activist," you probably think: angry purple-haired twentysomething, probably with daddy issues, screaming at an ICE agent. Political radicalism is driven by a profound unhappiness with life and, ultimately, with one's place in the world—a rebellion against a system that's made you miserable and a demand that it change to suit you better.

Hard-left activists get hysterical when things don't go their way. Pure anguish. If they could only tax the rich, open the border, or abolish private property, their personal unhappiness would be slayed. Radical politics is a projection of one's fears, insecurities, and inadequacies: I'm not the problem. Society is. There's a famous scene from *The Simpsons* featuring Principal Skinner saying, "Am I so out of touch? No. It's the children who are wrong."

Stereotypes have exceptions, and Joe Carens looks like one of them. The University of Toronto political science professor seems friendly for a lefty—he's clearly amused to be talking to an off-air Fox News host, but his amusement isn't condescending, which is good since

I enjoy being the condescending one. On its face, his background is about as normal as you could imagine: "I grew up in the United States as a middle-class Catholic kid," he tells me. An Irish guy from Boston. Like most Massholes, he loved hearing himself talk.

Joe is described as "one of the world's leading political philosophers on the issue" of immigration. His book *The Ethics of Immigration* is popular in academic circles (meaning nobody's read it). But I read one of his essays. Joe argues, "borders should generally be open and people should normally be free to leave their country of origin and settle wherever they choose. . . . On what moral grounds can we deny entry to these sorts of people? What gives anyone the right to point guns at them?"

Our conversation begins. "I'm turning seventy-eight in a couple of weeks," he says. He has a thick but well-kept white beard and a shock-white head of hair. He's a smile-talker, so at least we have one thing in common. As a young man in the late 1960s, he studied theology at Yale Divinity School. "Then my religious beliefs changed," explained Joe. "I stopped believing in God." A theology school that turns Christians into atheists—not a good look for Yale. He couldn't drop out of grad school because "I'd be drafted." He either had to go to jail or to Canada. Instead, Joe dodged a bullet and switched majors. He was able to remain at Yale and study political science. While he was there, Martin Luther King Jr. spoke on campus. Joe missed it. He confessed this was one of his biggest regrets in life. "I wasn't tuned in."

From there, Joe "taught at Princeton for a few years, and then moved to Toronto for a job where I've been for the last thirty-seven years now, which worked out really well for me," he says. In 1968, he married "a fellow graduate student . . . in the Divinity School. We stayed married for thirteen years. Then I really fell in love when I was teaching at Princeton with a fellow Princeton professor" (the feminist theorist Jennifer Nedelsky).

"By then, my wife and I had . . . we hadn't separated, but we were at odds," Joe says. "I got divorced and got remarried. And that's stayed. So I've been married to [Jennifer] since '85. So quite a while now." To recap, Joe stopped believing in God, avoided Vietnam, got divorced, married a feminist theory professor, and moved to Canada, where he pushes open borders. Trudeau, you can keep him.

Along the way, Joe became convinced that the concept of borders—the lines we draw and enforce to delineate where sovereign states begin and end—was fundamentally unfair. Joe's dream is kind of a goo-goo one-worldism à la the hippie movements of the 1960s. "We're all vulnerable in various ways," he says. "What this whole topic reveals is a kind of fundamental problem with the way in which the world has been organized. It's just not fair to everybody. And we have a responsibility to transform it."

Joe sounds like a child. "Life isn't fair," I explain. "It's not fair in nature, sports, business, anything. Why base your political philosophy on something that doesn't exist?"

"Well, it depends on what you mean by political philosophy, and it depends on what you mean by it 'doesn't actually exist.' So the 'life's not fair' slogan, it depends on how that's used." I suddenly realize I am interviewing the Canadian Bill Clinton.

"Babies, you, and the people you care about are vulnerable. So, of course, you do what you can to protect them, but you feel angry when people hurt them. We want to live in an order in which people are treated fairly." Joe's 'baby' talk would make sense later when I found out about his childhood.

When it comes to fairness, I personally consider first what's fair to the American people, not what's fair to the world. Unchecked illegal immigration isn't fair to American workers or American taxpayers. Joe clearly isn't putting America First.

The paradox of Joe's open-borderism is that he appeals to American values to substantiate his claim. "Let's think about the fundamental values that America is based on," he says. "I was brought up learning about the Statue of Liberty. 'Give me your tired, your hungry, your poor, your masses, yearning to live free.' So that was a powerful image of what the country stood for, which I think has been lost in recent years." Joe's just made the case for a world without borders by appealing to the values of a particular nation—which, by its very nature, exists within borders. How did this guy get into Yale?

"Would you be okay with millions of Americans walking across into Mexico claiming citizenship, starting to take jobs from Mexicans, dominating their local politics, throwing money around? Mexico wouldn't think that was fair. Do you think that's fair to Mexico?" Joe doesn't want to entertain my hypothetical. He only traffics in his own hypotheticals.

"We have different notions of what the theoretical argument is and how the relationship between hypotheticals and principles works," he says. Now I'm annoyed. Pure sophistry. Joe pivots. "If we lived in a just world, the problem of controlling immigration would disappear because the truth is most people would rather live in the communities in which they grew up. They speak the language, and that's where their friends and family are." Bingo. But then Joe plays the blame game. "We've constructed a world in which it is not fair to most of the people who live in it that they feel desperate to leave home."

"Who constructed the world where people in Guatemala don't want to live in Guatemala?" I ask.

Joe says, "That's a complicated question. . . . I try not to engage in those debates." What?! The highly esteemed political science professor says he "just wants people to reflect." The professor hasn't reflected. He just wants others to. Yes, he has tenure.

Joe argues we must "transform the conditions of the global order so that life is reasonable for the vast majority of people where they are born and grow up." He's arguing for a liberal utopia, where every country is equal, and nobody wants to migrate, but if some do, they should have the legal right to waltz across the border and claim a different citizenship. I'm smelling some segregation in the air. Joe's perfect world is one where people born in Zimbabwe stay in Zimbabwe? No integration? Everyone stays put? Is Joe not for diversity?

"It's a better solution to change the conditions where people live and to reduce the pressures for people to move. And again, I don't think the United States could [say], 'Okay, we're committed to that, and we'll do that tomorrow.' That is not the argument at all. It's getting people to take seriously that aspiration." But if it's impossible, naïve, and detrimental to American prosperity—why should we? And if America put its own citizens on the back burner and tried to make life fair and equal in every other country in the world, what would that look like? Would our friends in the Middle East like that? How about China? Hey, Beijing, step aside while Uncle Sam makes your society more fair. Relax, this will only take a minute.

Has the distinguished professor thought any of this through? Of course not. "I'm a political theorist," he says. "I'm not focusing immediately on debates about public policy." Okay, Joe, you tell us the world should be fair, and we'll do the heavy lifting. Joe is trying to imagine a world where if you're born in either Baghdad or Boston, life is so good that no one ever wants to leave. Oh, and everybody has the same standard of living. When you ask Joe how he'd restructure the world to make things more fair, he says, "That's outside my area of expertise."

What is your expertise, Joe? Joe says, "I'm a philosopher." I started college as a philosophy major at Trinity College. Then I had a professor like Joe, and I switched to history.

How are you going to get people to stay in their own country when the United States keeps offering illegal aliens free stuff? Joe won't answer. He accuses me of cross-examining him. As I follow Joe's logic, American taxpayers should pay for housing, food, and college tuition for foreigners . . . in foreign countries.

The abolition of borders in practice, Joe admits, isn't something we're going to see anytime soon. It's "not something that can be done overnight," he tells me. "I'm not saying, 'Oh, well, the solution to our problems is open the borders today.' . . . I mean, there are some proposals on the table, but the idea would be to say, you know what? We have a responsibility to try to move in the direction of change." Move in the direction of change. Bold.

I try pinning Joe down for the last time. "If someone's in the country illegally and they get a DUI, should they get deported?" Joe says I've abstracted two items. Round two. "What happens if someone sneaks across the border and makes it to San Antonio? Cops catch them. No ID, speaks no English, lies to officers. They've been working for cash under the table at a big corporation, driving down wages, sucking up resources from the local community. What do you do with them, Joe? Send them back or let them stay?" Joe says he doesn't understand the question. He adds that I'm "characterizing the migrant in a negative way." I apologize to the imaginary migrant.

Joe says, "I don't want to play that game." It's not a game, Joe! It's the reality of what's going on!

Joe's response to pragmatic objections is to zoom back out to the cruising-altitude level. "I just keep insisting, the open borders argument, I say this repeatedly in everything I've written and everything I've said, is not an argument about what public policy ought to be tomorrow," he maintains. He doesn't have the perfect plan because a plan for implementation requires engagement with reality, and reality gets in the way of the utopia that exists at the level of academic abstraction. Joe's detachment from reality is purposeful. He's against "focusing on what's possible in the world." What he's about, he says, is "stepping back and seeing something fundamentally wrong with the overall structure of things and how can we move gradually in that direction."

At this point, I'm convinced Joe the Plumber (RIP) was smarter than Joe the Professor. You don't need to have a PhD to think the world would be better if we all had it good. What do we do with that bit of common sense? Everything out of his mouth is a vague generality. But Watters doesn't quit. "Okay, Joe, you're the president. You're not a professor anymore. You're a person, you're in charge, you're going to do things differently. What are the top three issues you're tackling?"

"We need to address the issue of climate change, and the United States is the problem." Oh boy. Never mind that China is the world's largest carbon emitter; Joe isn't convinced that having America as the world's superpower is good for the world as a whole. Imagine if Canada was the superpower? The second big thing Joe says we need to address is the problem of racism. (Also gender, equality, and sexuality.) He wants same-sex relationships to be acceptable worldwide. Remember, Joe is now the president of the United States, and global gay marriage is a top issue. And finally, number three, the big thing Joe wants to do differently is fix income inequality. Joe says he wants to give more money to Third World countries. Sometimes they steal it, but who cares? Joe wants capitalism to benefit poor countries.

I'm not mad at Joe. I'm disappointed. When he had the chance to step up to the plate and really show me something, he whiffed. An

Ivy League–educated professor who's spent decades reflecting on the major issues of humanity, Joe gives me boilerplate. Climate change, racism, and income inequality. How do we solve these problems? Joe doesn't know. A job is waiting for him at MSNBC if he wants one. Even sadder, Democrat politicians are heavily influenced by professors like Joe. Pointing in the direction of fairness and virtue . . . without a workable plan to get there . . . while slamming the status quo as inherently unfair . . . is what the shallow left represents.

Wait a second. Joe is pretty privileged. Pretty elite. Peak privilege. What's his role as a privileged person to help the vulnerable?

"Joe, do you feel guilty about your white privilege?"

Joe admits he feels a little guilty about his privilege. Ivy League–educated, straight, white male, able-bodied tenured professor living comfortably in North America. Joe says he does feel conscious of his privilege, and he "doesn't deserve it."

"I'm a white male, but I don't want there to be male privileges," he declares. "My wife is a feminist theorist, so I am deeply committed to gender equality." He doesn't explain how he demonstrates his commitment to gender equality. Maybe he does the dishes, and his wife mows the lawn, I don't know.

Joe says he sees racism every day in academic life, "in all kinds of ways."

I didn't know the University of Toronto was awash in racism. It's weird since it's likely staffed entirely with progressives. I ask Joe how he fights racial injustice at his university. He claims he confronts it. I ask for an example. Joe's example wasn't what I expected.

Joe explains that a fellow professor was turned down for tenure, and he's helping them with the appeals process. Not really the Selma March. I ask if this professor was black. No, Joe says, but "they identify as a person of color." How does Joe know they were rejected for tenure because of their race? Joe doesn't know, and admits "they might have been turned down for other reasons." So Joe's assuming they were denied tenure because they were a person of color? Unclear. But Joe is an ally of a professor who identifies as a person of color on a tenure track.

It appears Joe's asking the entire world to restructure everything to be more fair, but Joe's not doing much in his own life to fight injustice at all.

Does Joe have another example of how he personally fights injustice? He digs deep and scratches his bearded chin. Aha! Yes, he does!

Someone was going to be appointed to a position at the law school, but "some donors objected because that person had written about Palestinian human rights." I ask, and yes, Joe concedes they were Jewish donors. After this kerfuffle at the law school, a report was written. Joe wrote a critique of the report. How many critiques have you written about internal law school reports summarizing squabbles with Jewish donors? I didn't think so. These are the brave sacrifices political science professors make in Toronto.

I ask Joe what his thoughts are on Israel, and he says, "Look, I have lots of Jewish friends." Careful, buddy. "Look, I think Israel's got deep problems now, and the treatment of Palestinians . . ."

You know the rest.

Joe's guiding principle—a constant refrain throughout our conversation—is fairness. He longs for a world that's fair. "What I try to say is, look, if we find ourselves in a world, we have to reflect upon whether we think the institutions that exist, however they came about—are these just or fair or are they not? And if they're unfair, we should try to change them to make them fairer. So that should be the question. The world you find yourself in, you didn't create it no matter who you are, but you have to decide whether you're going to perpetuate it or change it."

I have a hunch something happened to Joe. That something might be why he's focused on fighting unfairness.

I take a shot. "Were you ever molested as a child?"

"I'm not one hundred percent sure. I think I was sexually abused. I do think that happened, but I don't have clear memories. I've been in therapy, so it's not something I can point to. This happened to me at this time, but it did affect my stance in the world, I think." A Catholic priest is "one possibility, but I haven't got the specifics about it," he tells me. "So it could have been a family thing. I'm sure it wasn't my father, but there was an uncle who's a possibility. I'm not sure. I do think it was probably connected to that because I have a psychological aversion to being in Catholic churches. That makes sense, psychically, in that connection."

A renunciation of God after an alleged assault inside of a Catholic church would explain a yearning desire for fairer institutions. A fair institution would protect the most vulnerable. Babies are vulnerable. Was Joe molested as a baby? Who else is vulnerable? "Your tired, your poor, your huddled masses." His striving for strong institutional protection under the banner of universal amnesty makes sense in the repressed memory of an alleged Catholic Church–related child sexual assault.

When people experience trauma, they often remove themselves from reality. It's too painful. They have to detach to protect themselves. Joe's aversion to the unfairness of the here and now; his preference for abstract possibility over practical reality; and his focus on what could be over the nature of what is are all functions of a man who finds comfort in a world of dreams, rather than the world as it is. It's a compelling dream, in the final analysis. But it remains just that—a dream.

2

The BLM Supporter

Emily is getting divorced. She's also being sued by everyone in her entire family . . . except her brother.

"Do your lawyers know you're doing this interview?" I ask her.

"No," she says. "They don't need to know everything."

Her lawyers would beg to differ. Because once Emily starts talking, she doesn't stop. And she doesn't give a BLANK. A volcano of attitude, her personality erupts all over you. She'll spill her guts. I'm shocked she hasn't been cast somewhere on reality TV yet. "My energy is nervous energy," she says. "Really, it is."

Pretty, white, in her thirties, she's been "a beauty and fashion publicist for, I don't know, twelve, thirteen years." Her main client is "Crackhead Barney." I wasn't familiar with her work, but Barney's a black woman who dresses up and harasses conservatives. Here's an example of her "work." She films herself lying down in front of a group of progun demonstrators, decked out in green face paint and a purple wig, moaning, "Hnnggghhh . . . shoot me with your load, baby." "Despite the name, she's not a crackhead," Emily assures me. "She's a performance artist. She's wild. And she intimidates the right wing all day."

Emily, who bills herself as an antiracist activist, doesn't see the ridiculousness of a white woman promoting a black woman playing a crackhead. Emily is literally making money off fake black crackheads. "As a white privileged woman—I will say as well, very privileged, I grew up privileged . . . I never asked to be born, but I was born into a family, a conservative family, very, very conservative. This goes against anything that they would ever stand for." There's more than a little pride in her voice. "So we don't talk anymore."

On paper, Emily makes sense. "I married a finance guy. I did the whole white girl thing—the whole track that my dad had for me." After that, she "did the whole stay-at-home mom thing for a few years" too. These "whole [X] things"—you know, the lifestyles lived by millions of Americans—are usually described alongside dismissive gestures and a knowing smirk, as if to say, I was young and naïve back then. Now I know better.

Emily's sister is an influencer, she tells me. "So a huge part of that also contributes to why I'm doing what I'm doing. Because she gained all this notoriety in New York City for doing drugs. And she's pretty, and she's white, and she comes from a good family. She gets all this press. You would never see that with a black person, for instance. It's pretty privilege. It's white privilege." I'm starting to get the sense that Emily's antiracism has a lot more to do with hating her family than hating white supremacy. "The two of us started to beef online over Covid," Emily says. "And again, she's in the papers and in the *New York Post*, of course, all the time, who I protest actively. We go to Rupert Murdoch's house, we've protested all over them, which is kind of fun."

Emily and her sister were raised "in this stone, cold mansion—Tim Burton–style, with these stone walls and doors, and everything had these sharp corners," she says. "It was really creepy. It was a Frank Lloyd Wright house. It was kind of like living in a prison, and if you spoke up about anything, [my dad] just would totally retaliate on you. So, he just never wanted us to have friends. We had these ridiculous curfews, couldn't be on the phone, and it was just these rigid rules for no reason. But we knew our friends didn't have those rules."

You can start to see where the hatred for authority is coming from.

Emily's parents were a trip too. Her dad was a psychiatrist; her mom was a psychotherapist. "Talk about privilege, we used to go on these five-star vacations to the Dominican Republic or wherever the hell . . . sponsored by Pfizer . . . and meanwhile, my dad's just like . . . He's a drug dealer. What's the difference? He just has a degree from Duke." She had sleeping problems when she was six, so her "dad sends me to a therapist, and they're crushing up my pills in applesauce . . . as early as I can remember," she says. "My dad wrote prescriptions for my sister for Adderall, and she became an Adderall head." Emily was raised in a pharmacy. "We had drugs, the Prozac, the Viagra all over our house. Dad gave it to friends, family. At one point, he was Washington, DC's top psychiatrist because he prescribed so many drugs." Call it what you want, "the system," "the man," Emily felt oppressed. Her father "wasn't big into females using their voice. So over the last two years, I've learned how to use my voice in different ways."

Emily's left-wing activism began as a revolt against her parents' authority: "Growing up, my dad always told me how to not drive in black neighborhoods. He always wanted me to be two cars behind the car in front of me, so I had to have an exit strategy, if somebody came to rob me or beat me up. Did I really need to be afraid?" Later in life, she'd "bug out" when she drove through black neighborhoods.

When both of your parents are shrinks, everything looks like a disorder. "You couldn't eat a waffle without them thinking that, 'Oh, comfort food, you're depressed, aren't you?' Or I would want to sleep in when I was a teenager, and it's like, 'Oh my God, you must be so depressed.' No, I just want to sleep in. It was unbelievable. And they're both narcissists to the full degree, so it was always about them. So, just pills, pills, pills and just diagnosing us with 'this is what you have, this is what you have.'

"He did all kinds of crazy stuff," Emily says of her dad. "Just anything to shut us up." He "was also incredibly abusive, physically. Only with me. And I think a lot of that was because I had this voice. I had this lip. I mean, I couldn't help myself. When something didn't feel right, or he was doing something wrong, I had to call it out. . . . So I had two siblings, and I was always the one that got my ass kicked, always." He "would beat the crap out of me. And a lot of it had to do with the anger he had towards my mom. But he would take it out on me because I was this very loud-mouth kid."

One night almost turned deadly. "I picked up a knife, and I said, 'If you come closer to me, I'm going to do something with this knife.'"

After the knife incident, Emily's dad made a move. "I was kidnapped in the middle of the night and sent to this therapeutic boarding school in Utah called Cross Creek Manor, and it's run by Mormons. They're a for-profit institution, so your parents pay for you to go to these things. They pay people to kidnap you." Apparently, "Paris Hilton did a documentary about this last year. It's called *This Is Paris*, because Paris was also sent to one of these things. It's to shut you up. It's literally to shut you up."

At the time Emily was sent away, she was fourteen. "I was a virgin, and I'd smoked pot a few times," she says, and wasn't suited for the "boarding-school-slash-jail run by Republicans." You "literally don't wear shoes. You don't eat with silverware. You can't watch TV. You don't go outside. It's a cult. They brainwash you. You're completely, totally brainwashed. You have no contact with the outside world. They read your mail before it goes out. You have to do seminars and programs to get out. And the things they make you do—they make you beat towels to get anger out and scream. You would have to strip naked to prove your worth and your self-esteem. . . . You get thrown in isolation rooms. You're strip-searched. It's like jail, and I was only fourteen. I was pretty freaking innocent." Emily says she felt abandoned and suffered from PTSD.

"I got pregnant when I was fifteen. First guy that I was with, boom. Got pregnant." When Emily returned from Utah after a year, "my dad allowed me to hang out with one boy from my past—one," Emily says. "And that's the guy that I lost my virginity to and got pregnant with a few weeks later. Can't make this shit up. He chose this person. In a way, it's funny. Maybe my whole life has been like, how can I piss off my dad? Maybe that's just kind of connected with me subconsciously because I didn't really like this guy. He was just the only option." Immediately, she was shipped off to another "lockup school" out of state, in Pennsylvania, all girls.

But not before she had an abortion. "My dad's whole thing was trying to create these perfect little Republican conservative daughters," she says. "But he was a hypocrite about it. My dad is the most pro-lifer you've ever met. But when it comes to his kids, no, he's not. Oh, you're going to get that abortion, you get that abortion, honey, and you're going to keep quiet, right?"

Her mom—"a shopaholic," Emily says—took her to get the abortion. On the way back from the abortion, her mom went shopping. "I remember going to Planned Parenthood, and when we were done, we walked out, and she saw a brand-new Nordstrom Rack that had just opened. And she couldn't help herself, and had to take me shopping at Nordstrom Rack while I literally had a diaper on, I swear to God, because of the abortion. That's just how her mind works. My mom just really always thought about herself." Emily's mom also "has diabetes and an eating disorder on top of it, so she would never eat. She would pass out in the middle of Nordstrom, just on a Tuesday, and you have to run to Starbucks and get her a sugar packet, rip it open, and down it. So, that happened after the abortion too, in Nordstrom Rack."

It's at this point that I ask Emily if I can option the rights to her life story. She laughs. But I'm serious. Pill-popping shopaholic mom passes out at Nordstrom Rack on the way back from taking her daughter to Planned Parenthood. Hollywood would gobble this up. Shame on me for thinking how profitable a dark comedy like this would be. Shame on me for casting Kristen Stewart as Emily. Shame on me for imagining a bidding war between directors Wes Anderson and the Coen brothers. *Shame.*

Emily went to the University of Maryland. "My dad was so disappointed. So disappointed. The goal was to get one of his kids at Duke. He's a Blue Devil." Emily, her sister, and her brother never made it to Duke. "Not even close. He also wanted us to be doctors. I could never amount to what he wanted me to be. It was impossible. So I majored in sociology and family studies, again, to my dad's dismay."

Where does Emily's brother appear? "He's out of all of this; he's just kind of the third kid, and he just disappears." Her brother is a teacher. Never amounted to what her father wanted. "My dad used to say, 'Oh. If you had been a doctor like me, you could have gotten any woman you wanted.' He would say stuff like that to my brother." Reminder: the brother is the only family member *not* suing Emily.

Emily eventually married a guy who was the son her dad always wanted, the son he never had. "My brother ultimately just started to disappear, so when [my dad] met my ex, who loves sports, who loves college sports, oh my God, who's in finance, who makes money, golfs, they became best friends." Emily is perceptive enough to realize the obvious. "I married my dad, ultimately. I swore that I wasn't, but I did."

Emily's ex didn't have a ring. "He proposed with a Ring Pop." How sweet. "I got married at City Hall. I was seven months pregnant. My dad convinced me to get married. I didn't want to get married, and my dad convinced me because that's just what you do, so that's what I did. Then he gave me two hundred thousand dollars for a house in exchange in lieu of a wedding, so he would always use his money as a way to get me to do things, and it worked.

"Then I had a huge, swanky baby shower."

"How swanky?" I wonder.

"At Lafayette in SoHo." Swanky. "It was open bar, and we had everybody there." Everybody.

The marriage fell apart. "He worked 24/7. We started to disconnect. He started to cheat over time."

Now Emily's getting a divorce—"which is really fun," she tells me. Her father was dead set against it. "A lot of my divorce also had to do with the fact that my dad was going to lose my ex, right? So it's selfish. It's like it has nothing to do with his daughter. It has everything to do with the fact that he's going to lose a friendship, and he doesn't have that many friends." And now "I ruined my dad's life again." That last sentence is delivered with a not-so-subtle hint of satisfaction.

The split sounds nasty. Divorcing her husband is how Emily got into activism. It began "when I hit my ex with a hairbrush," she says nonchalantly. "The police came and told me to leave the home. Once again, that was never something I should have done. Had I known my rights, I never would've left the home." But "I got slapped with an abandonment charge" because "I did what the police told me to do. So a huge part of my work now, when I'm policing the police, is exactly because of things like that." Emily was a stay-at-home mom for five years. Now her children have been taken away from her. It's difficult to pay for divorce attorneys. She's not good with money. Her dad is suing her. And she missed an important court date. Still, Emily doesn't dwell much on not seeing her kids, five and seven, which strikes me as odd.

The divorce began right around the time that George Floyd was killed, "so all of that generational trauma" from her conservative upbringing "just hit me like a ton of bricks. All the stuff with Trump just brought it up to the surface." From there "I started getting into protesting. . . . I just found protests. And then I started to unlearn all the bad stuff that I was taught and how it impacted my life." Emily is dismantling her white privilege, one BLM protest at a time.

"When I got to New York, everything was closed, and the only thing that was going on were protests. So I would just be walking around with my headphones on, and I would see this massive protest, and I just jumped right in. That's when I started to find my voice. Then I'd find another one the next day, and another one, and another one. I mean, it's literally what kept me sane."

I asked Emily if Black Lives Matter was like a family.

"It was." Emily purged (or was purged from) her real family and found her voice and a new family on the streets of social justice.

"Dad cut me out two years ago as soon as I started in Black Lives Matter. He thought that everything that I was doing online was completely crazy, called me mental. They've been telling me that I need to go into a mental institution. Again, my whole life. I've been in mental institutions, many of them. My dad sent me there. My sister too. That's what they did to us when we were around. He would just send us to institutions all the time. I mean, we were tested as children by robotic clowns in mirrored rooms. I mean, we were just always being tested and thrown into labs. We were just like little guinea pigs at their disposal. I think it makes him look like some kind of ideal parent, like he's trying to help his kids."

Emily reveals she's been institutionalized and medicated against her will her whole life. "You don't get shoes. You don't get silverware. You're just medicated against your will. I couldn't even tell you the drugs that I was taking. I had to take what was given to me. I mean, it was just a line. You just pound the pills back. I was robotic probably for a year. Most of my life. I was probably robotic because I was on all these pills."

Now Emily is free. Oh yeah, and Emily's also dating a black guy and living in the projects in the Bronx. Talk about a change of pace. "I started dating a guy from Black Lives Matter, and he just happened to live in the projects," she says casually. It was "when I was divorcing—I had all this time on my hands." (Hence the activism.) "I've never dated a black guy. I've only dated white guys because I was only allowed to date white guys. So it was very exciting for me that a black guy would be interested in some white girl." When she moved from a wealthy neighborhood to the Bronx, Emily felt like she had to impress her new boyfriend: "I didn't want to look like some snobby white girl. So it was like, I just started, over time, dressing down, wearing more sweatpants, no makeup. I didn't want to stick out like a sore thumb . . . I didn't want people to think that I was just this privileged girl."

I have to ask. "Are you going to get married to this guy and have a baby?"

"I mean, my God." Emily giggles. "Can you imagine?"

"That would be the ultimate revenge on your father."

"Oh my God. You want to document it? You want to come along with me? I'll bring you in the hospital room." Hard no. But that's Emily. Blurting out reproduction racial revenge fantasy film offers. Bravo's Andy Cohen would kill for this. Real ex-housewives of the Bronx.

"Do you feel kind of guilty that you're white?" I ask. Yes, she does. "I don't speak Spanish. Every time I go into a store, and I can't speak Spanish with that person, I feel like, 'Emily, you're in their neighborhood. Don't gentrify the place.'" Emily the reluctant gentrifier. "Sometimes I don't like being white. It's funny you brought that up, just because I see my privilege all the time. In my building, the way people treat my boyfriend, for instance, they don't let him in the building." I have a feeling that people in Emily's Bronx building don't buzz her boyfriend in not because he's black, but because he's a stranger who doesn't live in the building. But I don't push.

Emily feels perfectly safe in the Bronx because she has white privilege. She pities the people who live there who don't look like her. "You see what children have, most of the kids don't even leave the house, like literally ever, because the parents are too afraid of their children getting shot."

"Do you bring your children to the Bronx?" I ask. "No," admits Emily. "Not yet."

"So you're worried about exposing them to violence?"

"Well, that's kind of my point. There is no violence. I don't know what the media is showcasing." The Bronx has the highest crime rate in New York City.

"Emily," I say, bewildered, "you said a lot of the people in this neighborhood are afraid to let their kids outside because it's so dangerous."

"Well, I think in their minds, that's the idea, but I don't actually see things happening. But I just know the kind of oppression that's happening in the Bronx. When you walk around, there are no kids outside. There's barely any women outside." Emily doesn't see the violence, or fear the violence; she just "knows" the "oppression."

"I guess I can't really speak to exactly why that's happening"—that's true—"but when I have talked to people, a lot of times it is they don't want something happening to their child. I don't feel like that when I'm in the Bronx personally, but I can't speak to that because I'm not a black woman with a child. Would I have my kids outside? Yes, I would, in the Bronx. I would take them out there in a second. I mean, really would. I feel like I know my surroundings very well."

The food sucks in the Bronx too. "When you go into a bodega, they don't have fruit there for the children to eat. You go into a Bronx bodega, and it's like brands you've never even heard of before. Little Debbie doesn't exist in the Bronx. If you can find Little Debbie in a bodega in the Bronx, you are killing it, like for real. These are things that I pay so much attention to."

Little Debbie is a processed food pastry brand featuring "honey buns" and "oatmeal cream pies," with a borderline illegal amount of sugar and preservatives. Little Debbie makes you Big Debbie. The Bronx bodegas are doing a service by not stocking them.

"Emily," I probe, "they don't have fruit and vegetables in the Bronx?"

"I mean, there's fruit stands and stuff. I actually did a TikTok on this." Of course you did. "The oppression in the Bronx that I see, I don't know how anybody could move up in life." Somehow, J Lo found a way.

Emily is rattling off the kind of college-campus-style BLM activist lingo—"privilege," "institutionalized racism," "dismantling systems," and so on—but it's a second language. She's like an American foreign exchange student in another country who's amazed and delighted at how exotic and marvelously different it all is. "If anything, I found [the projects] to be more welcoming and warm than that in Manhattan," she tells me. "To be honest, the stores there are full of so much magic, and they have things that you would never see anywhere else in the world—the African markets. Again, so I just got into it. I got into all the art and the people and the community service mutual aids. We would do mutual aids once a week. But in terms of police—the policing too, the way just the dirty cops that are in the Bronx, the way that they treat people in the Bronx. Just everything just opened my eyes."

Emily's an open book; politically speaking, she's a radical, but it's tough to shake the feeling that her radicalism isn't a kind of prolonged teenage rebellion. Recently "I got arrested in an abortion protest, but I felt really proud of that," she boasts. "I feel like I'm the Jane Fonda of protestors."

She admits that protesting "saved" her. "I'm part of all the networks, so if we hear of a drag queen story hour protest, I'm going to go to that. We look out for flyers, and I support every single one that I can get to." Protesting saved her from her ex-husband and her parents, it seems. "My dad *is* Trump," she explains. Yup. That explains a lot.

Emily's politics are a rejection of the cartoonish nightmare funhouse-mirror version of America, conservatism, patriotism, masculinity, whiteness—you name it—that she attributes to her father. They're a rejection, in a fundamental sense, of the world she felt she had been expected to join. George Washington "never impressed me much," she says. "Never." (But she does "like Abe Lincoln," she says. "Thumbs up.")

She sees white supremacy as a kind of dark magic, hidden in every ligament and organ of American society. So you can see the appeal of the kind of activism that compels followers to "tear down" a broken system; that sees the kind of bourgeois, white-picket-fence, Wonder Bread suburban lifestyle that Emily grew up in as an insidious cover for evil structures of oppression and power; and that resents authority—particularly the forms of authority that employ the use of force, like cops. Above all else, Emily and her new friends do not like cops. Not one bit.

Oh, and white people. They don't like white people. Which is funny, given the fact that, you know, Emily is white. But it was entirely reasonable for the activists to be hostile toward her at first due to the color of her skin. She nods gravely. "I was white. I was hated. People did not like me because I was white. That's just the truth." In the BLM movement, "I was one of the very few white people, and I just don't think that they felt that trust with me because we were fighting against white people."

We were fighting against white people. Whiteness, for Emily, is all-encompassing and omnipotent; it's both a superpower and a kind of kryptonite. On the one hand, it allows Emily to go places and do things that she says black people can't do: "Let me tell you something about my white privilege," she says. "What I do to police is very different than what most people are doing. I know that my privilege is very real: the way I can go up to cops, in their face, and they don't do anything to me— but if you're a black person, they'll brutalize them and arrest them." At the same time, that privilege functions as a kind of disability—a lower place in the activist hierarchy that Emily, for some reason, seems to embrace. "I did find that as a white person in a black movement—in a black-led movement—that was where the education had to come in," she says. "I really did need to learn how to be put in my place."

"Are you going to teach your children about their white privilege?" I ask.

"Yes. Oh, one hundred percent." No hesitation. "It just has to be part of their daily life."

"So, do you think the United States is a racist country?"

"Yes, I do. Very. I think that we don't know how racist we actually are. I really think that. It's just so deeply embedded in our culture, what we do in terms of the education system with children. Weren't we going to get rid of Columbus Day on the calendar, and turn it into Indigenous Peoples' Day?" We did, I tell her. More than one hundred cities—and a number of states—have done just that. Emily pauses: "Oh, did they?"

"Emily, as an Italian, are you proud of Columbus?"

"No, because I think that he was a bad man that took credit for something that he didn't do. Black people are the founders of this country, if you ask me. They're the ones that built the railroads. They built all of the structures. They did the work. All the creativity, all the things that America was built on, started with black people, and white people just came along, took it, and called it their own." I think the English, Scottish, Irish, Germans, Spanish, Chinese, and others may have "done the work" too. (Although white people "get some" credit for fighting a bitter, bloody civil war to free the slaves, she admits.)

Emily is surprised when I point out that black people in America have higher standards of living than black people in just about any other country in the world. "I didn't know that actually, to be honest with you," she says. "Again, making mistakes is part of learning, right?"

Emily is a recent convert to the left-wing religion; she has all the theological zeal but stumbles at times in rehearsing the dogmas. But her lack of concrete knowledge is, in and of itself, a testament to the absurdity of the ideology. She is adamant that the New York City Police Department, for example, is not a majority-minority police force. (Fact check: it is.) "I just looked at the stats on this." She nods knowingly. "They're not. It's white males still dominate the police force. I just did something on this." My assistant pulls up the demographic statistics: 42 percent white, 31 percent Hispanic, 16 percent black, 10 percent Asian. Emily pauses. "Really? Forty-two percent is white?" Yep. "That's interesting. I seem to see a lot of, I don't know. I'll look at that afterwards because, yeah."

I ask about New York City's black Democrat mayor. "Eric Adams, African American mayor. Is Eric Adams upholding white supremacy?"

"He's an ex-cop, so yeah," she responds. "Like, not all cops are bad, right? But they're bad because they're part of a racist system, right? That's how I go about it, right?" Emily seems to be softening, almost feeling out whether it's okay to not hate all cops. This is progress (kinda). "I think I'm just in a place in my life where I'm angry at the white man. But see, I still love. It's not every white man. It's not. It's just if they fall in a certain category, and I'm working on that, really, I am. I think I do have too much hatred in my heart. And I'm not a hateful person. I'm really not. Just in the moment."

We've had a breakthrough. Emily is realizing that her political ideology could be based on the emotional trauma she's working through.

"Well, if I was growing up in the hood, I already know for a fact that I would've become a gang member. Why do I know this? Because all of these people who become gang members are the lost children. They're all kids. All of these kids that are shooting people in the Bronx are exactly what I just told you. They're kids. They have no parents. They find community within each other. They're like the Lost Boys."

Emily gets deep.

"I've always felt like kind of a lost child, which is why I connect, I think, with the LGBTQ community so much because I just was never really accepted for who I was. I always had to be somebody else in order to make my family happy. So I never really got that full authentic childhood experience that I think a lot of other kids did because I was living in survival mode and constantly trying to people-please and make my parents happy and fix things."

"Do white people get any credit?" I ask.

"We do," she says, sighing. "We get some. We do. I'm not, I don't want to like, sort of what I talk about . . ." She gets quiet for the first time. "But I think you're, yeah, you're right. And I'm going to look into that too, and do more research. I think what I'm saying is a little bit broad."

It's hard not to sympathize with Emily. Her life is a mess. She's lost her kids and her husband, and her father just served her papers. "They hired a private detective and found me. I don't know, this shit is crazy, so it's been very hard to just Zen out. But I go to meditation classes and sound baths and things like that. I've gonged. I've gonged energy out. I do it."

I tell Emily what I do to relax (walking, stretching, reading). We bond.

"So why don't you run for president?" she asks. "I would potentially be open to voting for you."

"You're going to vote for a white male?"

"Yeah. No, listen, that's what I'm trying to put on the table. I don't hate all white males. You've changed my perspective today. I was thinking maybe I was going to be grilled. I've watched your stuff. I don't actively watch Fox News, but I've watched your segments before. I don't know. You all can get hard over there."

We can get real hard. She's right. But I'm listening now, and it's starting to make sense.

3

The African Nationalist

It took Ayo Kimathi about forty minutes to start talking about the Jews. But once he got going, Jews were all he wanted to talk about. Coronavirus? The Jews. Vaccines? Jews. The Ku Klux Klan? Jews. Mass immigration? Jews. Gangsta rap? Jews. Pedophilia? Jews. The Patriot Act? Jews. The Bolshevik Revolution? Jews. The Holocaust? Somehow, also the Jews. Obama? Jewish-funded controlled opposition. (Same thing with the NAACP—"It's not a black organization, never has been. It's a Jewish organization.") If all that seems incoherent to you—why would the Jews be operating both the KKK and the NAACP?—that's because you just haven't seen the bigger picture: "The way that Jews operate, they always on both sides," Kimathi says. "There's not going to be anything politically that's relevant in the world, any topic that you discuss where you're going to see Jews on one side, where there's not a Jew on the other side." It's a "great formula" where "you're never on the losing side, because you're on all sides all the time. This is part of the modus operandi." He's writing a whole book about it: "It's called 'Jews Are the Problem.'"

Ayo describes himself as an "African nationalist"—he rejects the term *black nationalist* because it's too associated with homosexuality.

"I'm a black person who sees black people as one nation of people, no matter where we are on the planet. I believe that we should be securing our own interests." Tall and wiry with a shaved head and bright eyes, Ayo is well-spoken and energetic. He's authoritative, like a father. A father who's never been wrong. The race warrior was raised by a single mother in southeast Washington, DC. "In my young age at one time, my mother reached out to my dad and told him, 'You need to meet your son.' So he said he was coming over. I'll never forget that day because of the excitement of that happening, but he never came that day. That was a rough day."

He didn't meet his father until he was twenty-seven. His mom gave him a list of men with the same last name one day and he sat around cold-calling when "one of the people said they knew who he was. I told them he was my father, and they told me what his address was. I just went one morning and knocked on the door, said, 'Hey, I'm your son.' He opened up, him and his wife, and we talked and laughed. I felt like it was important because I got to see the man who brought me into this world, and I felt like that's something I think every child would benefit from that kind of thing. I think it was a pivotal moment in the sense of I'm no longer the guy who has that empty space of not knowing who his father is."

"Do you still feel resentful of him for what he did?" I ask. "Do you understand him leaving?"

"I never felt resentment in that way." He shared with me that his mom never talked badly about his absent father. That softened the blow of abandonment, but he remained somewhat empty in places. "I do know that there are missing elements in my personality. For the man I am, for what I do, for our people, when people look from the outside, I'm quite a guy. I do some things nobody would do. I take positions people do not take, but myself looking inward on myself, there are missing pieces. And I can see almost all the missing pieces that I see in myself, who I would want to be, most of them are not having a father in my life. So I don't have resentment, but I do have a better understanding of the critical nature of having a man there on a daily basis, because there are things that you just can't replace what you get with a man there who cares about you and who loves you."

Ayo admits, "I would've been a better man in my estimation had I had a father there, but I probably wouldn't have gone into this." "This" being the whole black nationalist Jew-hating thing.

So Ayo not having a father around to love and protect him made him dedicate his life to loving and protecting the entire black race. Is Ayo a father? Yes. "I was married, two children. That didn't work, and I can say fairly that some part of that is I'm so married to the mission of saving my race that, to some degree, I may neglect some things that a father or a husband is supposed to be doing and concentrating on." Ayo neglected his family just as he claims his father had.

What's it like being married to a black nationalist? Not easy, apparently. "She left me," Ayo admits. "Part of that was because, quite frankly, I'm committed to racial survival in a way that, unless you have that same absolute sense, a person would not understand. I put myself in harm's way for my race regardless of what the consequences will be because it's the only thing that I live for. I live this mission. That's all-consuming. To actually live with a person who that's all they talk about and that's all they think about, and that's all they do all the time . . . is hard."

Ayo was married to the game. "My focus is on saving the race of people, and nothing is bigger than that for me." Can you imagine the pillow talk? "Sorry, honey, too busy to make love when there's so many whites to hate." Ayo says he's sacrificed a lot to save the black race. Money, security, his reputation. It started making sense why his wife filed for divorce. Yet, at times, Ayo seems genuinely wounded by the perception that he's an extremist—or that the things he believes are alienating to people, including his family. "If you go on Wikipedia, I mean, they make me out to be like, if I saw this guy, I would stay away from him." (Finally, a guy whose Wikipedia page is worse than mine.)

Washington, DC, mayor Marion Barry was Ayo's hero growing up. "Southeast DC was rough, and I'm not the roughest, toughest guy, so it was a very difficult . . . but Marion Barry was like a lifesaver, man." Ayo remembers as a teen making $3.25 an hour while "a white guy over there was making $32K." This "white guy" was a grown man with seniority and experience, but Ayo blamed racism. That's when Ayo's hero forced city money to his own race. "When Marion Barry became mayor, he said, 'Thirty-three percent of all contracts go to black people.' He called it 'a minority contract.'" Joe Biden took that torch and carried forward Marion Barry's legacy of equity. Hunter carries a torch too.

Marion Barry's real legacy is defined by crack. In 1990 the mayor was caught smoking crack in a hotel room with his girlfriend, who happened to be an FBI informant. His famous words during the takedown: "That bitch set me up!" Ayo still aches over the scandal.

"We looked at it like, oh, Barry, why'd you let them get you like this? We know that they set you up like this because they don't want you doing this, but why would you let them get you? We were upset at her for setting him up. We were upset at the FBI, and then we were disappointed with him because it's like, come on, man, we need you."

"So you believed the bitch did set him up, but you're also disappointed in Marion Barry for allowing the bitch to set him up?"

"Yes," says Ayo. "A lot of Trump people feel that way too, about Donald Trump." That's one to chew on.

"She did set him up. I understand it, but I don't say ['bitch'] to any of my sisters. I won't use that word, but I'll also say, what people don't know is that they came to her, the federal government, and told her they were going to take her children from her. So I'm not justifying what she did, but you come to somebody and tell them that . . . she was in a bad position too." Is it possible the FBI threatened to take "the bitch's" kids if she didn't snitch? Yes. Is it also possible Ayo has no idea what he's talking about? Also, yes.

In the early 2000s, Ayo quit his job as a small business specialist for the Navy to self-publish his first book, *War on the Horizon: Black Resistance to the white-sex Assault*, under a different name. After a few years of touring and delivering lectures under a pseudonym, Ayo took a job at Immigration and Customs Enforcement (ICE). But in 2013, reports from the Southern Poverty Law Center outed Kimathi, who was by then operating a website titled "War on the Horizon" that called for the killing of whites and "black-skinned Uncle Tom race traitors"— and featured an "enemies list" that included Rev. Al Sharpton, Barack Obama, Oprah Winfrey, Whoopi Goldberg, and Lil Wayne. Understandably, Ayo was let go from his cushy $115,000-a-year gig in the US government. The Secret Service even arrived at his house and "grilled me and everything like that," he later told a radio show host.

Why would a black supremacist put the first black president on an "enemies list"? Ayo was immediately suspicious of Obama as a senator from Illinois. The freshman from Chicago, by way of Hawaii, hadn't even sponsored any legit legislation, had no street cred, and suddenly was running for the top spot. "No black people even knew who Obama was. We're not talking about somebody like Jesse Jackson." Apparently, Obama was a puppet. "When you look at his cabinet, who surrounded him, what you have is the Jewish overthrow of the United States of America by proxy through the magic mulatto who they groomed, brought out of nowhere, financed through the roof, and then sucker punched white America into believing [they weren't] racist anymore," he tells me.

"But white America did a counter-coup, and I've got to admit it was pretty impressive what they did with Trump. That was something." In fact, Kimathi has a far more sunny attitude about Trump than his predecessor—Obama didn't do "anything about these murders of black people from the law enforcement," he says. "We had less of that when Trump got in. The money for black colleges, Trump came in and showed how easy it was to fund the black colleges. So, we began to see after 2016 . . . there's something deeper for us to evaluate here." Trump, Ayo says, "didn't even get a chance to actually be the president he tried to be, because the entire time he was in office he's fighting false allegations." And "when you take a look at it . . . let's be honest, who's leading the charge against Trump and his false conspiracy? [Adam] Schiff." And . . . we're back to the Jews. "This is a Jewish program that's being implemented for the destruction not just of America, but of the entire world."

Now forty-eight years old, Ayo, whose Facebook page enjoys nearly ninety thousand followers, serves as the spokesperson for the Straight Black Pride Movement (SBPM), a "coalition of groups" that argues "that homosexuality is 'European sexual insanity,'" *Ebony* reported in 2015. An Afropunk writer who attended an SBPM meeting in Boston in 2017 reported hearing that "homosexuals are pedophiles, along with claims that the Black LGBTQ community acts as an agent of white supremacy to decimate Black culture," and that "Black people cannot be born gay and . . . being gay makes you un-African." It's an odd meld of hard-left black nationalism and Christian social conservatism that scrambles the wires in the brains of a lot of standard-issue Black Lives Matter sympathizers. "His theories may be on the fringes of public discourse, but they form the intellectual underpinnings of a push that threatens to take hold among those who are genuinely concerned about the state of the black family and who want to see it strengthened and celebrated," *Ebony* worried. The SBPM "page is filled with beautiful photos and videos of smiling heterosexual black couples, parents with their children, Black people joyfully dancing at a wedding. What could possibly be the problem with that?"

While it's certainly true that Ayo is on "the fringes of public discourse," he represents a small but active tradition within a subset of American black political thought. The disgust at homosexuality, transgenderism, and other forms of "cultural degeneracy," and the allegations of their links to Jewish influence, have been a defining component of Louis Farrakhan's fifty-thousand-member Nation of Islam (NOI) since the group's founding in 1930. (The famous black nationalist Malcolm X led the NOI from 1952 to 1964, and the boxer Muhammad Ali was a member.) The NOI's bizarre theology holds that the black race is divine, that whites are a subhuman race created by an evil wizard named Yakub, and that humanity is living in the end times, approaching an apocalypse that will be brought on by a race war. The group opposes homosexuality, transgenderism, and the integration of blacks and whites; Farrakhan has attributed homosexuality to "Jewish power," argued that "the Jews were responsible for all of this filth and degenerate behavior that Hollywood is putting out: turning men into women, and women into men," and raged against "the Satanic Jews who have infected the whole world with poison and deceit." While the group is relatively small and marginal within the black community, it's more influential than you might think: Tamika Mallory, one of the lead organizers of the Women's March, has been embroiled in controversy for what critics call her close relationship with Farrakhan—as well as allegations that she shares his antisemitic views (which she denies)— and repeatedly refused to condemn him. Al Sharpton has taken trips to Africa with NOI members. And in 2018, a photo of Barack Obama smiling with Farrakhan at a 2005 Congressional Black Caucus meeting surfaced.

Kimathi cites one of the religious sect's key antisemitic texts, *The Secret Relationship Between Blacks and Jews*, which argues that Jews were primarily responsible for the Atlantic slave trade, as a major influence in the maturation—his term, not mine—of his political thought. "I used to blame you, buddy," he says, gesturing at me as a stand-in for the entire white race. "When you see my older work, if you ever see it, you'll say, man, this guy's hard on white folks. And I always blamed you guys." His "instinct" was: "White, I mean any white—white male, female, child, anything—they mean harm to me," he says.

I have to ask, "Are you threatened by a white baby?"

"That baby now is cool, but when that baby gets twenty-five years old, my child is going to deal with somebody who doesn't want them to get the job because they're black. That was where I was. Where I'm at now is a little bit different."

That different place, more or less, is just substituting "Jew" for "white." "I'm at a point now of maturity where, okay, genocide is actually occurring," Ayo says. And "what happens is I look for the answer, and I can never find an answer any different than the answer being Jew." Rather than looking at all whites as the same, "now I look at them and say, 'Am I dealing with a Jew, or am I dealing with an Anglo?'" Jewish power, for Ayo, is all-encompassing.

Even "the Holocaust didn't set them back," he tells me. In fact, "the Jews launched a war against the Germans first." Hitler, the victim of Jewish military aggression? Even more subversive, Ayo claims, "Jews created starvation, they created . . . The sexual stuff that we see here in America is merely a mirror image of what was downtown Berlin after World War I. We're talking about pedophile clubs, we're talking about homosexual clubs, we're talking about the interracial stuff. We're talking about prostitution, gay gangs walking around snatching people's sons up. We're talking about the kind of things . . . Everything we see happening in America today, every single thing you see right there in Berlin."

Suddenly, we start hearing qualifiers. "I don't support Hitler, but . . ." We've entered Kanye West territory. "But before long [Hitler] had erased the poverty, they created their own economic system, he got off the Rothschild central banking system, he resurrected the whites of Germany to become powerful. In six years, they had their own Volkswagen, they got their own car."

Then he went there. "Again, I'm black, I'm not pro-Nazi, they don't like black people. But I got to say, just from a researcher's perspective, this guy was pretty amazing at what he did, and much like anybody else that you just don't like. I'm not saying Hitler was great, I'm just saying if I were white, me, I would love Hitler. Not because of the things he did against Jews per se, but because what he did. He said, 'My story, my struggle.' He'd talked about what happened to his nation, how he went to the bottom and he lifted them out of it, it was amazing what he did. That's not the story you're going to get from the Jews because it doesn't serve their interests, and people will be offended by me saying it. I'm just telling the truth. I've done the research. This is just the facts."

Touting Hitler was a curveball. Time to redirect. "Tell me what it's like being black in America."

"Oprah Winfrey did a program many years ago, and she had a white guy on who was like, 'Black people complain too much. It's nothing about being black, you guys are just talking trash. There's no real issue.' He made an agreement to be black for one week."

"Oprah put a guy in blackface for a week?"

"Look, I would've said, 'Hey, what's up brother?' I wouldn't have known the difference."

"I've never seen that episode of *Oprah*." (Or any *Oprah* episode.)

"Well, here's the thing. It ain't much of an episode because he was supposed to do it for a week. I think he did it for an hour and Oprah sat him down and said, 'Why did you stop? You promised to do it for a week.' He said, 'I just couldn't do it. The stares, the looks,' and he wasn't happy to admit it, but he was like, 'I can't imagine what y'all are dealing with.' He couldn't do it for an hour, that's the best as I can give you. We've become so conditioned living under a situation of genocide that it's everyday life for us. That's just a life we live, whether we know it or not, and we just deal with it however we deal with it. But it is tremendous anxiety whether we acknowledge it or not; it's tremendous anxiety."

A college student went on *Oprah* to describe what it was like when he was black for a week in Florida. He had taken pills to make his skin dark and shaved his head. Oprah didn't put him up to it. Ayo is not really a fact-driven guy. We knew that. The college student did tell Oprah he experienced discrimination, though.

Ayo has "tremendous anxiety," just like all blacks. And he speaks for all black Americans. The all-knowing, all-feeling Ayo also speaks for white Americans. "You have this cavalier attitude like the world is yours, and why are we here?" Conservative whites are more honest about their racism, he explains. "'I don't like you. You're black, I don't like you.' They don't have to say that, but you know it, they're not trying to hide it. The liberals are more clever. The liberals tend to want to pretend to be friendly and smile more, but they tend to have, many times, more evil agendas because they're not honest, they're not up front."

"What do you think the liberal evil agenda is?" I ask.

"Well, the question would be," wonders Ayo, "are you talking Jews?"

It became comical how Ayo inserted Jews into every equation. But I was determined to discover a situation he couldn't scapegoat.

"What about black-on-black crime?"

"Black-on-black crime is more a function of the normal state of affairs with any group of people, when you remove resources from them and then when you insert harmful culture." There's the red flag. Someone else "inserted" something deadly. "But since the eighties, since gangster rap culture, which again, I know you're sick of hearing it, but I'm going to keep going back there, I'm just going to throw this out and keep running, but if we look at who financed that, Jerry Heller working through Seagram's and Interscope, Jews who finance this culture.

"But if you look at the effects of crack in the black community, and now opioids in the white community in America, you will see a similarity. Again, I know you don't want me to do it, but who was found guilty of the opioid crisis? I'll let you say, so I won't say it. Who was that?"

"The Sackler family?" I asked.

"Yes."

The Sackler family built a pharmaceutical dynasty in the United States that contributed to the opioid crisis. The family business pled guilty to criminal fraud charges involving deceptive opioid marketing. They've paid enormous fines, and litigation continues to this day. I had no idea the Sacklers were Jewish. I looked it up. They are. Walgreens also settled massive opioid lawsuits. The founder of Walgreens isn't Jewish. The executive chairman isn't Jewish. The CEO isn't Jewish. The CEO is actually a black woman. I'd never googled whether people were Jewish before, but I gather it's something Ayo does a lot.

Ayo goes to great lengths pinning things on Jews. Someone doesn't even have to be Jewish. They just have to sound Jewish. "George Zimmerman, he wasn't even going to be tried, if it wasn't for the Black Panthers going out there and putting a bounty on his head. He killed a young man walking home. A young man's walking home to see a basketball game, just minding his business, he kills him in cold blood, and what happens? He didn't get charged with anything."

Wait a second. "Wasn't he Hispanic?" I ask.

"His name was Zimmerman, help me out," says Ayo. "What kind of name is Zimmerman?"

Here I go googling again. Zimmerman is Catholic. It's time to confront Ayo.

"Isn't it convenient to always be able to blame the Jews?" I ask. "That's the answer for everything you see throughout the entire world. It's so easy to say, 'Oh, it's the Jews. It's the Jews. It's the Jews.' Do you find that's limiting your ability to see other sides?"

Ayo says it's the Jews' fault he blames the Jews.

"Black Americans far outnumber the Jews," I add. "Why aren't black Americans dominating the world when there's only a tiny amount of Jews?"

Ayo pauses. He reflects. Then he blows my mind. He heaps praise on the Jews.

"I mean, it's fantastic what they've done. I'm going to give them credit for what they've been able to accomplish. It's amazing." Ayo appears to respect the Jews' ability to divide and conquer. "We want to preserve our blackness; whites want their whiteness. Jewish nationalism is different. It seeks to overthrow every other group's individualism and splotch and merge those together, but to leave only Judaism as its only thing separate and distinct from the others. That nationalism seeks to destroy all of the forms of nationalism for Jewish dominion. It's about the dominion of the Jew. What they've done is they've brought the world at this point to the point of complete ruin. Now, it won't be ruined for them. They will have complete total dominion if their plans go through properly."

Ayo apparently respects both Hitler and the Jews. Both attempts to racially dominate the world he can appreciate. Game respects game.

Ayo claims he's older and wiser than ever. "I actually have grown to the point now, because of the way the world's moving, that I have more in common with white nationalists now than ever before in my life, which is a strange place to be," he admits. "I actually talk to them as much as I talk to anybody else now, and we get along. We agree on a lot of things." There's precedent for that too. In the 1960s, Malcolm X and the NOI attempted to make common cause with the American Nazi Party, led by George Lincoln Rockwell. Both favored racial separatism, and opposed racial integration in all forms. They also shared a hatred for Jews. Rockwell praised Elijah Muhammad, one of the first leaders of NOI, as "the "Adolf Hitler of the black man," and gave a speech making the case for alliance to a crowd of twelve thousand black NOI members. ("You know that we call you n*ggers," Rockwell, dressed in full Nazi regalia, told the crowd. "But wouldn't you rather be confronted by honest white men who tell you to your face what the others all say behind your back?") At one point, "the Klan even reportedly offered more than 20,000 acres of Georgia land to the Nation of Islam, intending to kickstart an exodus of American blacks to segregated homelands," the *National Post* wrote. Marcus Garvey, another prominent black separatist and one of the inspirations for the "Black Power" movement, provoked outrage from more mainstream black leaders by meeting with and praising the KKK, arguing that "I regard the Klan, the Anglo-Saxon clubs and White American societies, as far as the Negro is concerned, as better friends of the race than all other groups of hypocritical whites put together."

In white nationalists, Ayo sees some kindred souls. "Because you guys, if there's anything I've ever seen that y'all believe in"—not sure if he means all whites or just white nationalists here—it's "y'all Constitution. You're just not going to let this thing go, and you'll fight for it." That, Ayo says, presents an opportunity for an alliance—whites and blacks together, holding hands and singing "Kumbaya," to fight the all-powerful Jews. "We're not the one trying to draw you into war to kill your brothers and sisters in Russia. You just can't blame us for that. We're not the ones who are sticking six-month-old children in the arm with injections that have been proven to be genocidal and to kill people. We are not the ones doing that. So, we're not the problem."

"So, you see a day possibly where blacks and whites can get together and fight against the Jews?"

"I'll say it like this," says Ayo. "If we don't, both races are going to be exterminated."

It's almost as uplifting as MLK's "I Have a Dream" speech.

"Can you name three things that whites have done really well that you're proud of?" Throw me a bone, Ayo.

"I wouldn't say I'm proud of anything but . . ." Ayo is deep in thought. "Now, let me ask you, are you talking about white folks in general? Are you talking about Jews? Help me out."

Eventually, he confesses he's proud of "our" Constitution. "Your forefathers wrote a document that helped us free ourselves because we could say, look at your document. It says, I'm supposed to be freed. Your document said . . . That document, I will acknowledge. This is one time I would like to steal something from white folks. Y'all have stole a lot of stuff from us. I want to steal this from you. If I can find a way to take credit for the Constitution . . . I give your guys credit."

Yes, the "white folks" did create the Constitution. We can be proud of that. Ayo never got around to naming the other two "white things" he's proud of. I would have accepted golf and bourbon. Although, first, I'd have to check if Jews were involved.

Ayo pauses at one point, as if as an afterthought, addressing me and my research assistant who's on the Zoom: "Let me just ask, just to be clear, are either of you Jews?" I'm not Jewish. My research assistant says his father is Jewish, but not practicing. "Okay. I just wanted to be clear, either way it doesn't matter." Ayo nods. "I'm just telling the truth." With those formalities out of the way, he picks up where he left off: "To understand the Holocaust, we would have to look at the Bolshevik Revolution. . . ."

Still, he resented whites almost from the beginning—a resentment that he brought with him to Concord Academy, a prestigious (and largely white) preparatory boarding school in Massachusetts, which he attended on a generous scholarship. And it wasn't just whites; it was homosexuals too. Ayo recalls his angry outburst when Concord Academy became the first prep school to form an LGBT student group: "The language I used, you can't use that kind of language now," he says. Ayo reminisces how he bullied people and called them "f*ggots."

"There was this lesbian female, and I don't know how a female could be so frightening to people, but I will admit she had everybody afraid. And she was Jewish." Ayo proudly retells how he "jumped up" and got in her face one time "until she backed down and was female again."

He stood out at the traditionally pristine, staid prep school. "They wanted more diversity," he says. "Well, they got what they wanted." The education, from a traditional standpoint, "was excellent." But from the perspective of the quality of life day-to-day, "it was the most racist, difficult environment."

"I started learning how white racism operated being at a liberal school."

Are liberals more racist?

"It's a different type of racism, and it's a painful racism because it's done with a smile. And if nobody tells you what it is, I'm not going to lie to you. It can destroy you. I almost got destroyed, but I didn't." It appears that Ayo almost got expelled too. Before graduation, he remembers a teacher who told him, "I'm so glad you're leaving because you're going to hurt somebody here."

Ayo tells me he'll "never forget" being publicly corrected by a Jewish student in one of his classes. "It was one of the most important classes I've ever took. I took a course called Subliminal Messaging. Now, I'm not going to get into it, but who controls Hollywood and everything? We know it's the Jews. Okay? So, of course, it is a Jewish thing. They're the ones that understand it better than anybody. I didn't know none of that stuff. I just thought it would be fun. And I never forget, it was one of the most embarrassing moments in my life, but it taught me humility." (A lesson Ayo has forgotten.)

"There was a paper that they wrote that was talking about one thing, but it looked like it was talking about something different. And I was a bit of a jerk coming from Southeast [DC]. Not a tough guy, but I was tough there among all the white guys. So, I'm supertough now. So, I'm making fun of what they're talking about in the class because I'm not understanding. And I'll never forget, there was a Jewish guy. And he looked at me and was like, 'That's not what it's talking about. It's talking about this.' And he showed me. And when I actually realized that I had read something that was clearly talking about one thing and I was way over here sounding like an idiot . . . I was an idiot and a jerk. And I realized how dumb and unaware of what I was dealing with, for the rest of that class I never opened my mouth. I shut up and started learning. I said, let me shut up and pay attention. And what I learned there is everything isn't what you see on the surface.

"It was the best thing that could have ever happened to me because I ended up learning things." (Whether or not they were the right things, I'm not so sure.) "It just taught me the lesson of humility. Don't always think you know everything because you don't."

Mind. Blown.

"Do you realize what you just said?"

"I'm listening," he said. "What?"

"That a Jewish guy humiliated you in the classroom because he pointed out that not everything appears to be as it seems."

"It just told me the lesson of humility," he said, the irony totally lost on him. "Don't always think you know everything because you don't."

A Jewish student taught Ayo a valuable lesson: Don't lash out like a tough guy when you don't know something. Don't try to make up for ignorance with confidence. Relax and listen. You'll learn something. Your first instinct isn't always right.

Ayo experienced this formative moment—he calls it a moment of "humility"—and what was his takeaway? He judges everyone by their race or religion and assumes he's always right and knows everything. He blames a Jewish student for enlightening him. You can't make this up.

Ayo blames Jews for the destruction of the black family. He blames Jews for his dad leaving, not his dad. The anger he feels toward his dad is transferred to Jews. He's protecting his dad from accountability the same way his mother did. He blames Jews for his marriage ending. Blames Jews for losing his job. Ayo accepts no ownership. Black America isn't responsible for anything of its current condition. Ayo has constructed an ideological excuse for everything and dressed it up as "research." Ayo isn't dumb. He's been wounded and protects himself with a false sense of authority. Claiming the crown as the father of the black race. Protecting blacks against dangerous forces he's created in his own mind. Like a father protects his children. Something his father didn't do for him, and which he hasn't done for his children.

Strangely, I don't feel threatened at all by Ayo. He doesn't trigger fear. As despicable as his beliefs are, he's calm, easy to talk to, and can smile with you. But violence seems to lurk beneath the surface. He speaks highly of Nat Turner, a black slave who led a bloody rebellion that killed fifty-five whites.

"Do you think right now that violence would be a rational response from black America?" I ask him.

"No serious general takes anything off the table as it relates to accomplishing their mission. I would say whatever's necessary for me as a black person to defend and protect the interests of African people on this planet, I'm more than willing to do. I want to do it." Ayo adds that white folks are the problem with planet Earth. Although, at this point, he says, it's the Jews committing the genocide.

I'm left with one final question. What's more powerful, love or hate?

"Is interracial breeding off the table?" I ask.

"Off the table, absolutely."

"What if you fall in love with a white woman?"

"I don't believe a person falls in love. I believe a person chooses to engage with a person, to be in a situation to make a decision."

"So if you see a black man get married to a white woman, get her pregnant, have children, what would you say to him?"

"I'd say, 'That's how we end up with Obama.'"

4

The Anti-Work Inactivist

I kinda got someone canceled. It wasn't my fault. (Nothing ever is.) But someone lost their position because of me.

Doreen Ford is an "anti-work" activist. She appeared on *Jesse Watters Primetime* in 2022 and bombed. It was a catastrophically bad interview. (For her. I handled it perfectly, of course.) As a result, Doreen was canceled by her own community. Doreen was head moderator of a hard-left internet forum "for those who want to end work, are curious about ending work, want to get the most out of a work-free life," and so on. (Tagline: "Unemployment for all, not just the rich!") The interview was such an embarrassment for Doreen and the anti-work movement, they stripped her of her title. Now Doreen works even less. Which I guess is what she wanted. You're welcome.

The anti-work crusade exploded during the pandemic. "Antiwork—also known as the refusal of work—is nothing new," Vice News wrote in a December 2021 profile of the internet forum. "It's a radical political philosophy with roots in Marxism and anarchism, developed by a handful of 20th and 21st-century thinkers united by a vision of a society where people no longer have to work. . . . [The forum] has become a release valve for people all over the world looking to vent about bad bosses, ask for support in leaving their jobs, or simply share memes to pass the time."

"Political philosophy" might be too generous a term here.

Doreen Zoomed into my show that night from a cluttered, poorly lit room wearing a black hooded sweatshirt and glasses. This room was confusing. I saw a microwave and an unmade bed. A dresser and a breakfast table. Did Doreen sleep in her kitchen or cook in her bedroom? Unclear. Everything about Doreen was unclear. Unwashed hair, hoodie, makeup probably applied without a mirror—my producers told me Doreen was transgender, but they didn't tell me her identity didn't include looking like a grown-up.

I introduced the anti-work internet arena as "a safe space for like-minded people who want to do as little as possible and still get paid." Doreen said this was a "misconception." She tried to clarify. "We're a movement where we want to reduce the amount of work that people feel like they are forced to do . . . and don't want to necessarily be in a position where we feel trapped, you know?" Doreen emphasized she "still wants to be rewarded" but "not feel trapped."

I told Doreen I didn't understand and asked her, "Are you encouraging people to be lazy?"

"Sir, no." Wow, she called me sir. "So, I think laziness is a virtue in a society where people constantly want you to be productive 24/7. And it's good to have rest."

"How many hours is a solid workday in your ideal society?" I asked.

"I mean, I personally work. I have like a twenty-, twenty-five-hour workweek, which I think is fairly good. So, I would like less work hours."

What does Doreen do for a living? She tells me she's a dog walker. But dog walking twenty to twenty-five hours a week is too much. She'd like easier hours. You never ask a woman her age, but I'm not sure if Doreen is a woman, so what the hell. "And how old are you, if you don't mind me asking?"

"Sure, I'm thirty."

"You are thirty, okay." A thirty-year-old dog walker. A part-time dog walker, actually. "And is there something you want to do besides being a dog walker? Do you aspire to do anything more than dog walking or is that kind of your pinnacle?"

"I love working with dogs. If I had to do this the rest of my life, you know, I wouldn't be super complaining. Dogs are wonderful animals. But I would love to teach. I would love to, you know . . . work with people and stuff like that."

Doreen works with dogs, but eventually, she'd like to work with people.

Now I'm curious. "What would you teach, Doreen?"

"Philosophy, mostly." Tell me more, Socrates.

"Just instruction of philosophy, critical thinking, reason, stuff like that." You know, stuff like that.

I told Doreen, the thirty-year-old part-time dog walker/aspiring philosophy professor, that I'd love to take her class one day, not before noting that a philosophy professor probably has the same hours as a part-time dog walker.

"To each their own, they say. It's a free country." I'm a gracious host.

"Sure," says Doreen. "Yes."

"Not everything is free, but it is a free country." Smiling, I went to commercial.

Doreen got eaten alive. Here's what the lefty tech site Mashable wrote at the time: "The anti-work subreddit went private Wednesday following a lousy Fox News interview between anchor (and notorious tool) Jesse Watters and one of the subreddit's moderators, Doreen Ford. Watters and other Fox News hosts have argued that the subreddit is helping to fuel the Great Resignation, in which millions of workers nationwide have left their jobs. The interview was not a great look for the burgeoning online movement."

On the day it aired, some 3.6 million viewers watched this "notorious tool" interview Doreen. Millions more saw it on YouTube. Even the anti-workers themselves were appalled: "That interview was so embarrassing," one r/antiwork user wrote, "it made me go back to work." The forum temporarily shut down. The community itself descended into internal bickering and finger-pointing: "Longtime users expressed frustration and rage at the interview," the Guardian wrote. "Ford, who at one point during the segment referred to laziness as a 'virtue,' had set the movement back, they believed, by being made to look like the worst stereotype of r/antiwork." Ford was promptly relieved of her duties as a moderator.

The *New York Post* described the disaster this way. "These are tough days for the 'antiwork' crowd. Along with bedsores, sagging muscle tone, Cheetos stains on clothing, and a profound sense of unjustified entitlement, another occupational hazard for the occupationless has just emerged: Contact with the outside world. As a result of three minutes on Fox News Channel, the I-refuse-to-be-useful crowd have just seen their movement knocked off its axis by a nuclear level of ridicule."

The anti-work crowd savaged their leader Doreen: "Doreen, honey, you need to change your appearance. This is coming from someone who looked just like you. You cannot have a messy room, poorly lit conditions, messy hair and expect people to take you seriously." Another wrote, "At this point, the face of r/antiwork is a lazy, unprepared, unappreciative dog walker." My personal favorite: "If only the CIA was as competent at tearing down 'leftist movements' as infighting leftists are."

One of the criticisms that anti-workers made of the interview was that Doreen was not a good representative of their movement. ("The interview mostly focused on Ford instead of the movement as a whole, and it makes the movement look like, well, a joke," Mashable acknowledged.) So, I figured I'd give them another shot. And that's how I ended up talking to Brittany (not her real name).

Brittany is married with children. A buxom blonde, high ponytail, friendly face, brimming with flip, experienced suburban mom confidence, well earned through years of juggling work with logistical family management: meals, homework, pets, practice, laundry, driving, dishes, bills, spills. She survived ten years in human resources and now serves as the president of the Parent-Teacher Association and volunteers at her kids' school.

"Anti-work for me is . . . work when you need to . . . so, you get to decide what works around your schedule, and not having other people tell you what you can and can't do."

Brittany wants a world without bosses. "People don't quit the company. They quit their bosses." Brittany speaks with authority. "The real meaning of life, in general, is to be happy. Life, liberty, and the pursuit of happiness." (Brittany has a tattoo that says "Pursuit of Happiness." I didn't ask where.)

If my résumé was the same as Brittany's, I'd be anti-work too. "My first taxable job was Burger King over by the old airport." That one. "It is actually flame-broiled," confides Brittany. "It was minimum wage, seven twenty-five an hour. I had that job. I went to school. And I was in color guard. I was trying to save up money because we went to the Fiesta Bowl in Arizona.

"Someone working at Burger King or someone working at any of these other places, no one's going to remember those people when they're gone. But yet we're killing them by stressing them out. Depression is at an all-time high. Anxiety is at an all-time high. Suicide's at an all-time high. And most people are stressed-out because of their work life. And if they quit their job and what is killing them, then they have no money to live by, because this is the only option we get. Do you understand the amount of stress that people are getting put under? It's killing them, literally. And they're still people. When you die, the money doesn't go with you. You know what I mean?"

Totally, Brittany. The estate tax is downright evil.

After fast food, Brittany moved up into the hospitality business. "I used to work at a hotel where I worked night audit, and a gentleman came in with a gunshot wound. Been at a hotel where somebody committed suicide. Yeah. Hotel industry is not for the faint of heart."

Where was the gunshot wound? I wonder.

"It was in his stomach. And he didn't speak any English, so it was really hard. I was asking him, call 911, stuff like that. He was telling me no. I did it anyway because that's not something I want on my conscience."

"What about the suicide? How'd he do it?"

"Drowned himself in the tub," Brittany says nonchalantly.

"You saw that?"

"Yep."

"Was your boss unconcerned?"

"Well, of course he was concerned. The water was dripping through the walls and stuff down three floors of hotel."

Forget the dead man, there's water damage! Not a great manager, to my untrained eye.

The suicides and gunshot wounds didn't make Brittany quit. Her boss did. "I got the H1N1 flu. And the exact response to me was to 'come into work, or I'm fired.' And I was like, 'I guess I quit then because I can't drive.'"

Brittany's stint in HR for a decade left a bad taste in her mouth. "Even in HR, I've had employees say inappropriate things to the HR person. Things that they shouldn't have said to me. And I'm like, 'Dude, do you know who you're talking to? This is a terrible idea. Do you want to work here?'"

"What do they say to you?" I ask.

"Things about my butt and stuff like that."

I ask her how she handles the butt stuff. She tells me the first strike's a warning. Second strike's trouble. (Forgiving but firm. I respect that.)

"I got summoned for jury duty . . . actually a murder. It was really cool."

I'm so jealous.

"It was a mistrial, or whatever because one of the jurors started blabbing about the case, saying that they didn't know about it when they did, so we all got mistrialed. That was a second mistrial on that one."

Whoops.

"But the entire time [my boss] is like, 'You need to get out of it. You should get out of it.' And trying to make me feel guilty for doing what is court-obligated for me to do."

Brittany bemoans the "important" things she's missed because of work. "Important things like my daughter graduating kindergarten, you know what I mean?"

I didn't even know there were ceremonies for kindergarten graduation.

"The amount of times that we go and we miss all of these things, for what? The companies don't care about the people anymore. They care about their bottom dollar, the bottom line."

I'm tempted to tell her that companies are people too. The Supreme Court said so. But why antagonize her? She's on a roll.

"People need to talk to human resources as much at ten p.m. as they do at nine a.m. in the morning. Why can't I work different hours for this amount? As long as the communication is there to say, 'Hey, I got some stuff going on. This is when I'm going to be in. We can schedule around that.' Or I can take a call while I'm at a doctor's appointment. That's not a big deal. But it's not like that. They want you there all the time, chained to a desk. You can't get away. And then their answer to this stuff is, 'Let's have a pizza party to show how grateful we are for you.' It's like, 'Ooh, pizza. Yay. Make us flabby, so we end up getting some kind of illness, and then we're out longer.'"

Brittany should know better. There's no alternative to office pizza parties. Managers can't order fast food because that's disgusting. Less disgusting options (but still borderline) like Mexican and Italian require one worker to go around with a menu (or via email) asking people what they want. That's time-consuming and embarrassing. Plus, most women won't announce they'd like chicken parm with garlic knots for lunch. But if you just order pizza, the guys will eat a few slices (toppings boost morale) and the ladies will have "one slice." A few ladies won't eat any pizza and silently judge everyone. That's fine. We're silently judging you too, babe. Also, no utensils are needed; you take the slice from the same circle (go team!) and sit around (or stand!) watching each other all eat the same thing with their hands. No fight over who ordered the chicken tikka masala and didn't eat it. Isn't this fun!? But the crucial benefit to the office pizza party is no cleanup. Empty boxes, goodbye, no mess. What does Brittany want to order for the office? Sushi! Good luck.

Brittany's husband was a managing business partner at a Firestone "for ten-plus years, and he was killing it." As a part of his job, the family "went to the Bahamas and Hawaii for free." They had "over a hundred thousand dollar a year income between me and my husband," and they currently live in the house that her husband grew up in—"Financially it does help to have something that doesn't cost an arm and a leg every month," Brittany cedes. But Brittany wasn't happy. Her husband "was gone seventy-six hours a week," she says. "He did not raise the first part of my kids' lives because he was always at work. That's the sacrifice he had to make so we could live in a certain way. And to me, my kids would rather see him and have their dad there than to not have him there. So, what good are you as a parent if you're not a parent?"

When Brittany quit her job, her husband stopped working too. "When I said my husband didn't work, people look at him like he does nothing. And they're like, 'Well, what does he do all day?' I'm like, 'Well, he runs the kids around. He helps out friends. He volunteers for the community.'"

Brittany's husband went back to work. "He does automotive and sales right now." Brittany only requires one thing: "He has to love me unconditionally."

Those are the vows, I guess.

"Yes, is it cool getting out of a nice car when you're out on a date with your husband? Yeah, that's cool. That's fun. But we got to start assessing why we're doing those things, because most people that have all of this stuff, they're stressed-out because of what it took to get it. Or they're genuinely actually unhappy, and they think these things are going to fill that void."

Brittany admits she "loves Apple stuff." "I'm talking to you on a MacBook. I have an Apple Watch, I have an Apple phone, I have an iPad, things of that nature." She's not "filling a void" like other people, though. Brittany declares she "doesn't need it." Although, she confesses, she likes to shop. "That is one of my favorite things to do. But if I can't do it, then I can't do it. Most of America, one in four people I think it is, are hoarders." Those people are buying happiness. Brittany would give up her goodies "in a heartbeat" if she had to, she says proudly.

"The weight of a man is heavy," Brittany preaches, "and it often goes ignored."

Finally, a woman sees it.

"All of this pressure and stuff on you guys, the number one killer of men is heart failure from something called the widowmaker. And that's due to stress. And if you ask the women, they want you, not your money."

Brittany has obviously never lived in Manhattan. "And if they want your money, you're in the wrong relationship." Preach, girl.

"I would rather live without electricity than not have my husband," announces Brittany.

I wonder if her husband feels the same way.

Let's put Brittany's anti-work agenda to the test. How would it work in the real world?

"Okay, Brit, what do we think about a four-day workweek?"

She's all in. "Nobody ever really gets too much done on Fridays anyway."

Brittany believes everyone should be paid by the hour. "Somebody literally put people on salary to take advantage of them. You know what I mean? So I would say everyone is hourly."

So Brittany is talking about a four-day workweek, remote work optional, and hourly wages. Remember, she's a former HR manager, so this is her bread and butter.

"What are we thinking about in terms of holidays?" I ask.

"I don't see any reason why anybody needs to be working on holidays anymore. The banks don't work during holidays; the federal government doesn't work during holidays. Why are the common people working during holidays? Gas stations, you could do prepaid at the pump."

Problem solved.

I drill down on paid vacations. "So we're doing Christmas, July Fourth, we're doing Thanksgiving, we're doing Easter, we're doing Memorial Day, we're doing Labor Day, we're doing Martin Luther King Day, and we're doing Presidents' Day and January First."

"If the holiday applies to you, take it off," she exclaims.

"Kwanza?"

"If it applies to you, take it off."

"What about Festivus?"

"If it applies to you, take it off."

"Jewish holidays? Ramadan?"

"Applies to you, take it off."

"Do you see that this would be ripe for abuse?"

Brittany doesn't hesitate. "That's discrimination, so they're going to do it anyway."

Brittany supports four weeks of paid vacation, and she's addressed the holiday situation, but what about personal days?

"This whole personal days, sick days, mental health days, vacation days, it all needs to be lumped into one. So maybe I would say six to eight weeks total, thereabouts. If you need to take a day off, you need to take a day off. I shouldn't have to go through the wringer to tell you what's wrong with me. I just need a day. Leave me alone."

I explain that other countries have gone down the anti-work road before, and it didn't end well. "Greece has declared bankruptcy like three times in the past," I tell her.

"Who?"

"Greece, Brittany. The country."

"Oh wow."

Not registering.

Now that we've established a four-day remote-optional workweek with up to eight weeks of paid time off ("leave-me-alone days"), where do we stand on maternity leave?

"Well, definitely women should have the right to take up to a year. Speaking from personal experience, postpartum, and the depression, and the hormones, the stuff that goes with that, sometimes it is a better idea for them to be home, because they can't help anyone if they're pouring from an empty cup."

I hear that. "What about paternity?"

"Paternity, I feel like honestly they need to have the same amount of time as a woman."

"Brittany," I ask, "if I get my wife pregnant and then she has the baby, we're both off from work for a year?"

"It's up to you, why not?"

I'd have a dozen kids if Brittany were in charge.

Brittany's anti-work mentality is rooted in personal family misfortune. "If you're depressed, you put on your big-girl panties or whatever, and you just suck it up and deal with it, and you work through it. Is that effective? I don't think so. It didn't work for my brother."

Brittany lost her brother in 2020 from a drug overdose. "Heroin was his drug of choice, but heroin apparently got too expensive during that time, and he turned to methamphetamines that were laced with fentanyl. When he died, he had meth, fentanyl, cocaine, marijuana, and some other kind of meth in his system."

Drugs are a problem for her other brother too. He "has two kids, got a divorce, and it's been, for a lack of better words, a shit show with that." She just found out her "shit show" brother has "a third child." Her family is "a *Jerry Springer Show*." Her sister doesn't work. She has four kids, one adopted, with a husband who got injured in the military and now doesn't work either.

"So them watching my dad work so much and almost die a couple of times from it, it's almost like they had an aversion to it too. They were like, 'I don't want to do that, I'm going to die from it.' Long story short, they got into some other stuff that they shouldn't have been in, and that's what's going to take him out, but not my sister. She doesn't do anything bad.

"Dad broke his back when I was two," Brittany remembers. "They told him he wouldn't walk out the hospital, but he wanted a cigarette so bad that he walked out of the hospital to have one, so I guess that was a good thing about smoking . . . but my dad has never not had a job. I was raised in a conservative household. Man goes out, provides."

Her dad has had "three heart attacks, two strokes, three stents put in his heart, one put in his leg, and they're all saying it's because he's so stressed-out from working." Brittany recalls at ten years old her dad "crawling out of his bedroom because he was having a heart attack and I didn't know what was going on. I remember getting dropped off at school, and me and my dad never argue, ever. And we argued that day, right after that he had a stroke. Found out there was issues going on." Her dad "missed everything" she did growing up because he was working all the time. "I did color guard. He missed all the performances."

Her dad was a courier. "He would pick up bank stuff back in the day when it wasn't electronic anymore. And I would go with him just to spend time with my dad. I wasn't supposed to, but that was the only time I got to see him. I remember getting woken up at three o'clock in the morning because he needed me to help him bleed the brakes out, and I was the only one that knew how to do it in the house, and I had school the next day."

"You were pretty lonely growing up," I observed. "You didn't have the father in your life that you desired."

"Mm-hmm."

"Is that what you're trying to re-create now with your current marriage? And with your current family? Kind of doing what your parents didn't do?"

"I would say in modesty, I guess."

Work almost killed her father. And not having him around killed Brittany. As she sees it, she has one brother in the grave, another with one foot in, and they were victims of her father's work life. Brittany's anti-work ideology is a reaction to this. The anti-work agenda doesn't make sense, but when seen through her past, it does.

"I was raised by my mother to try to go find somebody that had money. Not to find someone that was going to make me happy. The basic needs of a human are shelter, food, love, and safety. That's it. That's all we actually need. Everything else is just extra, but that extra comes at a price.

"So my mother did not work. She doesn't even have a driver's license. It's so old-school."

Sometimes I wish *my* wife didn't have a driver's license. For insurance purposes. Call me old-school too.

"My dad had to declare bankruptcy," explains Brittany. "My mom liked to spend too much money. I love my mom dearly, but she does like to go shopping, and he has no ability to tell her no. And he definitely didn't have any ability to tell me no when I was young."

If men would just say "no" more often, America would be in better shape. "No" you can't swim against women, Mr. Thomas. "No" you can't pitch a tent on our sidewalk. "No" you can't erase the nation's history because you're ignorant and bored. Deep down, people want to hear "no." They need to hear "no." We all remember what happened to the children of parents who never said "no."

The reason Brittany's dad couldn't say no? He was one of eight. His parents experienced "financial struggles most of their life." Brittany says her father was "deprived" growing up because his Catholic parents "tried to live within their means," so it was hard for him not to spend money the minute he had some. It's always fun to blame poor financial planning on your parents.

Brittany says her dad buys things because he thinks "somebody else is going to think it's cool." Like cars. "Could he afford that car? Probably not. I mean, he still makes bad financial decisions.

"He was talking about the other day putting a reverse mortgage on his house, and I was like, 'That house is paid off, don't you flipping dare.'"

Are there reverse mortgage ads running on Fox News? No reason to check.

"It also doesn't help that my mom inherited a hundred thousand dollars, and my dad won seventy-seven thousand dollars on a scratch-off ticket, and it was gone in three months. Yeah."

"My mom's purse collection kills me. I'm a little jealous," admits Brittany.

Her "husband's parents got a divorce over money." *The Jerry Springer Show* extends to her in-laws. "My mother-in-law's . . . ex-husband got into fraud," and "had loan sharks coming after him and stuff like that. He passed away from a suicide. He actually rammed his truck into the back of a semi on purpose . . . because he was about to go back to prison." Now, "my mother-in-law, she is hyperfocused on money, and she worries about it constantly. A lack of money is now a trigger for her because of the experiences that she went through with my husband's dad."

Loan sharks killing your husband has a way of hyperfocusing the mind.

Brittany insists she's content despite the chaos and pain surrounding her. "I have never been more happy in my entire life," she tells me. "Until recently, I didn't know what happiness was. And now I truly do.

"I feel like everybody has the right to make their own choices." But those cases, she maintains—the people who actually like their jobs—are "the minority, not the masses. The masses are the ones that are having the problem."

Has Brittany considered how millions of people not working, you know, is supposed to work?

"Things might get more expensive if we eliminate all of these productive hours," I explain gently. "Do you see a need for the government to step in and provide more services?"

"Things are getting expensive already because of people's greed," she says assertively. "It's not because the government is providing more for the people or less for the people. Things are expensive because the CEO wants a twenty-million-dollar home."

Right or wrong, Brittany starts sounding like Bernie.

Railing against "gluttony," Brittany explains that "people just generally want all of the things that we don't need." "In caveman days, we could survive with no electricity and no water, with a giant monster behind us."

I think she means woolly mammoths.

"And we didn't have half of the stuff that we have. Yeah, we had a shorter life expectancy because we couldn't test the water and stuff like that. But at the same time, everything humans touch turns to poo because of all the industrial standards and stuff like that, making the stuff that we don't need."

Shorter life expectancy? Whatever. Poo.

Brittany's getting into a good lather about consumerism. The consumer in me moves me to speak up.

"Well," I say, "what if you really want a guitar and no one's making guitars?"

"You can make your own. It's not that hard. I've seen somebody do it with a cigar box before."

You could make a guitar out of a cigar box, but would Jimi play it at Woodstock?

"A squirrel buries their nuts in the ground, and everything is fine. We can't do that. We have to have a refrigerator that has Freon in it."

Honey, the Langtons are coming over for dinner! Where's that beef Wellington we buried in the yard last fall?

"So you're saying that the more humans are evolving, I guess, technologically, the worse things are getting?"

"Yeah," Brittany says. "We're just trading one illness, like drinking bad water, for mental health now."

"Well, the water's cleaner right now."

"There's bleach in the water."

"But people aren't dying from drinking filthy water in the United States," I tell her.

"Not that you can prove. I'm not a conspiracy theorist, but if there's bleach in the water, we've all seen the reports and stuff about the Tide Pods and the kids drinking bleach."

Brittany's "logic" is hard to follow. But I adore her.

"Okay, what about air-conditioning?"

"Air-conditioning. Here's the thing: we are doing stuff to make us comfortable because we think humans are not like animals. Did it occur to you that we might supposed to be able to migrate? We historically are fighting nature, and we are supposed to migrate from one place to another."

You mean summering in the Hamptons and wintering in Palm Beach?

"Every other animal flipping migrates for the most part, or they adapt to their surroundings. But we're adapting to our surroundings by building machines that are killing the planet. I don't know. Eventually, one day, we'll all learn because we'll either be here or we won't."

Brittany introduces the concept of "community-based lifestyles." She calls that "awesome."

"Like a log cabin situation?" I wonder.

"That might be the life for me. I know a lot of people can't do that. Like the little tiny homes."

Problem is you can't take a nice fat reverse mortgage out on a tiny home.

I explain how, throughout human history, we've aspired for "better," "bigger," or "more convenient." This drives innovation and growth, new breakthroughs and achievements, allowing more specialization.

"Well, that natural inclination is also being taken too far. That natural inclination could be the same as a man going out and trying to impregnate as many things as he can because the whole point is for life to continue. You know what I mean? But you guys fight that constantly, that urge to procreate."

Not Nick Cannon.

Now I understand Brittany. Brittany wants to dial back the work, the greed, the need for speed because it's pushing us to the brink, killing us. She wants to strike a better work-life balance. Stop fixating on material things, protect the planet, and spend more time with our families.

"Yeah, hopefully," says Brittany. "That would be great."

It sure would.

The pain and distress that people struggling with money experience is all too real—as Brittany herself has experienced. But whether or not it's because of the existence of work is a different question. One of the appeals of utopian ideologies like the anti-work movement is that they offer an easy culprit to point to as the source of human suffering. But their real beef is with human nature itself—with the imperfect world we all live in. That's what makes the anti-work movement utopian. Every society has work of some sort or another. It's difficult—and painful—to admit that the kind of struggles that Brittany's loved ones have suffered through are a permanent feature of the human condition.

People like Brittany have been sold a neatly boxed political vision that views society as a sort of math problem to be fixed, as if removing this or that variable could end the kind of suffering her loved ones have gone through. Throughout our conversation, she regularly references documentaries that she's seen as evidence for her politics: "I've watched a ton of documentaries," she tells me. "I don't think there's a documentary on Netflix I haven't watched or Amazon Prime. That's what it's about is just all of this luxury stuff and people not understanding the real meaning of—well, I guess my meaning . . . all the meanings are real meanings to someone."

She sounds more like a legit philosopher than any of the people I've interviewed claiming to be philosophers.

The meaning of life for Brittany is happiness. She claims she's happy now and has the tattoo to prove it. Brittany's "Pursuit of Happiness" tattoo fails to recognize one thing, though: happiness—real happiness—takes work.

5

The Vegan Instagrammers

Alondra is well-endowed. I only say this because she knows it—and wants you to know it. At first glance, her Instagram page is filled with shots of her chest: bikinis, crop tops, tight shirts with plunging necklines. But Alondra's grabbing your attention for a reason. "Come for the curves, stay for the words." And those words are "meat is murder."

Alondra, in one video, looks like a *Playboy* bunny. Then she tells you not to eat lamb on Easter.

In a belly shirt, Alondra holds a wild turkey in one hand and a sign in the other that reads: SENTIENT BEING NOT YOUR HOLIDAY DINNER #GOVEGAN.

Showing considerable skin, a picture of Alondra at a protest holding a sign saying: SKIN SHOULD NOT BE REMOVED, and another sign starring a rabbit: #FURKILLS.

Alondra shares her page with her boyfriend, Eric. But you don't see much of Eric. All you see is Alondra. Eric takes a back seat. And that's the point. It's about getting eyeballs.

I lay my eyes on Alondra and Eric, and they make an odd couple. Alondra is tall and voluptuous, with black hair and fierce eyes. She doesn't smile. Looks like a full-figured Chechen assassin. Then there's

Eric. Skinny, goatee, earring, shaved head with a backward baseball cap. Might lose to Alondra in a fight. He's cool. They're both cool in that low-key California way. But they aren't cool with carnivores.

They're "activists," Alondra says. "We just speak up for animals and educate people about what's going on." "Yeah," Eric pipes up. "Animal rights activist or vegan activist, just promoting veganism."

Eric's epiphany went like this: "For about a year or two before going vegan, I had this meandering idea about how what I do doesn't make sense. Because I had a dog at the time, and I had ideas like, 'Oh, it would be cool to adopt a pig.' And in my mind, I was thinking, 'How would I care for a pig while slaughtering and eating them?' And it didn't make any sense. And then I started thinking about my dog as well. I tried to make sense of it all like, 'Oh, I'll eat this one, but not that.' This is my friend."

One man's friend is another man's brunch.

"But Alondra came up with the idea for us to go vegan . . . so I went along with her. I thought it would be more morally consistent."

Alondra's conversion began, like all great crusades do, with a video on the internet: "We have a dog, and we've had him for a couple years," Alondra tells me. "One time I was on social media, there was a video showing what happens in the dairy industry. I saw it, but I couldn't finish it because it was horrible." A few weeks later, "My mother, she was going to bring me some food from a restaurant—flesh, animal flesh. And for some reason, at the time, the video that I saw—since it was the dairy industry, cows—I thought of the cows and I was like, 'Wait, what am I doing?' Because then I looked at my dog, and I was like, 'What's the difference between my dog and this cow that I'm going to consume?' And yeah, that's just when it clicked."

The difference is cows don't fetch. If it fetches, don't eat it.

"Alondra, what was the [dairy industry] video depicting?"

"It was a video showing dairy in reverse. It was showing a glass of milk and then how it's made. Do you know how dairy's made? I don't know if you know."

I don't know if I know either. "Well, I probably don't know the details as well as you do, but I think milk comes from cows."

"Yeah, it comes from cows," she says.

Nailed it. Except the quiz wasn't finished.

"But do you know why cows have milk come out of their bodies?"

I took a shot in the dark. "Is it the same reason that women have milk that comes out of their bodies?"

"Yeah," she says, "because they reproduce."

I'm on a roll.

"Yeah, basically what the video was showing was the reverse of the process, which is where they get the cows pregnant in order for them to reproduce so that milk can come out of their body, and then their babies get taken away, and they get killed because they don't want the babies to be drinking the milk that they're going to sell. Plus, selling the babies can bring in profit as well, and that's what businesses care about, profit."

Veal Milanese at a nice Italian restaurant can go for $29–$45. But a proper veal chop can run you higher than $45. Maybe just drizzle some olive oil, minced garlic, salt and pepper, a little rosemary or sage. Brown both sides. Nice and simple.

"How do they impregnate the cows?" I ask her.

"A farmer, typically what he does is he inserts his arm into the cow's anus who holds her reproductive system in place through there. And then he shoves a rod into her vagina, and the rod has semen that came from a bull, and that's how he gets the cow pregnant."

"He reaches his arm in and holds the female cow's what exactly?" I wonder.

"I'm not fully sure what the actual term for that part would be because I'm not a veterinarian or a doctor," Alondra says.

I can get a hell of a good look at a T-bone steak by sticking my head up a bull's ass, but I'd rather take the butcher's word for it—*Tommy Boy*.

Artificial insemination doesn't sound very romantic to me. I bet veal would taste better born from a bull and cow in love. Or even from a one-night stand.

"So they never let the bulls mate the cows naturally," I ask. "It's all artificial insemination?"

"That's not standard practice to do that with the bull," Alondra tells me. "Maybe some farms do that."

Farmers dim the barn lights, put on some Marvin Gaye.

"But I mean even if they do do that, it's completely unnecessary to continue the cycle of abuse and keep bringing baby cows into the world to send them to slaughter and all to exploit the mothers and then send them to slaughter as well. We could just drink something else, there's so many alternatives."

"What about organic milk? Is that any better?"

"No. If it comes from a sentient being, no."

Webster's Dictionary defines a sentient being as something "who perceives and responds to sensations of whatever kind—sight, hearing, touch, taste, or smell." Alondra and Eric have a different definition: something that "avoids harm." That's their moral distinction. Anything that "avoids harm" is off-limits for human consumption (or use). Fish, for example, "are sentient beings too," Alondra tells me. "They avoid harm. We could just easily not consume them. There's plants and alternatives." Veganism, she says, is about "causing the least harm possible."

I bet they harm mosquitos. Pretty much nobody just sits there and lets a mosquito feed on them.

I ask them about SeaWorld. They aren't fans. Dolphins performed tricks for me when I went to SeaWorld. Maybe I'm clueless, but it seemed like the dolphins were having fun. Who doesn't like jumping and splashing and balancing things on their nose? I bet the dolphins recognized me in the audience. Probably an honor for them to perform for me. They gave it a little extra that day, I could tell. I ask Alondra and Eric if they knew that dolphins are the only other animal besides humans that get high and have sex for pleasure. Fun fact. Yeah, dolphins get high. These young male dolphins—of course it's the young males who are the stupidest—will surround puffer fish that secrete DMT, which is that crazy psychedelic, when they're scared. And they'll surround them and poke them to make them scared and they'll secrete DMT and all of these young male dolphins will get really stoned. It's really funny. So, I'm against eating dolphins. That's *my* principle. I don't eat things that get high or have sex for pleasure. Or fetch.

I ask whether the Eskimos are allowed to eat salmon.

Alondra ponders the question. "Well, if someone has the ability to change, that's great, but . . ."

Eric steps in. "Yeah, we just all need to focus on where we're at, not where the Eskimos are at."

Vegan activism is more of a First World concern.

The vegans (veganites?) aren't fans of zoos either. "Yeah, we don't think that animals should be put into prisons that are completely not what they would be in in the wild." Zoos claim they're for conservation, but they're really about cash, Alondra says. Eric says zoos send the wrong signal to kids. "I see it as counterproductive because they're showing children that we should use animals for entertainment, and that will just lead to more problems with wildlife and sentient beings in general."

"Yeah," says Alondra. "Humans can learn about animals in so many ways. There are books, there's documentaries, so we don't need to go to a prison basically and just look at them be bored."

I'm not sure if Alondra's ever been to the Bronx Zoo, but when I went, those animals didn't look bored. They have a better quality of life than their wild cousins, who have to deal with poachers, predators, and diseases. When I watch nature documentaries, animals in the wild act the same way zoo animals do. It's like reality TV. I'm sure the Real Housewives of New Jersey act like that when nobody's watching.

Alondra disagrees. She and I aren't seeing eye to eye on a lot today. "That's why a lot of them constantly go around in circles, or they display behavior where their mental health is basically affected."

"Yeah," I said. "I lived in a small apartment once, and I felt like I was a zoo animal."

I get a laugh out of Eric. Nothing out of Alondra.

"This morning, I read my young son *Curious George*, the guy with the yellow hat. Is that book not a good book to read to children, *Curious George*?"

"I don't remember the full story," Alondra says. "But I know that he's a monkey, right? I don't know."

"Yeah, that's all I remember," says Eric. "That he's a monkey."

I explain. "He bought him in Africa, the pet monkey. He brings him all the way here. And then George is so curious, he keeps getting into trouble, but he always ends up getting rescued, and he's a very lovable monkey. Is that kind of a bad message to send to my son?"

"I don't know," Alondra says.

Eric thinks long and hard. "The origin of George may be questionable, but once you're caring for a monkey, you're caring for them."

Alondra still isn't sure. "I don't know, it's a fairy-tale book. It's not a—"

Eric interrupts, "Yeah, it's kind of like a fun fictional book."

"Yeah, it's not . . . Yeah." Alondra seems confused.

"Well," I add, "Michael Jackson had a pet monkey."

"Who?" asks Alondra.

"Michael Jackson."

"Jackson. Oh, okay. Yeah." Come on, Alondra. The King of Pop. "We don't really support having wildlife in your home because it could just be in the wild. We don't support paying for them to make wildlife have babies to raise them in captivity. We think that's cruel."

"So when Ronald Reagan, he was an actor before he became president, he used to have a monkey that he costarred in major films with. You don't like monkeys in Hollywood?"

"No," Alondra says. "We don't like animals in film when they're forced to perform for humans. Because it's basically like the circus, when they make them do tricks for humans. There's a lot that goes on behind the scenes to get them to perform, and it's completely unnecessary."

Alondra, wait until I tell you what goes on behind the scenes in Hollywood to get *humans* to perform.

"And also nowadays, due to technology advancing, there's CGI and there's so many things that we could do where we don't have to have these animals that are behind the scenes tortured in order to get them to perform for humans."

So Alondra wants to put animal actors out of work. She has a lot to learn about politics.

"Do you guys ride horses?"

"No, we don't. We don't ride horses, no." Alondra speaks for Eric most of the time.

"What about for transportation? Isn't that better for the environment than getting into a Ford Bronco?"

"Yeah, we're not in the eighteen hundreds," reveals Alondra, "so we don't want to cling on to dated narratives that could harm others. It sends a message that they're here for us to exploit."

"Yeah," says Eric. He does a lot of agreeing.

I'd love to be "exploited" like a horse. Like a premier racehorse. They treat racehorses better than most humans. Constant grooming and pampering. A dietitian. A personal trainer. Millions of dollars invested in elite horses. Those horses look happy. They get to be outside all day. The jockeys are pretty light. A few laps. Then a massage. Some amphetamines before a big race. Get some TV time after you win the Derby. Don't forget about the stud fees. That's when the real fun begins. I'm not saying I'd eat a horse. I don't eat animals I bet on.

Alondra strongly disagrees. "I don't think enslaving and conditioning into performing for the benefit of someone else is treating better. I think that's slavery basically."

"I've seen [horses] break legs on the track or just get injured on the track, and they bring this green tarp over, and they kill them right there," Eric says. "Olympic athletes would never face that treatment."

The Russians would if they could.

"I got one for you," I tell them. "What about the one that killed al-Baghdadi, you know, that ISIS terrorist? We sent that beautiful, I think it was a shepherd, into that tunnel?" (It was a Belgian Malinois.)

"Wait," says Eric. "We sent a horse to kill al-Baghdadi?"

"No, no. We sent the German shepherd."

"Oh, a dog. Okay."

"Conan, and he smoked him out of his hole. That Baghdadi was a bad dude. You don't think we should have these German shepherds embedded in some of these military units to help us track down terrorists?"

"Well," Alondra says, "I think that humans can progress. They can always progress and have advanced technology in different ways to help situations, like the one that you described. I don't think that it's completely necessary to have animals do things for us when, like I said, we could do it by having technology advanced and different methods. We could use our brain to come up with different things that we could do."

Conan got a medal for the al-Baghdadi raid. The K-9 was honored at a White House ceremony. Conan wagged his tail next to President Trump. Where I come from, that means a dog is happy. A president would look pretty stupid bestowing an award on a robot dog. What a waste of time. Alondra doesn't get it.

"What about these drug-sniffing dogs? What about these fire dogs that are embedded with these fire companies that save lives? What about these dogs up in the Arctic that have that little barrel of drink under their gullets, and then they race out, and they help you if you're stranded on a sled?"

Alondra and Eric just want "progress." Until then, dogs will chase down criminals who burglarize their homes, and Alondra and Eric will just have to be grateful.

Then things got personal.

I described my diet to them. Lots of lamb chops, strip steaks, pork chops. Eggs for breakfast. Eric said I "lacked empathy and respect."

"And justice," added Alondra.

I explained that I wasn't aware of what happened inside slaughter-houses (although I assume there's slaughtering). But then admitted that, even if I was aware, I'm not going vegan.

Eric was harsh. He said I was demonstrating "a mixture of apathy or possibly just wanting to be cruel."

"Wanting to be cruel?"

"Yeah," Eric said. "Not respecting your victims and not caring."

I didn't want to be cruel; I just wanted dinner. My dinner wasn't a victim. It's more of a gift from Mother Nature. Thank you, Mother Nature. This beef Wellington is succulent.

I offered an apology for my meaty diet.

Alondra refused to accept it. "Yeah. Well, it's not really about . . . saying sorry to us because we're not really the victims. We're not the ones that were tortured and got brutally murdered to end up on your plate. But yeah."

"Yeah, maybe like a lamb," said Eric.

"Yeah," said Alondra, "to the victims that you paid to be killed."

So if someone's eating chicken, "would that make you an accessory to murder?"

"Yes," Eric declared.

"If I went out and bought milk, would that make me an accessory to murder?"

"Well," said Alondra, "it would mean that you're paying for abuse and the murder of sentient beings knowingly. And also, like I said, there's alternatives. You could just buy the alternatives instead. And you wouldn't want what is happening to the victims to be done to you, right?"

"Right," I agreed. "I do not want to be artificially inseminated, and then milked."

If I'm going to be inseminated, I'd like to be wined and dined, get to know the inseminator first, find out if he's ambitious, strong, votes Republican, stuff like that. Being milked seems tedious. I've seen what women go through when they breastfeed and pump. Nipple soreness, fatigue, and infections: those are just a few of the undesirable side effects of being milked.

I asked whether I could be arrested for drinking a milk shake.

"Well, no," said Alondra. "We don't live in a society that is currently majority vegan, unfortunately. But that's why there's activists and a lot of people that are progressing and changing in that regard."

"Would you like to eventually see something like that? If people are going out and slaughtering animals and eating animals, would you like to see people face charges for that?"

Alondra says yes. "If we live in a world that meant the majority is vegan, they're against abuse and murder like that, then I guess that would be consistent."

Eric says certain laws are already on the books. "People right now are being charged for crimes involving dogs, and people don't really complain about those actions of punishing dog abusers and dog fighters. But yes, this would be something new in the society where someone would be charged for abusing a cow for dairy."

Police!! Put the milk down and step away from the vehicle!!

I think I understand this now. "All right, Alondra, you feel that animals are basically at the same level as human beings, correct?"

"How someone views others on a ranking level is pretty irrelevant . . . if your actions cause harm to them and cost them their lives." She gives me an example. "Most humans view their own family as superior to random humans that they see on the street. But that doesn't mean that because they value their family more, that they're going to randomly harm other humans or take their lives. That doesn't mean that. So regardless of your view on superiority or whatever, your ranking system with animals, I don't think your view on them and their rank justifies harming them and killing them."

"Yeah," says Eric. "We find it a little more complicated to rank species against each other in terms of any parameters. We just try to respect them, no matter what species they are, just try to show them respect."

I'm getting a little nervous. Under these rules, I get indicted for disrespecting a pig.

"You couldn't get Congress to ban eating meat unless there's sort of popular support for it, right?"

Eric admits, "We don't live in a dictatorship."

How about this, I ask. "Would you guys be in favor of a vegan dictatorship?"

"No," says Eric. "I think just in general, it comes with its own issues because it's just one individual." Eric worries that when the vegan dictator dies, and his son assumes power, he could be "a meat eater, so that wouldn't be great either."

Eric's right. A vegan dictator's reign would be short. The populace would be hangry. Assassination attempts galore. Plus, the deep state would never allow a vegan dictatorship. The meat and dairy lobby is too rich and powerful. If I ever became a lobbyist, I'd lobby for Big Meat. The perks would be delicious. And when you take a congressman out to dinner, my client *still* gets paid. The one rule I'd have would be this: If the congressman orders his steak well-done, we can't do business. It shows a lack of respect for the animal.

Alondra turns the tables on me. "So, Jesse, what's stopping you from going vegan?"

"I love to eat meat, and it's something I've always done," I tell her.

"So, do you think pleasure justifies abuse?" Alondra asks me.

I saw *Fifty Shades of Grey* once with my wife. I heard the book is better than the movie. But I'm not getting into my personal life with this woman.

"It's a really good question," I admit to her. "It's a really good question. I'll have to think about it for a little bit."

Extreme vegan protesters can be annoying. Especially when they're outside your restaurant. Alondra tells me about a demonstration outside a restaurant on the sidewalk "to spread awareness about what goes on."

"There was a situation where there was a farmer," says Alondra, "or so they claimed. They said they farmed pigs, and they were mad at our demonstration. They were upset, and they threw . . . Because they were eating at the restaurant, I guess, and they came out and threw a lemon at us. They were just really mad that we were there, and they were saying that they eat pigs and blah blah and . . . Yeah."

"Did the lemon hit you?"

"Yeah," she says. "I think so."

That lemon didn't avoid harm. You know what that means.

"Do you worry if the whole country goes vegan, you're putting lots of people out of business?" I ask.

"Well, there's always a way around it," says Alondra. "And as we progress, we could try to adapt to what's going on with the times, leave dated things behind. Just like with landlines, most people don't really use that anymore, like house phones. They mostly transitioned to cell phones. And other examples can be made. I just don't really have some right now. Yeah, there's always businesses that they could get into the vegan businesses and have companies that create alternatives and have restaurants that are vegan, so there's always a way around it."

"I get the landline thing," I tell Alondra, "AT&T's still in business. They're actually doing pretty well, even though people gave up their landlines."

"People can still be in the food industry," she says, "but it could be vegan. There's always a way to adapt with the time and progress."

Reality check time. "Some of this terrain is unfriendly to crop farming. It's more geared toward raising cattle or raising sheep or whatever you're doing. If you get rid of that, I don't think you can just plant corn in that soil. There is going to be a significant transition for millions of Americans who are in this business. Do you have any empathy for them or not?"

"All the animals that we bring into the world require crops as well," says Alondra, "so those crops already exist anyway."

"Yeah," says Eric. "Animal agriculture is insanely inefficient, so I believe that there are many extra jobs being filled right now that don't necessarily need to exist because there's already enough crops, like she said, to feed us, but we're just feeding it to animals instead."

Everyone gets to eat animal feed. Got it.

Despite the stereotypes of vegans as a left-wing movement, which are mostly accurate, there's a weird vegetarian and even vegan conservative subculture. Arthur Brooks, the devoutly Catholic former president of the conservative American Enterprise Institute, is a vegetarian. Ben Shapiro, of all people, has said friendly things about veganism before. There's even a "Vegan Conservatives" group in the United Kingdom, which describes itself as "the vegan and vegan-friendly caucus of the Conservative Party."

"I don't like that liberal stereotype because we don't fit into that," Eric tells me. "I know . . . there's a lot of conservative vegans, and I don't feel like they should be called liberal just because they're a vegan." "We don't really identify with liberal or conservative," Alondra adds. "We mostly just focus on what we feel makes the most sense, so that could be certain things from either side. But yeah. We don't like the whole identity politics thing that liberals do all the time, and other things."

As for Biden versus Trump, Eric says: "I didn't really like either side." ("Yeah," Alondra agrees.)

Eric maintains he had a "normal childhood." He grew up in the San Fernando Valley area of California and "remembers a lot of fun times with family."

"Is this your career?" I ask. "Or do you have a traditional job on the side?"

"I have a traditional job, and I am pursuing things on the side as well, as far as education and career goes."

Eric won't open up to me.

I try Alondra. "What do you do for a living?"

"I work . . . Yeah, I have a job. I'd just rather not say what my job is."

"It better not be for Burger King."

"No, it's not." Alondra and I aren't clicking.

"You guys shop at Whole Foods?"

Alondra says no. "We buy whole foods like rice, beans, all that. Lentils, pasta."

"Lentils are actually very filling," I add. "I love lentil soup."

"Yeah," says Alondra. "It's good."

We're really vibing now.

"Give me a week in your life. Give me some meals, what you guys like to eat."

"Oatmeal with peanut butter and cinnamon and fruit in the morning and then for lunch . . . I don't know, it varies. But we like pastas, or I don't know, tacos."

"Yeah," Eric says. "Lots of garbanzo beans."

"Yeah, chickpeas and tofu's good too, we like it."

"Yeah, tofu," says Eric.

I ask about Beyond Burgers, the plant-based beef. They aren't loving it.

"Do you ever drive by McDonald's and get a whiff and get hungry?"

Nope. McDonald's sells salads. They'll do that. No vegan Big Macs. Yet.

"Is it hard to be vegan?"

"No," Alondra says. "I personally don't think it is at all because what the animals go through is way harder. They are in cages suffering, and then they get their throat slit. I don't think that eating alternatives is harder than that."

Alondra is a barrel of laughs.

Eric's "an atheist," he says—"I was raised by a Catholic family. I can't even really remember, but they were religious, and I would go to church with them. But yeah, now I'm atheist." Alondra too: "Yeah, I'm not religious either. I was raised really religious. My family still is really religious, as well."

I tell them that hearing their personal stories helps me understand their goals better. "Well, I really don't typically share personal things with humans, for the most part—with humans that I don't really know," Alondra says. I don't know if that means she shares personal details with nonhumans, but if it does, I get the appeal—when you talk to a cow, the cow can't talk back. That's the difference between cows and humans. News at eleven.

I wonder what's behind Alondra's guard. What Eric sees, and I don't. I hit them with the M-word.

"Are you guys going to get married anytime soon?"

"Yeah," she says. "Maybe."

"Yeah," says Eric.

They glance at each other. Now it's weird.

"Uh-oh, all right," I say, sensing something. "How long have you guys been together?"

"Twelve years," reveals Alondra.

"Twelve years, Eric, and you haven't proposed?"

"Well, we'll keep that private," he says. "That topic, the marriage topic."

Thaaaaaaaat just about ends it. I thank them for their time. Tell them they talk the talk and walk the walk. I respect that. Alondra thanks me for listening and says, "It's been a pleasure." They want me locked up for animal murder. They call me cruel. But they politely thank me. I'm missing something. I'm not sure I understand veganism. And that's okay.

I'm more interested in Alondra and Eric's relationship. They're committed to animals, but they won't commit to humans . . . to each other.

6

The Drag Queen

When Tyler appears on my Zoom, I spot a decked-out Christmas tree in the background. It's not even Thanksgiving yet. "I couldn't wait," he tells me. "I'm just so excited."

Tyler's a drag queen.

"Did you erect that tree just for me?" I ask.

"Maybe," he says with a grin.

Tyler's flirting with me. But something even more controversial is afoot. Tyler announces he erected his Christmas tree in October. As a stickler for tradition, I've always held that trees don't go up until after Thanksgiving. Let Thanksgiving breathe. There's plenty of time to celebrate Christmas, all December, in fact. Don't rush the holidays. But the more I think about it, why do we coddle Thanksgiving? Awww, poor Thanksgiving, give it a chance. Enough coddling! Christmas is a powerful holiday. It can't help itself. When the Christmas spirit moves you, it moves you. If that happens to be before Thanksgiving, so be it. I'm not apologizing for Christmas anymore. Stop holding Christmas back! If Thanksgiving can't hold its own, it shouldn't get special treatment. Thanksgiving is great. Don't get me wrong, it's my second favorite holiday, but not only does Christmas also have football, it has family, presents, trees, festive red and green clothing, Santa, and its own music. Christmas even has villains! (The Grinch.) Plus, Jesus was born. To be honest, the other holidays aren't even in the same league. I bet Thanksgiving is a little embarrassed that we coddle it so much. No more treating Thanksgiving like the press treats Joe Biden.

"Ooh, my ensemble," Tyler coos in a faux-effeminate tone. "I made this little Christmas dress a few years ago, and I felt like it would be appropriate. I'll give you a little stand. I'm not wearing my pads or heels or anything 'cause I didn't think you'd see me from the waist down, but . . ."

Tyler stands and twirls for me. His hair is fully done up like a woman and he's wearing a thick sheet of makeup.

Tyler also has a beard, so—in terms of biological sex, at least— there's no real ambiguity about how the Good Lord made him.

"Tell me a little bit about the beard situation."

"Well," he explains, "I am a boy more often than I am a lady, and I felt like it was a way that I could stand out from my peers and also still be true to my quirky, authentic self. I do get a lot of questions about it, and I love making people ask questions a little bit."

Oh, I have a lot of questions.

"Is the beard decorated in a Christmas spirit for this, or do you always have that kind of glistening look?"

Tyler's beard is dusted with what looks like tinsel.

"Sometimes I've grown my facial hair out a little bit longer. I like to do a little bit of a twirly mustache sometimes. Sometimes it's colored to match my hair, but I think the gold goes with the blond pretty well and the jewelry, so naturally . . ."

Yes, naturally.

Tyler's a "performer" at heart. But that doesn't pay the bills, so he works as an inventory manager and visual merchandiser for a local furniture retailer. His colleagues know about his situation. Most of them have been to his drag shows.

"So really mixing business with pleasure," I say.

"Yeah, always. Otherwise, why would I be in the business if it's not bringing me pleasure?"

That's what I always say.

Tyler started working as a costume designer in his teens. He loves to sew and says, "This has become an outlet where I'm able to do that and to share it with my community."

"So, this is a professional situation. You're designing clothing?"

"Let's say, semipro. Yeah, I am a talented queen, and I know what I'm doing."

Tyler is gay (not transgender) and lives in Salt Lake City, Utah. I ask if there's a "Mormon contingent to this situation," and he says no but adds, "I recently was at an event and some sister missionaries were walking down the street and they're like, 'Oh my gosh, you look so fabulous. We need to take a picture with you.' I'm like, 'I've never taken a photo with missionaries before.'"

Tyler's never done anything involving missionary. Which confuses me. The whole gender thing. I'm not as smart as I look.

"Okay. So, you prefer romantic relationships with men, and you identify as a woman though when you're in drag? Explain the whole process here."

"I do prefer to use female pronouns when I'm dressed as a woman, when I'm presenting more female. I don't really have a problem with any use of them for myself. I definitely have words that I don't associate with. I don't ever really feel like a dude or a bro. But, yeah. I do identify as a man, and I'm a man in a dress and a wig."

When Tyler dresses in drag, he's "in costume," and "embracing a different part of my identity and letting myself feel different energies in my body."

I don't know what he's talking about, but I bet Gutfeld does.

"So, you were born a man."

"Mm-hmm," says Tyler.

"And you've known you've been gay for how long? Early on?"

"Yes. Very, very early on. I mean, I'm sure that my parents knew very early on. I have photos of me in hats and heels and swimsuits . . . like over the fugliest eighties sweatpants."

When your young son wears heels, you just know.

"So, when you're 'presenting' female, you're just kind of embracing and presenting the female side of your character or your identity?"

"Yeah."

"Are you saying I have a little bit of drag identity within me that I'm repressing?"

"There's a phrase. We're all born naked, and the rest is drag. Drag doesn't have to be just males presenting as females. It can be anything on the spectrum. I know you probably sit in hair and makeup for a bit before you go on TV, and in a lot of ways, you're presenting a certain persona."

I'm Watters, and this is my drag show.

"And, you are playing a role, and it is kind of . . . It's still a costume. It's still something that might not always be completely you all of the time, but it is still a part of you."

Do I spend more time in hair and makeup than a drag queen? I'm not doing the math on that.

Now that I'm talking to a real-life drag queen, I have some very important questions.

"Is *queer* a good word or a bad word?"

"I tend to use the word *queer* when I'm talking about the LGBT community because it's a little bit less of a mouthful, and I think for the most part it encompasses a lot of people. It's hard not to step on somebody's toes all the time, and I know there are people that would probably take offense to that, but as long as it's coming from a genuine place of love and respect, I don't think that they should really have that much of a real issue with that."

Did you hear that? I have permission to say "queer." This is great. I've gotten approval from a drag queen. I've wanted clearance for this word because I don't like saying the alphabet (LGBTQIA2S+). We have the alphabet to form words with. Saying the alphabet defeats the purpose of using the alphabet.

Now for the big one. I've never been able to wrap my head around this.

"Tyler, what's the difference between gender and sexuality? Explain it to me like I'm a child."

(You shouldn't talk to a child about sex.)

"I think that gender and gender expression is the way that you want to present yourself and how you feel the most comfortable displaying yourself, your hair, your clothes. I think sexuality is a lot more who you're attracted to, what you're attracted to, and the way that some of your parts exist and what you choose to do with them."

I need to talk this one out. "So, I'm a male, and I dress in a suit, and I have a short haircut, and whatever. But then there's who I'm attracted to, who physically turns me on, who I want to be romantically involved with. That's my sexuality."

"Yeah," says Tyler. "Your sexuality and your assigned-at-birth sex are very different. And that's very different from your gender identity."

"Wait, you just, now, see now you lost me."

This is the problem with this stuff. It's the terminology. When someone says, "your assigned-at-birth sex," my mind falls down an elevator shaft. It makes it sound random, like who you assigned as homeroom teacher. Same with "gender identity." What does that even mean? Tyler tries again.

"Sexuality being like who you're attracted to. Your sex being how you were assigned at birth. And your gender identity, how you feel and respond to your gender and the things that you were given and what you do with that."

I think he's referring to "my parts."

"Wait, you just differentiated between my sexuality and the sex that I was assigned at birth."

This is where they lose me.

Tyler gives it another shot. "Yeah. You're a male, and your sexuality, you're a straight male. Your gender identity, you're a cis male."

Here we go again. "Cis male?" When did this become a word? Cis? Seriously? What does this mean? Am I slow?

(Yes.)

"So you are on this one end of the spectrum. Me being a gay man, the gay portion is my sexuality. I was assigned male at birth. My gender identity is a little bit more fluid. I don't necessarily want to confine myself to one box, and I don't want to confine myself to the other. And drag is an area where I'm able to meet in the middle and express both the masculine and feminine energies. Does that make sense?"

"I think I'm getting there."

(I'm not.)

My research assistant is on the Zoom too. He steps in. "Well, I think I'm not necessarily the authority on it in this call, but the basic premise is that sex is your biological makeup, right? It's based on your genes, et cetera. Gender is a sort of much more complicated set of social constructs. It's how we as a society conceive of what makes people men and women, or anything."

"So sex and gender are different?" I ask. He seems unaware that any of his opinions on this might be trendy now and worth canceling him by the time the book comes out. Who can keep track?

"Yes."

"Got it. And then where does the attraction thing come in? When you get turned on, where do we put that?"

"That's sexuality."

The conversation feels like junior year trigonometry class. Nothing makes sense, but I'm squinting and nodding. An hour later, I forget everything I've been taught.

"Am I gender fluid, Tyler?"

Please say no.

"That's a question that you have to answer. Personally, probably not." (Phew.) "It would be fun to see you walking in some heels, but that wouldn't make you gender fluid in any way."

Tyler wants to dress me in heels. I see where this is going.

I ask Tyler about how the drag show business works.

"Mostly everything is managed through social media. We have troupes and drag families that are able to perform for different events around town."

"What's a drag family?"

My family can be a drag sometimes.

"Drag families would be kind of the people that you associate with the most and perform with the most. It's basically like your chosen family. They're people that you can come to for advice that have your back. If you need to borrow something or need a safety pin, they've got you."

I have never needed to borrow a safety pin.

What are Tyler's rates? Booking fees usually start around sixty dollars per number. He's in a "drag band." Lead vocalist. "We just recently finished our nineties show, and we're getting ready for our third Christmas show this year."

I wonder what their drag Christmas show is called . . . *Don We Now Our Gay Apparel? Tis the Season to Be Mary?*

"What kind of songs do you perform?"

"I honestly love to sing rock songs. I think that it's fun, it fits my voice really well, and I like that sort of badass energy a little bit."

I make a request. After warming up his pipes, Tyler belts out "Life in the Fast Lane." The man has chops.

"Do the Eagles know you cover them?"

"No," says Tyler.

In his drag persona, he performs at "a lot of brunches," the occasional nightclub, and even "concert halls" and "outdoor venues," he adds. Tyler sings, dances, and interacts with audience members.

I ask if he's performed in front of children.

"I have. Yes, in venues geared specifically for families. I have now done three family-friendly shows. They've all been very impactful for me and for audiences."

This is where the real controversy comes in. Drag shows for children suddenly seem to be everywhere in America. Tyler knows I have an issue with this.

Toddlers to teens have seen Tyler perform. He says the audience for a "family-friendly" drag show would be: 1) straight parents with a child "on the queer spectrum," or 2) children with a parent or parents "on the queer spectrum." Tyler insists this is appropriate. "I think that what we're doing is really healthy for our community, and it's a wonderful form of outreach for people that don't otherwise get to see themselves represented, especially not in person."

The deeper question, of course, is whether the kind of fluid identity—in which gender is "a spectrum," the distinctions between boys and girls are erased, and one can wake up one day and choose to be a different gender than they were the day before—that Tyler represents and evangelizes for is healthy for children to be exposed to.

For Tyler, drag performances are about inclusion and representation. "I can say for me personally, as a little queer boy, I would have loved to see myself represented on the stage as a child," he tells me. "I think it can be very isolating when you don't feel like there's anybody that can relate to you, when you are kind of alone in your feelings. So, I think that it's important to give exposure."

I understand what it's like to turn on the TV and rarely see anyone who is like you: I'm a conservative living in America.

But respect—even "representation"—is not the same thing as normalization. Lots of Americans are fans of niche activities: drag shows, death metal, rugby, comic books, art house films. Being a good person means being nice to someone who loves comic books, but you don't have to respect them more for liking them. It's definitely not discrimination to make a television series that never once has a character who loves rugby. There is no need to normalize death metal by having bands rock and wail at elementary school kids.

If lots of women think drag is gay men mocking straight women, we have to respect that too. If a majority of Americans think drag shows are not appropriate for children, why can't we add that to the long list of things we don't allow children to do?

Tyler's views on gender, while increasingly popular, are still outside of the norm. And that's fine for Tyler, I guess, as far as it goes. But glamorizing and normalizing dressing up as the opposite sex—transmitting this to children as a public performance worthy of positive attention and cash compensation—is the behavior most of us disagree with.

Tyler argues that "family-friendly" drag shows are therapeutic. "There are so many times when we're in these venues where people can come up to us with their children, and they say, 'We've never been able to experience something like this before. We don't have a place where we can take our queer children or where we as queer parents are able to take our straight children and show them this element of community that we've been able to create.'"

There's more going on at these drag shows than the performance. There's a queer community family therapy session taking place.

"I get to talk to teenagers that might have come together with their friends, not having any other place where they could really go and be themselves fully without feeling judged. . . . That's really fun to get to interact with them and to hear what kind of things that they have to say and how they're learning to express themselves and their feelings.

And I think it's a great way for families to be able to have an activity to do with their children, that they can learn more about their children through, and that open their children up to be able to ask questions to their parents, and to their peers, or mentors, or us. Every child has a right to ask a question."

I have a question for Tyler: "Do you think what you're doing at your shows with families, with young children, is sexual at all?"

He says no. "When we are putting these shows together, we have a very vigorous screening process. We know what music everybody's going to be performing. We have to send in pictures of our costumes. We have to make sure that the whole thing is appropriate. We need to know how to respect the boundaries of the families that are coming to our shows."

I tell him to describe this family-friendly, nonsexual performance.

Tyler says he performs the number "This Is Me." "I have a very big vaudeville-style gown, the big feathery thing around my shoulders and an updo with feathers, and I'm giving that message of that 'this is me, and I don't feel ashamed for it.' And, there's nothing sexual in that performance at all."

Tyler, a man, dresses as a woman, and performs a theater act in front of queer families.

All I've personally seen on the internet of "family-friendly" drag shows has been "wildly inappropriate footage," I tell him. "I have not seen tasteful drag shows to children at all on the internet." Half-naked cross-dressing men grinding and gyrating in the faces of children.

"Have you seen some of these performances, Tyler?"

"I have seen some of these videos, and some of them honestly were pretty shocking to me. I do know that that is not the most accurate representation of the community as a whole, and I do believe that some people have made mistakes, and they probably need to take a better look at what they're doing and who their audience is."

I'm glad Tyler at least agrees with me on this.

"I don't think some of the dancing or some of the outfits are age-appropriate," I tell him.

Tyler begins to deflect. "We just went to a Lizzo concert a couple weeks ago, and there were some children sitting right behind us, and the opener comes out, and she's singing all of these really, really vulgar songs and dancing very provocatively, shaking everything around. You know, all the parts are out. And, I look at just entertainment in general and the way that it does have the potential to sexualize children. It's not just drag. It's not any one specific thing, but it unfortunately happens in entertainment and the media."

I agree with Tyler about the entertainment industry in general. But Lizzo, a sexually explicit female hip-hop artist, doesn't advertise her concert as "family-friendly." The nasty drag shows we've seen footage of do. It looks like parents taking their kids to a strip club. Just because it's billed as "family-friendly" and the strippers are in drag, it's still like a strip club.

Tyler remains defensive. "So, would you feel uncomfortable watching children enjoy a halftime show with cheerleaders dancing around with their sort of scandalous costumes and miniskirts?"

The Dallas Cowboys Cheerleaders are a wholesome institution. How dare you, Tyler. Plus, you take your son to watch the Eagles beat the Cowboys. That's the main event, not the halftime show, which takes place on the field, not in your face. The cheerleaders aren't gender-bending either (although some bending occurs). After the halftime show, the cheerleaders don't swing by the stands and talk to children about their gender. The cheerleaders don't give families lap dances, but I'm sure those sick Cowboys fans would enjoy that.

I ask Tyler if he believes drag should wait until late teens, since these performances could influence a child's developing sexuality. Tyler tells me all the children he's performed in front of, queer or not, have come away with a positive experience. "They love the music. They love the dancing. They love the sparkles. I think there aren't really any questions about gender. They may say, 'Why do you wear these dresses?' And, my answer to them is, 'Because, it's fun.' I mean, I was a costume designer, so I've looked at costume history, and men have been wearing suits for over one hundred years, and that's been the standard of dress. Women get to wear all sorts of fun things, and I don't think that it should be completely reserved to them."

The only women's clothing that looks fun to me? Sweater robes. I don't think that's what they're called. But thin sweaters that look like blazers or jackets and fall down past your waist. I guess for men we'd call that a cardigan? I always try on cardigans, but they never fit right. If they'd make them thinner and longer, kind of like an oversize deconstructed cashmere shirt, that would work. I wouldn't go out with it. I'd wear that around the house in the winter. As a layer. Sort of a smoother, longer slinky pajama top with buttons that drape chill and clingy. Loungey. That's my idea of a "fun thing." Brooks Brothers should get working on that.

You have to draw the line somewhere with these performances. As far as kids are concerned, "What would going too far look like, Tyler?"

"I don't personally feel like a bar setting is a great place for children to ever be. Definitely not lap dancing; don't put any of your parts in their faces. If you want to go up to where a child is sitting and do a cartwheel or get into the splits, that's just gymnastics, essentially. I don't think that that's really anything sexualized. So that's probably where I would draw the line. I know that we need to be open to having these conversations with people in our own community and letting them know when they've probably crossed the line. I know that there are a lot of parents in that moment that wouldn't necessarily be able to express to these performers that what they're doing isn't okay. So I love that we're able to have these discussions and that this is brought to the attention of our community. That we need to be more aware of what we're doing and be representing ourselves in the best light that we can. Because the upbringing of our children is so important. We want them to live happily mentally and emotionally, and we don't want to come in the way of their development."

It pleased me to hear Tyler say this. Although men wearing wigs and lipstick doing "splits" in front of children isn't how I'd define "gymnastics."

It takes two to tango too. Tyler concedes this: "I don't think that everybody has done the best job in representing our community, but I do feel like it is the responsibility of the parent to establish boundaries for their families and know what is okay depending on the age of their children."

Tyler seems well-adjusted. But from when he was young, he knew he didn't fit in. How?

"I knew that I wasn't like other boys my age. Not being into balls, and trucks, and cars, and sports. Enjoying playing dress-up and playing with dolls or singing, dancing, being more of a performer type of child. It made me feel a little isolated because, at the time, that wasn't necessarily something that was brought into the light."

"Were you flamboyant as a middle schooler?" I asked.

"I was in the performing arts. I don't think that I was your typical ultra-flamboyant child. But I don't think that I was necessarily fooling anybody. I felt very normal in the way that I presented myself. I was just trying to present normal so that I wouldn't have to be bullied."

"Did you ever try to be straight?" I asked. "You know how people try really hard?"

"Yeah," admitted Tyler. "There were two sisters that I dated, and it didn't really work out with either of them. I kissed one of them, and I started laughing and ran away. I was taking voice lessons from her mom at the time. Then later on, I went to date her younger sister. When she asked if she could kiss me? I just said, 'No,' and drove away."

Guys dream of dating sisters. What a waste.

"When did you kiss a guy for the first time?"

"That would be my senior year of high school," he tells me. It was some guy in the drama club. "I just remember texting this guy and having all of these superlong conversations about how 'We don't understand the way that we feel. Feeling isolated in our sexuality and not having people that we can go to. Not being able to have open conversations about how we're feeling,' that was really hard. So even though parking our car down at the river bottoms and making out for a little while might have been fun, there still was a lot of trauma that comes from that. Because in that moment, you're finally letting yourself be who you have always known that you were and wanted to be. But I felt too ashamed to be able to."

This is why drag queens love Elsa from *Frozen*.

My first kiss was in the squash courts at the Philly Cricket Club. Summer in between fifth and sixth grade. No drama, no trauma.

"When you saw other boys throwing the ball around or doing their thing, were you like, what are they doing with that ball?"

"Well," said Tyler, "my parents will say whenever I was signed up for tee-ball for a while, they would just see me out in the outfield picking flowers. Not super-interested. They tried, and I played soccer for a while and wasn't very good at it. But it was nice to get out and run around."

If Tyler were on my team, and someone hit a line drive to left field, and he was picking daisies, I would have been pissed. If you're the coach, you have to bench him.

It's too bad Tyler wasn't into sports because he's built like an athlete. Six feet, 175 pounds (I asked for his measurements out of professional curiosity, of course). He lifts. He says he's fast. "I'm still very competitive," he says, "and I want to be the best performer on the stage every time.

"Yeah, I mean, my parents have told me when I came out of the womb and the doctor saw my neck, they're like, 'He looks like he can be a linebacker.'

"My brother actually plays for a Major League Baseball team, so I've had a lot of sports in my life, but it's not something that's really interested me at all."

Whoa. That's significant.

"He's two years younger than I am."

"Was that difficult for you growing up?" I ask him. "He's a star athlete, and you have no interest in sports whatsoever?"

"Yeah, it definitely was," Tyler admits. "It still is a little bit, honestly."

"Do you have a competitive spirit about you and your brother?"

Tyler definitely does. "I mean, that's where my competitive spirit comes from."

I explore this. "[Your brother] is now a major-league ballplayer. I mean, that obviously triggers some feelings of competition, interfamily competition, brotherly competition. Is that maybe a reason why you've pursued this kind of performative profession?"

"I wouldn't say that it's not a reason that I do, because I've been a performer my whole life. I've been singing my whole life. So, it is kind of something that to me feels very natural and something that I would enjoy doing regardless. I mean, I've been performing longer than he's been in the majors, but I haven't been performing as long as he's been playing baseball."

Tyler is keeping score.

Was there bullying?

"There definitely was always some bullying from both sides, which is very normal. But yeah, we didn't always see eye to eye. And I know he's frustrated me many times. I'm sure I've done the same."

I ask Tyler if his Major League Baseball–playing brother is open to his lifestyle.

"I believe so," he says with hesitation. "I don't think that he's been to one of my shows. I know that my parents have been to multiple. His wife has too." But Tyler says his brother is busy during the season, and Salt Lake City doesn't have a team, so he doesn't come through.

"Are you disappointed he hasn't been to one of your shows?"

"I think it would be fun. I think that he would enjoy it. Especially if he came to one of the drag shows. But, at the same time, I haven't been to any of his baseball games."

That's a bombshell.

"He plays in the majors, and you've never been to a single game?"

"Nope."

I ask the most important question a guy can ask. Who could beat who up?

"I would say that I still could [beat him up]. We wrestled quite a bit, honestly, as kids. It was one of those things where 'Kids go wrestle, go get some of this energy out.' I don't know that I fully felt defeated, ever. I know how I could get him into a position where he was sort of immobilized. So that was fun."

Life is funny. Two brothers. One's a married pro ball player. One's a gay drag queen. They're both physical specimens, highly competitive public performers. They were rough with each other growing up, and now neither has attended the other's game/show. How did Tyler's sibling rivalry factor into his drag show career? Is Tyler's mentorship of queer children at "family-friendly" drag shows a reaction to the childhood loneliness he experienced in Mormon Utah? Maybe. Hopefully the brothers stay close, because I'd like to hit Tyler up for free tickets if his brother's team makes the playoffs.

7

The Radical Feminist
Sex Worker

Sky is a prostitute. She lives in Las Vegas. She wants to legalize prostitution. She propositions me during our interview.

"Okay. Let's say in theory, either your wife was cool with it, or she wasn't going to find out . . . one of the two, whatever you prefer."

I prefer neither, but go on.

"Let's say prostitution was fully legal right now. Let's say I just wanted to pay you because of who you are."

I'm Watters, and this is my world.

"Just like, let's say a reasonable amount. Let's say like a hundred grand, because I want to give you oral sex, because I think that it might help my image if I get to say that I gave you oral sex, and just the opportunity to do that might be worth one hundred thousand dollars to me for your twenty minutes. Would you do it?"

"No."

"Why not?"

"One hundred thousand is way too low."

Sky laughs. "It's too low. I love you."

She's white with dirty-blond hair, pulled back tight in a single braid. Sky has a pleasant smile, nice teeth, a healthy round tan face, good skin, and a deep masculine voice. She's fit. It's rude to ask a woman how old she is, but I'm guessing early forties. She talks so much I can barely get a question in anyway. "I'm on Adderall," she tells me, but she sounds like a person on cocaine.

She was born in Bakersfield, California. "My dad—a Cornell grad—was a world-renowned oil engineer, so when I was very young, he flew us to other countries to grow up so that he could come home every night to us. So I spent five years in Jakarta, Indonesia, and then we moved to Singapore for a couple years."

"That must have been hard for you as a child to be moved around," I said. "It's not like you're moving from California to New Jersey."

"I wouldn't call living with seven live-in servants hard, but sheltered, yeah." She never realized how privileged she was growing up. "I thought everybody grew up with a pool in their backyard and servants and fresh flowers and saltwater fish tanks."

Her family moved back stateside when she was in middle school and relocated to Reno, Nevada. "I came from an upper-class, white privilege family. My mother has never taken a hit of pot, never drinks more than one glass of wine at night. My family has very good manners, very old-fashioned manners. . . . I know about which fork is which, and all this stuff. I was raised to go to college and graduate and get a good job."

That never happened.

Sky dropped out of college to run a pyramid scheme. "I took that across the country and poured my heart into sales, which is where I found my love for sales. When I think of mixing it with selling what comes in between my legs, which is just the most valuable thing here on this Zoom call."

I would argue that what comes out of my mouth is the most valuable thing on the Zoom call.

Sky went to prison for cocaine trafficking when she was twenty-five. Obviously, it wasn't her fault. "The feds set me up," she claims. At the time, she was making $8,000 a month dealing. "And I did hold a pretty solid part-time job as like a cover. I was working at a beauty supply store, which is one of the places they set me up at. I actually sold cocaine out of the store."

Excuse me, miss, do you sell face powder? Yes, we have some in the back; follow me.

She was facing a fifteen-year mandatory minimum, but she had "high-priced attorneys, so a deal got cut." If her dad admitted he knew she was selling drugs out of his car, then "the DEA could legally confiscate the vehicle." It just so happened his car was "a Lexus IS 350 the feds had their eyes on." Her trafficking charge dropped from a level 3 to a level 2. Her short stint in prison was "humbling."

Before Sky was dealing, she was stripping. "When I was only seventeen years old, I remember eating lunch at Applebee's, and we ran into a couple, I'd say, more lower-class girls from high school that were stripping at the men's club, and they were, of course, under twenty-one. They started telling us how cool it was and how much money they were making in the VIP room, and it was just ridiculous, and so I rose to the challenge because I was interested in seeing what a strip club looked like."

Next thing she knows, she's at the strip club "interview." "I find myself doing a naked body check in the back where they're looking at you butt naked, giving you the approval or whatever. Making you feel like you passed some tests." Sky went to work "that night," underage at a men's club in Reno. "I didn't even have stripper heels yet. They basically threw me on the stage, let the girls teach me how to dance, and next thing you know, I was a certified stripper."

"What kind of moves were you doing?" I asked her. "Did they give you any sort of training?"

"I took jazz dancing growing up," she says, "so I wasn't a total amateur. It's kind of like the slower you move, the less mistakes you're going to be obviously making."

I tell her that's my strategy on the dance floor. "Just kind of limit the movement."

She laughs. Then blesses me with the certified stripper dance tutorial. "You kind of bend your knee toward the inside and drag the toe of your heel and do things with your legs and then sit on your butt and do the mermaid."

"The mermaid" is when you sit on your butt, hands planted to each side, swiveling your closed legs together in front of you like a mermaid. I only know this because I googled it, I swear.

"You kind of just waste time, and the guys don't care what you do. As long as you're not up there moving too fast, you're not going to get made fun of."

After a while, Sky quit stripping. "It wasn't working with my schedule. I didn't really like the blisters. It was just too much. I was either sitting down with guys that wanted to take me home after shift or I was getting talked to literally like I was some little girl. Like, 'What's a girl like you doing in a place like this? You don't belong here.' That would make me angry. I had an intense hate for men after stripping, of that experience. I guess I was insulted and offended. But then again, I was a firecracker. I was in great shape from volleyball. I didn't even have my fake boobs back then. I had my small A boobs, which the guys seemed to love, and it was fun. It's the funnest industry ever."

Around the same time, Sky got into crystal meth. "The guy that introduced it to me and my girlfriend told us it was ecstasy."

Hate it when that happens.

After prison, Sky started dabbling with crystal meth again. "I did end up with a problem where I was letting my boyfriend inject me and shooting it in my veins and getting so high I was obviously not the same person. But then I turned to Narcotics Anonymous, and they saved my life. I haven't touched street meth in almost eight years now."

"Congratulations," I tell her.

"Thank you."

"What does that feel like when they inject it right into you?"

"At the very first split second, you don't feel anything," she says, but "once the drug rushes through the first couple pumps of blood and hits your heart, it feels like an explosion of heat inside of you, and everything just starts moving really fast. It's like you almost have a pure attention to everything. You don't miss anything. Everything is sped up and quick and just . . . You don't really have reservations sexually anymore. You become extremely sexual when you take a hit in your arm.

"The first time you try meth, it's going to be an amazing experience. You're going to love it. Whether you're taking out the trash or working or going to a concert, you're going to say, 'Oh my God. What was that stuff? Give me just a little bit more.'"

"Wow," I say. "If it makes taking out the trash that exciting . . . Do not tempt me."

But I wonder. "Sky, how do you go from dating a guy? The next thing you know, he's shooting you with crystal meth?"

"Once you realize the power of the drugs, sometimes whole relationships can be based solely off a guy obtaining or holding methamphetamine. If you like methamphetamine and there's a methamphetamine dealer that's always got his hands on it. Now, you might find yourself in an entire eight-month-long dating relationship based on the fact that this guy has what you want. Maybe he just wants your company. Maybe he needs help answering his phone. It could be anything. You find what he wants. You give it to him. You're going to get free dope. Because the dope to a drug dealer is not so special."

Sky explains how dealers exploit, control, and oppress the masses for money and power. "You can really utilize dope to get people to do things that they would never do were they not on dope. If you really want to get something done, you ask the bottom, because they're the ones that need the diaper money. They're willing to literally hurt people for very small amounts of money. That's why you can't just write people off because the bottom, unfortunately, overpowers the top in numbers."

Despite coming from a privileged background, Sky identifies with the poor. "My feelings and my experience after I'd say about age eighteen really resonates more with people at the bottom. People that have to struggle and more with people that are involved with, let's say, drugs and prostitution."

Her "mentor," if you will, is involved with drugs and prostitution. "I dabbled with cocaine for a long time, using it when I was selling it. Then, one day in the strip club on New Year's Eve, I made a resolution with my drug dealer to stop getting high on my own supply and see how that would benefit my life. He, of course, didn't believe in using his own product, so he influenced me quite a bit. He was also definitely a certified pimp, like a real pimp. He made a lot of money a lot of ways off of exploiting women, but I would say the right way. He ruled with finesse and money and drugs, never violence. He was a different kind of guy. He'd have girls coming into the bar where we'd be hanging out at, at all hours, just bringing in money and stuff."

Let this be a lesson to all the pimps out there: it's better to rule with finesse than violence.

Their relationship blossomed like this: "I was the homecoming queen, I was real popular. He was this black football player. And I ended up becoming really close with this guy and spending a ton of time with him in the strip clubs."

Your quintessential American love story.

"On the weekends, we had a romantic relationship, even though he had another relationship with a female. He would call me his side chick."

It's so sweet.

The coke dealer/certified pimp "was one of the major influences on me in telling me that I should charge for my time, whether it be to provide the girlfriend experience or just have sex, there should be a cost." Like a self-help guru, he just wanted Sky to reach her full potential. When Sky told her mom her boyfriend "is trying to pimp me out," her mom was "beside herself," and prohibited her from talking to him again. "My parents really despised this guy that I was looking up to."

At the same time a pimp was trying to turn her out, her parents "found out I was dealing cocaine out of their house, and they gave me a choice that night. They said, 'You can either take all the drugs you have right now and flush them down the toilet in front of us, and you can stay, or you can take your drug stash, and you've got to go because we can get in trouble and lose the house.'"

Mom and Dad definitely didn't want to risk losing the house. A car is one thing, but a house?

Sky didn't hesitate. "I said, 'I'm not flushing a thousand dollars' worth of dope down the toilet.' So I left, found my own place."

Where did Sky move to? "I got a place in the same complex as what we would call the trap house. The trap house is the place the drug dealer keeps himself safe by distributing drugs out of. Which isn't necessarily where he resides."

Never live at the trap house. I'm learning so much.

Sky lived by the trap house for almost a year, "until the day we heard a bunch of pops go off, and we realized somebody's house got shot up. And it was, in fact, the trap house that was kitty corner to me."

Never live kitty corner to a trap house either.

Our conversation ran from raw to philosophical. Sky's book smart *and* street smart—basically a wealth of knowledge about things I never needed to know but was fascinated by.

"There's this side of feminism," she says, "that's arguing that prostitution is just the exploitation of women's bodies. Well, let me ask you a question. What do you think that's been happening this whole time? What do you think that's happening right now?"

Apparently, legalizing prostitution is empowering to women? "We're having to carry out this God-given gift of being able to sell what we're born with. It's like being born with an apple orchard. The government tells you, 'Well, you own all the apples in the land, and that's great . . . but you can't charge whatever you want for an apple . . . you can only give them away.' It's like, 'Okay. I can give this away, but it's illegal for me to sell it. Why?'"

Eve should have *sold* Adam the apple. That's what Sky's driving at, probably.

"You've ingrained this into me that money is the most important, respected, highly coveted thing in the United States. I'm going to be valued based on my units of choice, which are my dollars. Yet, you're going to tell me that the things that [men] seek the most often . . . I can't charge [men] for? Now I'm confused."

I'm confused too. Is this why women make us take them apple-picking every fall?

Sky explains why the government outlawed prostitution. Old white men, who run everything, didn't want to be overcharged for sex. "Since the beginning of time, we have been selling pussy, one way or another. . . . The government didn't outlaw prostitution to protect the prostitutes. The government was comprised of older white men. . . . Maybe their excuse was they wanted to protect the women. But I'll tell you what, they didn't want to get robbed. Old white men didn't want us to be able to exploit them."

Sky doesn't believe all men want prostitution banned to selfishly prevent sexual price gouging. Some men have "good intentions," maybe they're Christians, but really "it's called shame. The men are shameful because of sex. They don't want to hurt the woman because they are a real man. They figure they're protecting the women from these aggressive male predators that supposedly, if they just outlaw prostitution, these male sexual predators will just somehow go somewhere else." But look at what's happened, argues Sky. "No matter how many prostitutes they lock up on the strip every night, it's always the same number of them the next night, and they just keep coming."

The argument is psychological. The government lets women "do it for free" but won't let them "put a worth on herself." By denying women "self-worth" in the sexual marketplace, you deny them respect, and self-respect. This lack of respect invites violence. "You don't abuse someone that you respect, and you certainly don't respect someone that you can abuse. So, what I'm asking is stop making it so easy to abuse the women, give us a chance to charge for what we've got, then we'll earn the respect from the men, then we'll take care of the men because we'll be at peace." Sky says women will feel equal, rewarded, and compensated for "all this fucking work we've been doing for centuries . . . taking care of you fuckers sexually. You're telling me that's not a job, honey? It's been a job since day one."

It's been the man's job to take care of women since day one. And women take care of men, in more ways than one. Is that true? Nope. "When women, from the beginning of time, if you look at the animal kingdom, what have we needed you all for? We can hunt on our own. We can make our own food, right? In the animal kingdom, the only thing we need you for is reproduction, correct?"

"Well, we're pretty good hunters, Sky."

"You're good hunters," she concedes.

"Don't try to sell us short."

"But brother, you see my point; the burden falls on your species to procreate. So, for some reason, I got this gift where I don't feel that I need sex, and I've noticed all the men need sex, and they want it so bad that apparently that's the only reason most of them even talk to me is because they all have this ultimate goal of hopefully seeing me naked. So, this is a joy, in my opinion, life is easier for women.

"I see women taking over the world. I see us bringing our boys home.

I see a lot of love going on and a lot less war all because we just figure out how to legalize prostitution."

Sky sees legalizing prostitution as the key to ending abuse, inequality, and war. Also, the future is female. "The future will be like *Kill Bill*," proclaims Sky. "There will be women and they will own properties, and they will have multiple men, teams of men helping them because that's what's going to happen. You've already created a monster. Who do women have to look up to in America? I'll tell you who. Cardi B, Nicki Minaj, Kim Kardashian, those are our idols, Paris Hilton. Sex tape, sex tape, became famous from a sex tape, shows her pussy. Britney Spears, look at her flashing her cooter to the entire world. That's asserting dominance."

Sky's right. But that doesn't make it right. If women are going to be objectified and sexualized by society, her thinking goes, they may as well embrace it.

Prostitution, as the old saying goes, is the oldest profession in the world. Whether or not sex should be a commodity available for purchase is a question that different societies have taken a wide range of views on. Some have had sects that embrace what is called "sacred prostitution," integrating the buying and selling of sex into religious rituals. (In certain regions of India, lower-caste girls are "married" to Hindu deities, and service the male priests and worshippers in that deity's temple.) Others, such as ancient Greece, often treated the institution as a public industry like any other—during the Greek Archaic Period, Athens ran legal, state-regulated brothels, offering services from both women and young men. In the West, by the beginning of the sixteenth century, many Christian countries had begun to prohibit the practice, viewing it as immoral and destructive. But even within Christendom, the world's oldest profession was once viewed as a necessary evil: St. Augustine, for example, maintained that "if you expel prostitution from society, you will unsettle everything on account of lusts." Sky Alexandra isn't exactly St. Augustine.

The question remains the same: How would legalizing prostitution work? Brothels are legal in Amsterdam. There's a huge underground industry of trafficking poor women from Eastern Europe into the red-light district for profit. Even when out in the open, the reality for these women is dark and ugly. But Sky has an answer for everything. Since the government "can't easily tax your private parts," according to Sky, "the answer is cameras."

Willing to sacrifice privacy, Sky desires cameras in every brothel, hotel room, and private home. This way, the government could tax the sex and prevent violence. "The people in the house should have the rights to say, 'Okay, well something bad happened. So, now, government, you can see what happened last night from five to six p.m. in my bedroom. I give you access.' They already have access; there is no such thing as privacy. They can hear through walls. They can hear everything."

The feds can already hack into your phone, Amazon Alexa, your TV, your Ring doorbell, your laptop . . . and spy on you, so Sky says, "We don't have privacy anymore. Let's just admit it. So, it wouldn't hurt to just put everything out on the table, just give up to go up." The entire country turns into the Bunny Ranch and the federal government watches and taxes any sexual transaction. "The only government I would have faith in trying that out with," says Sky, "would be the American government." Respectfully, this is when I realize Sky is out of her mind. However, her plan would certainly help police recruitment since police would be paid to watch amateur porn all day.

"I'm sure the government could help us come up with some Facebook-type app where maybe every hooker is required to turn on the camera, and there's a live cop sitting in another building somewhere where he watches the sex live."

Tens of thousands of police officers would be coming out of retirement. "Honey, I'm back on the force. The chief needs me."

"But isn't prostitution already kinda legal, Sky?" You are charging, women are charging.

"If prostitution was legal, I'll tell you what I would be. I would be the next Heidi Fleiss. I would be running the coolest whorehouse in the world. We would have it all. It would be impeccably clean. We would have self-help classes and manners classes for the girls. We would start to educate them. Whatever skills they lacked, we would encourage them to learn horseback riding to reading, just to learning about business so you can talk to businessmen properly. You have to add value to the marketplace."

I've never known guys to want hookers on horseback, but everyone has a type.

"Unfortunately, the majority of prostitutes are uneducated," admits Sky. "We're being raised by the American school system here."

She gets no argument from me on that.

Sky has apparently done her research. "The brothels, nineteen percent of the women reported orgasms. Whereas, the call girls who are pretty much running their own business on their own, seventy-five percent of them are reaching orgasm. That's empowerment."

(My research assistant looked long and hard and failed to find this survey Sky cites.)

Lyndon Johnson's "War on Poverty" failed. Sky has a solution. "So, we need to get better at our trade. We need to offer better love, so to speak, the girlfriend experience. Our prostitutes can't just come with sucking and fucking; that's boring and caveman shit. We need to be real advanced with this. We need to seduce all the senses. We need performers and people with skills to be able to sell sex because that would give the power back to the people." (If you read between the lines, this is what *The Federalist Papers* was all about.) "So, that would give us a way to get out of poverty."

But behind the uplifting talk about female empowerment, there lurks a conniving attitude, a sinister streak, where Sky reveals, like an emotionless tactician, how simple extracting money from men is. "I've spent a lot of my life trying to manipulate men and see what I can get from them. I've learned the hard way that most men don't want to have to feel they need to pay for sex. Most men are seeking the human connection. They don't just want their dick stroked. They want an hour of conversation. They want something to work for. They want it to be a challenge. Essentially, paying for pussy takes all the fun out of it from a man's standpoint."

Fact check: true.

"I'm the type of bitch like now you're not going to catch me paying for a relationship again, but you're also not going to catch me having sex for any reason other than to increase my finances or increase my worth."

Sky busts out the crudest analogy ever. "You want to see something that rules the entire world in one picture?" It was an origami piece made out of a hundred-dollar bill made to look like a vulva. "That was what runs the world, money and pussy."

She's forgetting nukes. But I let it slide. Sky's on a roll. She explains "the game" to me.

"If you really want to turn a trick, if you really want a sugar daddy, if you really want to make money, you *don't* do it the illegal way. You get around that."

How so?

"It's very simple. It's like marriage. You ask for help. It's illegal to sell pussy, but it's definitely not illegal ever anywhere to ask for help."

Help is on the way.

"What do I do to take advantage of men now? I do it the right way."

You see, there's a right way to take advantage of men and a wrong way. I bet you didn't know that.

"First, I give them my time. I invite them to my house to see what I'm worth, to see about me. If I make them interested in me, I ask them about form, family, occupation, recreation, money. I touch all their points (figuratively) and find out what type of person are they. Are they analytical? Are they a whale? Do they like helping people? Do they just want to have fun? Does he just want to fuck? What does he want? I'm going to investigate first. Just like Stephen Covey says, 'Seek to understand before being understood.'"

Sky and I have so much in common. We both practice the art of listening.

"It takes time to make money off a man. I had a three-year relationship with the sugar daddy that became my fiancé. I never had sexual intercourse with him, not in three years. I got a ring on my finger. I drained his bank account, and he bought me a Range Rover."

Whoever said romance was dead?

"He's this fifty-eight-year-old, somewhat crippled. He used to be obese. He's deaf. He talks kind of like he's retarded. To me, I am a predator. I see my prey. I see that they're weak. I fulfill that weakness with my presence. I made this man feel like the king of the world for the last three years of his life. God forbid. He got liver cancer. He passed away when I was engaged to him. But I never had to sleep with him. I was in love with him. All I had to do was let him give me head a couple of times. Guess what? Both times I orgasmed. Was I attracted to him? No, not in any way, shape, or form. I was not physically attracted to him.

The thought of kissing him literally made me kind of sick. I would do it for him because I was in it for the money. I knew what he wanted. He wanted intimacy. He craved intimacy. I gave him just enough to keep him around, and I use that man for all that he's worth."

I like Sky. But I think she's a sociopath. And she ruins men like this constantly.

She tells me a story about her parents' neighbor. "He's eighty-five years old, he's dying, he's had five heart attacks; sweetest, old, innocent man ever. I shocked the hell out of him. I said, 'You want a naked lap dance for fun?' I turned on the music, country music, and I got stripped down butt naked. I had it in his face, everything. He was terrified. He was shocked. So I didn't ask him to pay for pussy, but I got antiques . . . I got three handmade quilts that his dead wife made. So yes, in a sense, I'm always seeking to see what I can get from the sexual interaction."

For Sky, life is Darwinian. Kill or be killed. Everything is a power struggle. All relationships are transactional. Violence is behind every door. If not violence, then money. The battle of the sexes is real.

"So a lot of men have this inflated idea of who they are. Even if you giggle, you laugh, now they think, 'Oh, I got a shot,' and they get this overinflated ego. You can sense it. You can feel it. So that's when I tell them, if they say something like 'Oh, if you had a time in bed with me, oh the time it would be.' That's when I pull out 'Well, that would cost you,' or something like that. Because I love seeing him flinch and feel powerless. Because then I say, 'Well, you want an hour with me? It'd be at least a grand. That's the magic number. About one thousand dollars, and I might do it.' And then they look at you in disgust. And I get joy out of that because now I've distanced myself from this predator in a way that makes me feel empowered and happy."

Like a shield and a sword, Sky uses prostitution to survive and protect herself. There's a deep lack of trust. "I've been raped one time in my life. It was by someone very close to me. I have to protect his identity because I respect him, and I did love him, but it's funny how betrayal will always come from those closest to you."

This hustle-to-survive instinct traces back to her childhood. "I was taught hard work. I was taught dedication. And I was always, in one way, shape, or form or another, taught that the most important thing in life that matters is money. That's what I learned from my mother, that's what I learned from my father, and that's what I learned from my brother. Even when I brought my dad fifteen thousand dollars in dirty drug money to help pay for my Lexus, he was proud of me. He didn't tell me, 'How did you get that?' Or question how I came up with it. He knew it was dirty money, and he was still proud of me because I made the money, because that's all that matters."

"I think that you just nailed it right on the head there," I tell her. "That's what it's all about. It's about money. And that's the way you were raised."

Sky lets slip that her mom is a "hard-core atheist." She says she feels sorry for people who don't believe in a higher power. She feels sorry for her mom, a hard-core atheist, hard-core Democrat. Her father "is the biggest Republican ever, loves Trump, my mom hates Trump, so we don't really talk politics in my house."

Sky's mother "is so submissive" to her father. "There were times when I was disappointed in her for not divorcing him because of either the way he spoke to her or the way he treated her. He never put his hands on us, never was physically violent. So, I love my father more than anyone in the world." But Sky's relationship with her mother is fractured and distant.

"Was your father disrespectful to your mother?" I ask.

"Verbally, yes."

"Verbally abusive?"

"If he had enough, all he had to do was get loud, which he often got loud, raised his voice, and he could stop any conversation he wanted at any time he so chose because he was the financial overseer in my family. He made all the money, took care of her forever. Now, was my mom a harder worker in a sense? Maybe, because she never stopped, she just never stopped. That's where I learned to clean. She changes the beds every day, everything has to be perfect, she always did all the dishes."

Sky learned early at home that money equaled power and respect. She identified more with her father, and was disappointed that her mother didn't unshackle herself from what Sky saw as an abusive marriage. Perhaps Sky's life today emulates the feminist independence that her mother never achieved in her eyes. Perhaps she's chasing money by any means necessary the way her father did. But disappointment permeates the whole family. Sky shares with me that "all of my family members" are "ashamed" of her involvement in the sex industry. "The stigma is heavy. The stigma is very, very, very heavy."

Sky's father still supports her. He bought her a house, which she lives in and rents out to men. "I live with five male roommates. To me, I'll never be lonely. My advice is just, yeah, get the money, get the power, get the respect. The first and foremost concern of women should be to learn to be more like gay men, save your money, save your fucking money, get the power back."

Sky recounts her litany of interactions with drug kingpins, gangsters, and federal agents with a cavalier attitude. There's no real regret; it's as if she's telling her story in the third person. Sex, for her, is the same way. Because at the end of the day, sex isn't about sex. It's about power. And Sky loves having power. Legalizing prostitution is about reclaiming power from the pimps and politicians—all men, in Sky's mind.

It's about autonomy.

Money, sex, and power are all the same thing for Sky. "It does turn me on to think about; it does make me sexually excited to think that a man would spend his hard-earned money on intimacy with me," she says.

In a way, all this is about revenge—a metaphysical, cosmic kind of revenge, notching a win for the ladies in the generations-long war of the sexes. This view of things is a kind of self-fulfilling prophecy: If you treat love as something that can only be measured in dollars and cents, then that's the kind of love you're going to find. If you treat men as rapacious animals, then those are the kinds of men you're going to get. Anything else requires a certain amount of trust—trust that Sky doesn't have. Men, in her estimation, are driven by a raw desire to take things from women. Selling sex is women's best shot at taking something back.

Sky isn't alone in this view, although she's more honest than most. Feminism, which once condemned prostitution as the exploitation of women, has now embraced "sex work." Listing "the reasons we need to decriminalize sex work," the American Civil Liberties Union argued: "It would . . . help sex workers access health care, lower the risk of violence from clients, reduce mass incarceration, and advance equality in the LGBTQ community, especially for trans women of color, who are often profiled and harassed whether or not we are actually sex workers." In *Teen Vogue*, feminist writer Tlaleng Mofokeng argued that "sex work and sex worker rights" are "the litmus test for intersectional feminism," and that "the impact of continued criminalization of the majority of sex workers, most of whom are cisgender women and transgender women, means that sex worker rights are a feminist issue."

It's obvious Sky wouldn't be able to live like this without her parents' considerable resources. She acknowledges this.

"You're very focused on class," I tell her.

"Definitely," replies Sky. She's come into contact with gritty street-level players that most people with her upbringing don't ever even contemplate. Racism is real in the streets, as Sky sees it. In the sex game, "white women are more highly coveted." To johns and pimps, a white woman can charge more, explains Sky. "We're looked at like a prize, like a trophy." She notices the inequality, and Sky's alliances are clear. "I'll tell you what a dangerous combination is, a black man and a white woman. That, to me, is a much more dangerous combination than a white man and a black woman because, you see, the white woman and the black man have the same enemy, and that's the powerful white man. All white women have been held down by their men, all of them."

"Do you mostly find yourself in relationships with white guys or black guys?" I ask.

"Black guys." Sky elaborates about the black football-playing pimp/dealer who "influenced" her the most . . . whom she was "deeply in love with." She adds, "I also have his initials tattooed on my side." He's "an incredible drug dealer, incredible pimp. He saved me from a bad relationship. I was in an abusive relationship with a white guy, and that was a guy that did me wrong in many ways. And along comes my hero, this big black 50 Cent–looking guy, dressed impeccably all the time. I'm talking Louis Vuitton, gold chains, you name it. He was the ideal pimp because he never once threatened me physically or violently, and he seduced me with everything he had. And to this day, I will still call him my best friend."

"You've put black men on a pedestal?"

"I like black men because they help my confidence because they see me as a trophy just because I'm white. So I already feel valued and respected. Even if they're incapable of real respect, they still look up to me just for being white and being around the crowd I'm in and around the people I have access to. They don't have anything."

"Do you feel that you weren't valued by your family growing up?"

"I feel I was underestimated, but never not valued. No, I always felt valued. I always felt like they loved me. I feel I hurt them a lot. I created wreckage in my past and hurt them to the point of distance."

Sky's brother, she says, is "a very powerful, influential man in Las Vegas. He's got everything I didn't get. He got the math smarts. He's like a hacker. He can hack into computers. He used to be a bookie. He set up through Costa Rica. The feds raided his house in Henderson a long time ago because he had so many guys coming in and out of the house that the neighbors had enough evidence that it might be a drug operation."

Sky doesn't seem close with her brother, even though she claims she isn't actively prostituting anymore in the traditional sense. "Without the necessary help, it is too degrading. It is too frustrating. It is absolutely bang-your-head-against-the-wall annoying." Sky keeps it classier. "We need to just focus on selling love. Let's call it what it is. To a lot of men, they don't want to have sex. They want to make love."

Does Sky really believe in love? True love between a couple eliminates violence. Real love creates value, respect. I ask her, if you cheapen sex and you make it just a commodity like anything else, doesn't that trigger more abuse?

"Love. What is love?" Sky asks sarcastically. "Love to me, I love money. So again, first and foremost, I see a man's worth in dollars. I see your worth in dollars. So that's just from my perspective, though. That's coming from a very selfish, cocky standpoint. But don't mistake my confidence for ego, because I am a Gemini."

Well, I'm a Cancer.

Sky gets feisty.

"So, your little feelings and whatever you're saying to me, it just doesn't mean much to me because I already know you are the inferior species to me."

Hurtful.

"So, in a sense, you never had control, you never will have control, and you can't have control is why you don't like this idea. You don't like the idea of losing this wonderful, classy idea of a woman somehow needing a man."

There it is. Legalizing prostitution is, for Sky, allowing a woman to fully control her own body.

What are Sky's politics? She's not a Republican or a Democrat. "I'm not even a gold digger. I am a professional at selling love."

What's the most important thing in life? "Money," she says. But also "choices." "A dollar is a unit of choice, whether you like it or not. So if you have a dollar, you can have McDonald's for lunch. That's your one choice. If I have a million dollars, I can fly to Tahiti and have some fresh fucking lobster. That's the kind of choices I want."

(The lobster in Maine is much better. She's thinking of prawn.)

"You're talking about the fact that men want women to need them, and that's true obviously," I say. "But I think men and women need each other. The problem with the view of sex, I think, that you're laying out is that it's not about needing each other in this deep sense. It's about a transactional relationship where you get together, you do something so that one party can get one thing and one party can get another thing. And there's no sense of the fact that men and women are actually made for one another."

Sky tells a joke. "A little kid asks his dad. He's like, 'Daddy, what's a blow job?' And the dad's like, 'Dinner and a watch.'"

We laugh.

"We're trying to get value for what you value."

Don't get her wrong: Sky "loves" men. "I'm so straight, it's not even funny. The only time I ever fuck with pussy is for the purpose of impressing the man that's there or making the man feel good. So I've had threesomes, foursomes. I've had sixsomes, you name it."

Also, legalizing prostitution isn't a one-way street. "I'm telling you, there will be a lot of successful gigolos in this industry once we legalize it. So there is hope for the men like never before because women are going to start to feel empowered enough to pay for their own sex, right?"

Hunter Biden could make his first honest buck.

Sky hits me with a story out of the blue that scares me. "I was manic," she says. She tells me one day she hops in a cab with her dog and heads down to the strip. "This whole time I'm planning, I know exactly what I'm going to do. I don't know why I'm seeking this thrill specifically, but I crouch behind a trash can, I take off all my clothes. I take off my shoes. I take off my socks. I'm sitting there crouching down behind this big trash can on the strip where it says RENO, BIGGEST LITTLE CITY IN THE WORLD, up in lights. Have you seen the sign?"

"Yeah."

"And I took off all my clothes. The dog wasn't on a leash, but she was following me on my heels because she was terrified and we went to the middle of the road, and I'm in the middle of the traffic, and they're going slow, and I'm butt naked, and it's the middle of winter, it's cold. And I just start joyously doing cartwheels and walking back and forth in the middle of the street, and people are taking pictures of me. A Mexican guy runs up. 'Can I take picture with you, chica?' And I'm like, 'Yeah, sure,' and I'm butt naked, titties out, probably definitely shaved cooter."

Oh dear.

"But that day, they gave me the choice. The cop came running over, he put his jacket over me, and he's like, 'Why are you doing this?' and I just looked at him. And he's like, 'Where are your clothes?' and I pointed to behind the trash can where I had left the clothes, the clothes and the shoes were gone, they had disappeared. So, I had to ride naked in the back of the cop van, and they took me to the mental hospital, and I had to stay a few weeks, but it's called thrill-seeking behavior."

Yup.

"So, when you're bipolar, sometimes when you get manic, you feel literally as important as if you were the president of the United States but most of the time, when you're manic, you feel like the whole world is watching you and everybody can see what you do."

Go on.

"If you hear a helicopter above, you think they're there watching you. It's almost like you look at an animal, and you think the government has a device that's in their head that's looking at you. It's almost like you're publicized, for anything you do. It's like I ran down the street naked for clout, for clout to say because I knew in my mind that would be the coolest fucking story to tell people that I just got butt naked and ran down the street in a joyous manner. And it was still, to this day, one of the coolest things I've ever done. And my brother came to the mental hospital, was just beside himself, my mother, everybody. I put my family through so much wreckage, but I know that, and they still love me as if I did nothing wrong and I just . . ."

"Do you feel like you're doing a lot of this for attention from your family?" I ask.

"Attention," says Sky. "I've always called myself an attention whore, so I like attention a lot, and I'm the baby of the family. I always got excessive attention. My mom overly mothered me and trained me and cultivated me to be this public speaker. And I used to win state speech competitions where I'd have to memorize the whole speech and deliver it in front of a crowd, and I'd win first place."

In this one regard, Sky's mom did a great job. Sky's a very captivating speaker. But sadly, she's disturbed. Maybe she's not a whore. Maybe she's an "attention whore" playing the role of whore. This manic episode, and the way she retells it with such glee, explains what motivates her behavior. Sky should stop trying to save other women and save herself. But nothing will make her reconsider her mission.

"Just imagine if you could save lives and get women out of boxes that are, right now, locked up in boxes and stuff. What if 9/11 wouldn't have happened if, let's say, prostitution was legal where bin Laden was? I bet you anything he wouldn't have been involved in trying to bomb the whole world."

"I don't know why Bush just didn't fight the war on terror by legalizing prostitution," I say.

"Now we're friends." Sky laughs. "Now we're friends."

Friends without benefits. And not to be a nitpicker, but Navy SEALs did uncover a fair amount of pornography in bin Laden's compound after the 2011 raid.

8

The Pedophile Explainer

If you're sexually attracted to minors, Steven Brown (not his real name) is here to help. A thin, middle-aged white guy with glasses and a goatee, Steven inserts his pronouns (*he/him*) in his bio. He was a lawyer, then says he left the profession to "do something better with my life" and joined the Prostasia Foundation. Most lawyers can do something better with their lives, well, except this.

The Prostasia Foundation claims they "protect children" by protecting the "rights and freedoms" of "minor-attracted persons" (MAPs). *Pedophile* is a term they want to get away from. Being a pedophile "does not mean you're a monster," "it just means you have a sexual attraction." "There does not seem to be any therapy that can change the attraction," but this doesn't mean you are "doomed to harm anyone." "If you are a pedophile, you are not alone," reads the foundation website. Most of "the stigma" associated with the term *pedophile* is because of "scare tactics" in the media.

Steven insists his work is based on "science" and not "moral panic and fear." I can't help it, but the way he talks reminds me of Dr. Anthony Fauci talking about Covid. The Prostasia Foundation was formed so we don't "throw human rights away just to protect children," says

Steven. Finally, someone sticking up for the human rights of people sexually attracted to minors. I thought this day would never come.

"The popular view is that it's impossible to prevent someone from offending against a child if they have that sexual attraction," says Steven. "But the scientists that we work with say, 'No, that's not the case. You can prevent someone from abusing a child, even if they do have the attraction.' And so one of the things that has made Prostasia's work controversial is trying to draw this distinction between the attraction and the action. The action of child sexual abuse is what we want to stop."

Society has it all wrong when it focuses entirely on punishing child sexual abuse rather than preventing it, explains Steven. "It's always got to be a higher priority to prevent [children] being abused in the first place, rather than just letting it happen and then arresting the perpetrators."

One great way to prevent child rape is to punish child rapists with stiff sentences so they can't rape any more children. But Steven has other ideas.

Being sexually attracted to minors doesn't mean you're "completely evil and depraved and sadistic," claims Steven. "Definitely, there are some offenders who are sadistic and psychopathic and have a lot more going on. But then there are other people who are just like the rest of us. They know the difference between right and wrong. And despite feeling these feelings, they don't want to go ahead and rape a child. And so it is possible for these people to be diverted away from offending."

Steven argues that you can't stop certain people from being attracted to minors, but you can try to stop these people from acting on that attraction.

It's very "difficult" for the minor-attracted person not to rape a child when "society is telling them, 'No, you're terrible. You are just as bad as an offender. Even if you haven't offended yet, eventually you will.' These kinds of messages that they hear from all around them are not helpful. They're harmful.

"We need to just let professionals who work with people who are attracted to minors, we need to let them do their job and to stop harassing and treating them as pro-abuse when they're not."

Who is harassing whom exactly?

"I regret to say that Fox News has played its part in the demonization of these professionals," Steven tells me. "And there are professionals who've had to go into hiding, who've had to change their residence, who've had to retreat from public life. And I myself have also received death threats. I've received horrible phone messages."

"You should see the death threats that I get," I tell him. "You have no idea." As a Fox host, I receive a staggering amount of death threats, a surprising number coming from my own family members, which really hurts and makes things awkward at holiday get-togethers.

How dare anyone demonize those who make a living defending the right to get aroused by infants? Getting turned on watching Nickelodeon is something you're born with, says Steven. "Medically, scientifically, there's some suggestion that it is inborn in a similar way. It develops without any choice." In a way, men who enjoy viewing child porn are the victims of circumstance. Like Lady Gaga said, they're "born this way."

Steven is clear about one thing: "In one hundred percent of cases, child sexual abuse is wrong, and no matter what the circumstances are, whether it's a runaway teen, whether it's a priest abusing their parishioners, whether it's a drunk father, whether it's an older sibling, or whether it is someone who has the attraction that they didn't choose, it's still just as wrong. So yeah, just to underline that point, again, the attraction is not chosen, but the action is."

I ask Steven, "Why are we calling it minor-attracted persons?"

"So *pedophilia* is the correct word to use where it's an attraction towards prepubescent children, that is, children before puberty. But I prefer not to use that word for several reasons. Firstly, because there's attraction towards older children, which isn't covered by pedophilia, teenagers. The older they get, the more normal it is to be sexually attracted to them. So when you get to sixteen-, seventeen-year-olds, it's not unusual at all for adult men to find teenagers attractive. Like if you ever went to a sports game and you had teenage cheerleaders, obviously it's natural for there to be some level of sexual interest there for a regular adult male. But they would still officially be . . . it would still be unlawful and wrong to act on that attraction. So you may not be a pedophile, but you may still be minor-attracted if you're attracted to older teenagers, or teenagers of any kind. So that's one reason why the word *pedophile* is not appropriate. The other reason is because in the public's mind, it means sex offender. So *MAP* is better, because *MAP* doesn't refer to a sex offender. It just refers to someone who's attracted to children, and not just to prepubescent children. It could be children up to the age of eighteen."

"Are you fully confident in saying that your average forty-year-old adult male, when he goes to watch his son play a football game, that if he sees a fourteen-year-old cheerleader with pom-poms on the sideline, that he's sexually attracted to her?"

Steven tells me to follow the science. "There's experiments that have been done."

What kind of experiments?

"They hook a device up to the penis and measure the blood flow, and then they show images of people of various ages and genders, and they measure the response. And so we know scientifically that there is a response for the ordinary adult to various ages of underage children. It may not be something that they want, it may not be something that they even enjoy or are conscious of, but there is a physical response that's generated."

Steven is arguing that when he goes to his son's high school football games, he might be so turned on by the fourteen-year-old cheerleaders, he won't be able to stand up and clap. There's nothing "pervy" about this at all, he says. "Finding a teenage girl attractive is something that you shouldn't have to freak out about, because it's just an instinct. It's just something that happens in your head without you choosing it." Adults lusting after ninth graders isn't unordinary, he says. Or shameful. What's wrong is "perving on the girls' locker room or [going] up to the girl afterward and [making] inappropriate remarks."

In Steven's world, actions speak louder than pervs. If I had persistent desires to murder someone, is that something I "shouldn't have to freak out about," since I'm not actually acting on that desire? The point of drawing this line is that it drains the attraction itself of a sense of moral shame. But the attraction is shameful. Sorry, but you should freak out if you feel attracted to children. And "destigmatizing" that, as Steven wants to do, is the first step toward accepting it wholesale.

Should we fear pedophiles? No. "Pedophilia is not very common," he says. "It might be one percent of the population who are primarily attracted to prepubescent minors." I'm not sure how honest people are in surveys like that, but okay.

"If you see one hundred people in the street, one of them is a pedophile." Steven delivers the stat like he's unburdening me of my fear of child molesters. It's had the opposite effect. This means while walking to work, I passed several men who wanted to have sex with my children. My gosh.

Don't stigmatize pedophilia, says Steven. "The way that we treat pedophilia and other forms of minor attraction with a heavy stigma can actually inhibit people from getting help. It can scare them away from getting help. A lot of, even therapists, if someone comes to them saying, 'Hey, I'm attracted to children,' they'll call the police, even if they've never done anything. Now, there are therapists who know better than that and who don't do that. But there is still a risk that because this hatred of the condition is so ingrained, that people just won't admit it. They'll just live with this, and they'll just let it fester inside them without getting help, because they're too afraid to tell anyone and too afraid to reach out for help."

What's the law here? Well, a therapist is required to file a police report if they believe their patient is a danger to others. If a patient tells his therapist he's thinking about committing a crime (molesting a child), the therapist must report. Is there a legal difference between telling your therapist you desire sex with children versus that you plan to have sex with children? Perhaps ever so slightly, a lawyer would argue. But this is a dangerous space. Therapists should err on the side of protecting children.

Stigmatizing pedophilia "is a form of identity politics," says Steven. He's concerned about the stigma of pedophilia infecting other sexual arenas. "Stigma spreads. So you may say, 'Oh, well, I'm only going to be stigmatizing pedophiles.' But then it grows to include trans people. Then it grows to include gay people. Because people's gut reaction of disgust or whatever about the attraction, it spreads. It never stays put. That's why you have drag queens. That's why you have all of these other LGBTQ groups who are also getting smeared as pedophiles. Not because they've ever abused a child or ever would abuse a child, but just because their sexuality is lumped in together."

The degenerate behavior of pedophiles, Steven worries, is bad PR for gays, lesbians, transgenders, and drag queens. Ironically, it's Steven's PR game that needs improvement. He was weirdly unable to give me a straight answer on where he stood on "age of consent" laws.

"The age of consent, where do you come down on that?" I ask. "It's eighteen in California and some states." In other states, "it might be fifteen, sixteen."

"Prostasia Foundation's position is that it doesn't involve itself in debates about changes to the age of consent, because that is not a subject that we want to concern ourselves with," says Steven. "We follow the law."

"Why wouldn't you, though?" I ask him. "The age of consent is a legal line . . . and you make a distinction between postpuberty and prepuberty. I'm surprised that you personally, or the group, doesn't have a read on that."

"I think it's not a scientific decision," he says.

Suddenly, "the science" no longer applies. Why?

"That kinda is a moral decision in a way. And so you can't get a scientific answer to that. You can't ask an expert what should the age of consent be, because it's really a question of risk. If the child is too young, then they might consent to something that is going to hurt them later on. They might regret it later on. And the younger the child is, the more likely that is, because children are silly and impulsive and they don't really understand what sex is. And so as a society, we need to work out what's the right balance to strike between teenagers being independent and making their own decisions and living with the consequences for their decisions, the balance between that and protecting younger children."

Steven begins waxing philosophical. "Is eighteen the right age? Maybe. In different times of history, maybe fourteen was an okay age. Or in some countries, I think it's still that age. It's a question for the society to decide. And there's no real right or wrong answer. It's just whatever age you pick, everyone has to agree to live with that. And if we think there are too many teenagers ending up on the sex offense registry for having relations with each other, then maybe the age is too high. But if there are teenagers who are ending up pregnant, and this is sort of normalized within society, maybe the age is too low. But I don't have the magic answer to that. Prostasia doesn't have the magic answer to that. So it's just such a hard question that the best solution is just to not enter that debate at all and just to accept whatever society has decided."

I tell Steven he's being "cowardly." I also tell him it's "odd" for him not to take a position since he's been "brave enough to dive into this [taboo] discussion" about the rights of minor-attracted people. Furthermore, age of consent laws are absolutely informed by science. "Scientifically, you can say developmentally, sexually, psychologically, or emotionally, this is the age that science believes teenagers are able to consent to sexual relations. You don't have an opinion on that?"

Steven responds strangely. "It comes down to risk," he tells me. "Not every time when a child is sexually abused, they end up suffering harm. Some children actually survive and may even look back at something that happened to them when they were under the age of consent and be happy about it. But you can't know that in advance."

This is the kind of concerning statement that makes Steven suspicious in polite society. He then couches what he just said. "There are many, many more examples of children who had early sexual experiences and regretted it. And yes, it really depends a lot on the circumstances. But regardless of the circumstances, there's a higher risk that they're going to have a bad memory or some trauma. So, I don't think it's cowardly. I think it's just acknowledging that we are not always good at assessing risk individually.

"And that's why we rely on society to set guidelines. The same reason why we have traffic laws that set a speed limit. I wouldn't trust myself to be able to know what is a safe speed limit. I am comforted by the fact that we have a number that someone has chosen, and presumably some experts have given their input into that. And it's a number that our society is comfortable with, and I'm happy to live with that. And so that's my approach to the age of consent as well."

Steven, an expert in the minor-attracted-persons industry, needs an expert to tell him what a minor is. Plus, his analogy doesn't fly. A cop isn't going to let you off with a warning if you're having sex with a girl just a few months before her eighteenth birthday. Maybe Steven and I have different driving styles. "I don't ever really look at the speed limit to determine, 'Oh, well, an expert told me that forty-five miles per hour is the legal limit.' . . . I drive the roads instinctually," I explain to him. I drive differently under different conditions. When I speed, I speed safely, and rarely notice the speed limit unless I'm in a hurry on the Garden State Parkway. The New Jersey State Police don't play. They treat every speeder like a pedophile.

"You're a member of society," I remind Steven. "You keep saying you 'pay attention to what society chooses' . . . so instinctually, as a member of society . . . do you think [the age of consent] should be eighteen? Do you think it's seventeen? Do you think it's sixteen, fifteen, fourteen?"

"Every child is different," he says. "And so there would be a different age of consent for everyone if there wasn't a single uniform age of consent, because everyone matures at a different rate. And so the whole purpose of having an age of consent is because that's a road that you don't want to go down. You don't want to have to make a judgment call, is this kid mature enough for sex? That's not a judgment call that anyone should be making, if for no other reason that they're probably not a neutral party if they're considering sexual activity with a child. They're going to err on the side of what they want, not what the child wants. And that's a bad thing. And that's why having an age of consent is a good thing, so that you don't have to make those determinations.

"If Prostasia were to become an organization which was to have debates about what the age of consent would be, we would get a lot of pro-abuse advocacy saying to lower it. And that's not the kind of force that Prostasia wants to be in society. It doesn't want to be seen as promoting more tolerance for sex between adults and children because our position from the outset has been we are never going to go there."

Steven's language is revealing. When he says "pro-abuse advocates," he's referring to child molesters. "Pro-abuse advocacy" is the sanitized term for the child molester lobby. The Obama administration called an Islamic terrorist shooting up a military base "workplace violence." When you talk like this, you have an agenda. Steven confesses that Prostasia "doesn't want to be seen as promoting more tolerance for sex between adults and children." Notice the concern with public relations.

"It's always going to be considered wrong if it's against the law," he says. "So that was a very conscious decision not to allow those sorts of debates." Remember, it's not "wrong" for an adult to fantasize about sex with kids, according to Steven; it's "wrong" to have sex with kids. Is it wrong because it's against the law? Or is it more wrong because it's immoral? What makes it more wrong, the illegality or the immorality? Steven doesn't say. He just doesn't want to "go there" on age limits, "because once you open up that door, there's no closing it." Steven doesn't like the optics of the debate. "Prostasia is wrongly seen already as being pro-abuser. That's not correct. But you can just imagine how much more that argument would apply if Prostasia was to entertain arguments about the age of consent being changed."

This still seems like a dodge. I call him out. "I understand from an organizational standpoint, from a defensive position, you don't want to go down that slippery slope. But you're not a member of the organization. You're just Steven, a guy here talking to me. And you're saying, I guess, it depends on the individual minor, whether they're ready for that. But we make calls like that all the time when it comes to setting ages for a driver's license, whether it's for setting ages for parental consent for an abortion, trans surgeries for children, sending them off to war at eighteen. You set age limits for all kinds of things, and people have opinions about those things. And you don't do it on an individual level, 'This person's not ready to go to war. This person's not ready to start drinking. This person's not ready to buy tobacco.' You still have a national age limit or a state age limit. Personally, you don't want to tell me sixteen, seventeen, fourteen, fifteen, eighteen?"

He ping-pongs it back to me. "What do you think it should be?"

"I think it should be eighteen," I say. As a father of three girls, the older the better. And as a father of one boy, eighteen is ample. He's a stud. We don't want any of his female high school teachers preying on him. Too tempting.

"I think eighteen is a good age," says Steven, "but it is arbitrary. If I lived in a state where the age was sixteen, I would probably feel that was okay. I wouldn't feel comfortable with sixteen-year-olds being pursued by much older people, obviously. That kind of icks me out. But should it be possible for a sixteen-year-old to choose to have sex with a partner of their choosing? Probably that's fine as well."

The age of consent laws in the United States range from sixteen to eighteen, with most states settling at sixteen. Most states also have "Romeo and Juliet" laws, exempting couples close in age. So we're talking about the age a teen can consent to sex with a full-on adult. In Europe and Latin America, the age of consent ranges from fourteen to eighteen. In other parts of the world, the age of consent can go as low as twelve. Several countries set the bar at "puberty." Others set the bar at "marriage," which doesn't sound like much of a bar at all.

"But it's not totally arbitrary, right, Steven? Because I assume you wouldn't be comfortable with it being ten, right?"

"No. Obviously. Historically it was assumed that puberty marked the age of sexual maturity. Nowadays, I think we understand child development better, and we realize that often they may have the signs of puberty well before they're psychologically ready to be entering into sexual relationships. So we now would say that an age of twelve or something is too young. But anything between puberty and eighteen, I think, is a range where countries can choose to set their ages of consent. In many countries of Europe, the age is fourteen. That seems young to me. That probably doesn't sit well with me personally, but there are different cultures where that is seen as being okay. And you can understand why they might want to do that, possibly just so that young teenagers are not going to have the risk of ending up as criminals for doing what comes naturally. But for me, I would go with sixteen or eighteen."

There you have it. Extracting the appropriate age of consent from Steven took fifteen minutes. Why so hard?

"How old are your children?" I ask.

"Eleven and fifteen. A boy and a girl."

"And you'd feel comfortable with your daughter at sixteen having sex with an adult male?"

"I think I would have the same level of discomfort as any parent would with that. Nobody likes to think about their children having sex, even their adult children sometimes. It's just something a parent doesn't want to think about. So that's the reaction that I have to it."

My next question rattles Steven. "Do you think a minor-attracted person should be a babysitter?"

"I don't think that . . . It really depends, I guess, on the individual. I don't think that . . ."

He pauses to think. I've struck a nerve.

"Because that question raises a whole lot of other questions," he says, "like do you know that you are hiring such a person as your babysitter or is it something that is secret in their head, and who's making the choice? Should the MAP themselves agree to babysit, or is it someone else? What are you asking?"

"It's not that hard of a question," I say. "Are you comfortable with a minor-attracted person being a babysitter?"

"I can't really say in the abstract because, like I said, all that means is that the person finds some under-eighteens to be attractive."

Actually, Steven said earlier that most adult men find under-eighteens attractive. Remember the high school cheerleaders? The science? He continues to struggle.

"If they're babysitting a three-year-old, then they're not going to be any risk to that person, are they? Because they're not attracted to three-year-olds. They're maybe attracted to fifteen-year-olds. I think it's a call that they have to make. If they're babysitting someone that they might be putting at risk, then of course they shouldn't do that. And they ought to recuse themselves in the same way that they shouldn't put themselves in a risky situation at school or at a sports event. Anyone who feels like they may be at risk of behaving inappropriately shouldn't put themselves in a position where that might happen. And so it comes down to personal responsibility at the end. We all have to take responsibility for not putting ourselves in situations where we might be tempted to cause harm."

Let's see where he goes with this. "So if you have a minor-attracted person who wants to be a middle school volleyball coach . . ."

"If they would be in close proximity to children that they would be attracted to, and if they feel like there's any risk that they couldn't control themselves in that situation, then that would be inappropriate for them. But you can't make a blanket ruling and treat all MAPs as the same because they may be attracted to different ages, to different genders. They may have different levels of control over their feelings."

Let's get personal. "So you wouldn't be okay with a minor-attracted person babysitting your eleven- and fifteen-year-old?"

"I wouldn't have insight into their head," he says. "I wouldn't really know what's going on. If they told me or if I had some reason to know that they were attracted to the ages of children that they would be babysitting, then I would probably choose someone else."

"Oh, you would?"

"Yeah."

"Why?"

"Because I do know that that is, regardless of whether someone admits to being minor-attracted or not, that's one of the most risky situations you can have. Leaving children alone with someone who isn't their guardian is one of the riskiest situations that children can be put into. And that's why youth pastors in churches are a particular risk of offending. And why sports coaches are a particular risk of offending."

"So you believe that minor-attracted people, adults, are potentially criminally dangerous towards children."

"Anyone is potentially criminally dangerous," deflects Steven. "That's not a useful question to ask."

"Are they more potentially criminally dangerous than someone without that attraction?"

"Yeah," Steven finally concedes. "There's an expert called Michael Seto who has a model of sexual offending called the Motivation-Facilitation Model. And according to that model, you need a motivating factor to offend, which could be a sexual attraction towards children, having pedophilia . . . so that's a motivating factor, but that by itself is not enough to create a risk of offending. You also need facilitating factors, and facilitating factors can include things like unsupervised access to children. So you have the motivating factor plus the facilitating factor, and that equals the risk of offending. So does existing in society as a minor-attracted person make you a risk to children? Not without those facilitating factors as well. So facilitating factors, in addition to the one I mentioned, alcohol can be a facilitating factor. Having other mental health problems such as depression and anxiety can be a facilitating factor."

"So a minor-attracted person, adult, is such a risk that they can't be left alone with children. They can't be—"

Steven interrupts me. "That's not what I said."

Yes, he did. Steven just told me "unsupervised access to children" is a "facilitating factor" for a minor-attracted person. "That sounds pretty dangerous to me."

"You shouldn't leave any unrelated adult alone with the child if you can avoid it," he says. "Because you have no way of knowing what's in that person's head."

"So I can't hire a babysitter?"

"Well, that's why we have background checks for babysitters. You've got to be really careful."

"Well, a minor-attracted person does not come up on a background check," I tell Steven. "Only a convicted person does. People don't do FBI background checks to hire babysitters. By the way, we can't even trust the FBI with our elections; you think we trust them with our children? The FBI let the Michigan State gymnastic coach molest gymnasts for years after the abuse was reported. Not happening.

"So you're saying you can't leave a minor-attracted person alone with a child, and they can't really drink alcohol because that—"

"I didn't say that." He interrupts me again.

"I thought you said that facilitated that urge."

"No," says Steven, getting flustered. "There are various facilitating factors that may apply to different people. You can't generalize. Some people can drink alcohol, some people can't."

I get angry for the first time. "Steven, I'm just mentioning the risk factors that you brought up, and now I'm a little more concerned than I was at the beginning of the interview because you said in the beginning of the interview that everybody has urges. Now you're saying you can't leave them alone with children."

"But I'm not saying that," he argues. "That's what you are saying."

"No, you just said that. You said you wouldn't let a minor-attracted adult babysit or be alone with children."

"I said I think if I knew that their age of attraction, their range of ages that they're attracted to was the same as the ages of my children, I wouldn't take that risk."

"Because it's risky. That they might rape your kid. You don't think that's dangerous? This sounds dangerous, Steven."

"We live with risk all the time, and so we have to decide what are the risks we're willing to take and what are the risks we're not."

"Are you willing to take a risk of having a minor-attracted person around your eleven-year-old? No."

"I wouldn't have. Personally, I don't allow any adult unsupervised around my children."

There you have it. Steven doesn't hire babysitters or nannies. He doesn't leave his children alone with a music teacher or a tutor or a tennis coach. Maybe this is why Steven doesn't seem especially worried about pedophiles hurting his kids. He's worried about everybody hurting his kids.

"This seems a little sort of evasive, though," I tell him. "We live with risks all the time, but some risks are more manageable than others. The premise of the question is, are minor-attracted persons, by virtue of their sexual attraction to children, more dangerous around children."

Steven finally surrenders. "If you're hiring a babysitter, and for some unaccountable reason, you happen to know that this person is attracted to your children, it would be unwise for you to leave them alone with your children because yes, there is a risk and unsupervised access could elevate that risk. So yeah, that would be risky. So I'm not denying, the whole premise of the conversation is that this is one of the factors that can lead towards the risk of offending, and that's why we need to make sure that this population has the support that they need to stay at living law-abiding lives."

I'm still not satisfied. "But don't a lot of minor-attracted people go out of their way to put themselves into situations where they're alone with children?"

"Do they?"

"Well, yeah."

"If you say so, because I don't think that there's any evidence of that."

"You don't think there's any evidence that there's a lot of minor-attracted people working with children in schools, in churches, in Boy Scouts, in youth groups throughout the country? You think they just avoid children at all costs?"

"No." Steven's stubbornness is questionable.

"You're saying that minor-attracted people don't necessarily seek out children to be alone with, any more than—"

"That's a generalization. No, I mean some do, obviously, some do."

"Steven, that's like saying alcoholics don't go to bars."

"I would be interested to see research on that, if there is research on that."

"Steven, with respect, you're saying it's a coincidence that a lot of these pedophiles just so happen to be working with children in the Boy Scouts, in the Catholic Church. . . . Come on, Steven. You're not seriously telling me that."

"I have no . . ." Steven sighs. Finally, he agrees "some of them" seek out opportunities to gain unsupervised access to children. "But what's your point?" he asks me.

"What's my point? The whole point of this is that you're trying to prevent minor-attracted people from being alone with children."

"Yeah." Steven just stares at me. Then he tells me that minor-attracted people are denied the therapy they need because society isn't open-minded enough to have these conversations. It's society's fault.

The project that Steven is engaged in is about eliminating the social distinctions between those who are sexually attracted to children and those who aren't. When those social distinctions—dare I even say "stigmas"—are eliminated, what's to stop the political and legal distinctions from disappearing next? If there's no moral difference between someone who wants to have sex with children and someone who doesn't, what's the reason for restricting one over the other?

"My point is this," I tell him. "You can say the same thing about criminals. Oh listen, these murderers, these rapists, these gangbangers, these sex traffickers, these drug dealers, if only they had the mental health support, we have to stop stigmatizing them. If only they had the mental health support, the psychological support that they needed, they wouldn't go about killing people, punching people, and stealing cars."

"So what's your solution?" Steven asks me, throwing his hands up. "I'm hearing a lot of criticism and not much by way of solutions. What's your solution?"

"I am gathering from you, from all of this evidence that you've presented, that these people can't be trusted and that there actually has to be an aggressive approach by society, punitive and preemptive. Restrict access to children, and when there is an offense, to punish harshly, because it's an urge."

I tell Steven I used to travel the country confronting judges who gave soft sentences to child sex offenders. *The O'Reilly Factor* created so many waves that forty-five out of the fifty states passed some version of Jessica's Law. The law was named after a nine-year-old Florida girl, Jessica Lunsford, who was kidnapped, repeatedly raped, and murdered by a twice-convicted sex offender who should never have been free at the time. Jessica's Law calls for a mandatory minimum twenty-year prison sentence if you're convicted of raping a child under twelve. First offense. The judge has no discretion. Long sentences are required because the crime is so heinous and because the rate of recidivism among child sexual abusers is high. Oftentimes, they will molest again if released back into the community quickly.

Steven jumps in. "You're wrong," he says. "Courts for a long time operated on the assumption that there was a high rate of recidivism. And a friend of mine who's actually an advisor to Prostasia Foundation, called Ira Ellman, looked into it and wrote a journal article that's been very well cited and has since changed the opinions of some of the judges who were writing these cases." Steven insists the rate of recidivism among child sex offenders is "not frightening and high." Steven claims the large majority of child molesters are "not unstoppable monsters." "Most cases, someone does offend only once, and they can be rehabilitated successfully. And most, in fact, are rehabilitated successfully."

I'm not swallowing the study Steven's pushing. I google child molester recidivism rates on the fly and the stats don't jibe with Steven's source.

"This is not a good statistic, Steven. The initial follow-up of the child molesters found that forty-two percent were reconvicted of a sexual or violent crime during the fifteen- to thirty-year follow-up period." I continue to investigate the recidivism rate among child molesters and most studies peg it at around 35 percent. That seems high to me, even if it means most don't go to prison a second time. Yet Steven tells me the studies I'm finding have been "debunked." He always has a factoid that makes child molesters appear less dangerous.

Even if we assume Steven is right, if you found out that only one in ten men who went to prison for raping a little girl were caught raping another little girl in the next five years, would you feel a lot better about men who rape little girls?

I ask why Steven pursued a career helping the cause of sex offenders. Most children, when you ask them, 'What do you want to be when you grow up?' say athlete, work on cars, be a doctor. Not Steven. He's found his purpose in life helping adults horny for kids. "You're trying to explain their side of things. You're trying to destigmatize their issues. That's an interesting calling."

"I wouldn't say that that's true at all. My mission is the prevention of child sexual abuse. And we just don't believe that the methods that our society uses right now are effective in doing that. Just treating it with this blind moral panic and just ignoring statistics and science is not helping to prevent children from being abused."

Every day we're flooded by new calls to "destigmatize" everything—obesity, youth sex changes, and so on. Those are debates we can have, if we must. But "stigma," properly directed, is a crucial part of any healthy society. In fact, cultural and political mores that draw a line between good and bad things, encouraging the good things and discouraging the bad things, is the basis of civilization itself; it's a line between order and chaos. Some people should be ashamed of their actions and ideas—and few things are more deserving of shame than wanting to have sex with children.

"*To Catch a Predator*. What were your feelings on that show?"

"Well," says Steven. "It's encouraged a lot of vigilantism that contin-ues to this day. And now it's people on YouTube who have their *Catch a Predator*-style channels, and they're not qualified. They're not backed by the police. They're dangerous. They can misfire, they can target in-nocent people, and even if they target guilty people, they can make it harder to get them brought to justice because you're not doing this as a police officer who knows what they're doing. You're doing it as an am-ateur, and you could be messing up the evidence or who knows what."

"But initially, Chris Hansen, after the first season, was working with law enforcement."

"And if that's the case, then some of those concerns go away. But I also then still have concerns about how we are turning this into enter-tainment. And it doesn't sit right with me that we should be creating entertainment fodder out of something so terrible."

"So you don't like the show *Cops* either?"

"Not really. Yeah, I think it's kind of exploitative."

Steven probably hates *The Bachelor* too. And *Real Housewives*. He's missing out on a lot of good TV.

"Were you abused as a child sexually?"

"No, not exactly," he says. "There were some things that we wouldn't get away with nowadays. I remember when I was in the Boy Scouts, and we were all showering together in an unenclosed space with adults there, things like that. So we wouldn't accept that sort of behavior these days. But I wasn't actually abused."

I ask Steven if he was ever inappropriate. "Did you ever do anything to a child? Or when you were like nineteen and she was like fifteen, did anything like that happen in your life that set this course up for you?"

"No," says Steven. "I was a very late bloomer. Yeah, I didn't even date until I was almost thirty."

I start laughing.

"I'm sorry, I didn't mean to laugh, Steven. You didn't date until you were thirty?"

"Yeah, I was very shy and a bit of a workaholic as well."

"You didn't lose your virginity until you were thirty?"

"I was in my twenties when I lost my virginity," he says, "but I didn't have a girlfriend until I was thirty."

Oof.

"You were thirty. What was that first time like for you? Was it har-rowing? You must have been nervous as hell."

"Yeah."

"That must have lasted thirty seconds. . . ."

Anyway. Don't want to be mean to Steven, the late bloomer. I'm glad he waited.

"Your wife, I got to ask. She's married you. God bless you two. She knows what you're involved with. Is this awkward at dinner parties?"

"I feel like you are approaching this as a shameful vocation, and I don't feel that way about it at all."

No shame in Steven's game. Not even a little.

"I feel like I'm doing an absolutely necessary service because I am willing to tackle a topic that has caused a lot of harmful, misguided hate and intolerance and abuse to flourish unchecked for so long. And I'm one of the few people who is willing to put their personal reputation on the line to fight back and say, no, this is not helpful. I have no shame at all about the approach that I take towards this topic. And in fact, it's served me well. I'm now a trust and safety consultant. I get paid by internet companies to take the same approach to their networks, to take an approach that's based on research, that's based on statistics and evidence rather than being based on gut response."

Internet companies have Steven, an advocate for minor-attracted persons, on their payroll. These internet companies receive requests from law enforcement. They manage chat rooms and enact privacy guidelines. When potential issues of online predators arise, don't trust your gut, Steven advises them. Follow the research Steven gives you. The studies that "prove" pedophiles aren't that scary. Have no fear, minor-attracted people: with Steven in your corner, the internet is your safe space. How comforting. Are these euphemisms—"online safety," "digital rights"—a way for MAP activists to disguise their agenda?

Steven is "proud" of his work. "I talk about this at dinner parties with anyone who's willing to, and I have no qualms about that."

Sue, this is Steven. Steven, this is Sue. Steven was just telling me he does PR for pedophiles. Sue and I were just talking about how pedophiles could use more advocates. Isn't that right, Sue? By the way, Steven, we're new to the neighborhood. Know any good babysitters?

Besides protecting children, Steven claims he's also protecting the rainbow. His secondary goal is to "protect the human rights of others who are harmed by our society's reactionary, non-nuanced approach to this topic. And that includes the LGBTQ community, it includes sex workers, it includes writers of fiction, and creators of art who are accused falsely of being pedophiles. . . . And so while yes, protecting children is the ultimate objective, it's also driven by a feeling of social justice towards these people." Steven blurts out, "I am a progressive. And yes, I think that the political right has captured the issue of child sexual abuse and pedophilia and turned it into a weapon of the culture wars. And I think that that's wrong. I think that it shouldn't be politicized in that way. I don't think that we should be calling our political enemies pedophiles and groomers. I think that's absolutely harmful and that it causes a lot of innocent people to suffer."

Steven strikes me as a Dick Morris for sexual extremists. He's a political consultant. He provides talking points, research, and communications strategies for people on the sexually abnormal spectrum. But this isn't a two-way street. Steven compares himself to a lot of progressive groups who have never endorsed his approach. The more mainstream LGBTQ community isn't comfortable being a part of the minor-attracted persons movement. The queer scene doesn't want Steven "defending" them. With disappointment in his eye, Steven admits most of the left is "terrified" of the MAP movement. But it's not his fault; it's society's fault his work is "too radioactive."

Just take a look at Prostasia's website, and you'll see what radioactive means. The group is lobbying against further child porn restrictions and, in some cases, lobbying for loosening of restrictions on child pornography. Steven is lobbying against the CREEPER (Curbing Realistic Exploitative Electronic Pedophilic Robots) Act. This legislation would ban the sales of infant-sized sex dolls. These child sex dolls are available online. They have settings that simulate rape. Steven is against the CREEPER Act . . . and against any restriction of pedophile cartoons or child rape fantasy fiction.

"So art and fiction should not be criminalized as child pornography. If it doesn't harm a child, then it shouldn't be treated the same way," he says. Steven prefers all resources going to stopping actual children from being abused. "Cartoons don't harm anyone."

"So what about if you got a graphic image of a kindergartner getting raped and it's computer-simulated, it looks real as hell, Steven. That's not child porn?" I ask.

"No," he argues, "because no one's harmed. If no one's harmed by it, then we have no business banning it."

"I'm obviously the greatest listener in the country and very open-minded, and super-nuanced, which is why I'm spending time listening to you and not judging whatsoever," I tell Steven. But there's an anger building inside me. Theoretically, I understand Steven's position on all this. But it's repulsive.

"Who funds your research?" I ask him. Always follow the money. "Where does the money come from?"

"Well," he says, "Prostasia files taxes and discloses the sources of its revenue. And some of those are anonymous donations, so I can't reveal the sources. In general terms . . ."

"Some are anonymous donations?"

"Sorry?"

"They're anonymous donations?"

"I can say where some of the money has come from because that's on the public record. We had a grant from a charitable foundation called the Just Beginnings Collaborative, which also funds a lot of other child abuse prevention work. So that's one of the sources. We also had a grant from another foundation, which I'm trying to remember the name of right now, but I can't, but I can get back to you on that if you want."

"You have no idea where this money's coming from to fund this research?"

"Yeah, I know exactly where it's coming from," he says defiantly. "I'm just not telling you exactly where it's coming from because I respect the anonymity of some of our donors, and they have absolutely every reason for that because of the way that we've been targeted as a group. It's absolutely reasonable that our donors would want to remain anonymous because they don't want to be targeted in the same way that I've personally been targeted."

"Maybe it's the cynic in me," I tell him, "but you always can get what you pay for, if you know what I mean, Steven."

"I don't know what you mean. This research is peer-reviewed, we're not paying for results, we're paying—"

I interrupt. "I know there's been a lot of peer-reviewed research recently that I think you and I can both agree it might have turned out differently than what the facts were."

"Peer-reviewed" doesn't have the cachet Steven thinks it does. Thousands of "peer-reviewed" research papers on everything from global warming to Covid to junk food have turned out to be garbage. This research is often funded by the industry that profits from the paper's conclusion. And the "peers" are just other researchers who rely on the same research grant money.

"Listen, I understand your position," I say. "I really do. And I don't want to be antagonistic, but there's an evasiveness to some of your answers where you're being a little squirrely. There's a reason why society treats pedophiles the way they do. And you know that reason."

Steven holds his ground. "I'm never going to apologize for taking this stance that we need to think less about the sexuality and more about the action, because it's the action that harms the child, and it's the action that needs to stop."

"And I would like for you to give me a little credit for being so open-minded and such a great questioner."

"Okay. I mean, I didn't much like the way you tried to pin me down on the babysitter thing, but otherwise, I think you did a great job."

"I'm not on board with it," I tell him. "But I totally see what you're saying. I think there's something that we're all not saying, that you're not saying, that's a little concerning."

"Do you want to spell it out?"

I explain to Steven that the money flowing to the MAP lobby is suspicious. Paying for research could be "academic washing." Draping a legitimate academic study over a filthy concept for better PR. This money could be a "front" for "forces involved in this space that maybe you're aware of, maybe you're not aware of, that aren't good, Steven."

"I know, that sounds . . ."

"And I think you know exactly what I'm talking about," I tell him straight up.

"It sounds a little conspiracy theory."

That's what they say when you're over the target.

"Listen, you know that that's there," I tell him. "I don't want to push it, but it's there." I'm trying to be respectful.

"If there are forces like that," he says, "then I don't see them. I see a lot of speculation, and the closest that maybe we got to that was [Jeffrey] Epstein, right? Because people were protecting him. Someone was protecting him. Some people were protecting him. So, if there is some kind of conspiracy going on, I think it's got to do with money. And that's not money that Prostasia is seeing."

"You would agree," I say, "that there are wealthy men, and that there have been wealthy, powerful men, not just in the United States, but all over the world, from the beginning of time, that have an attraction towards younger women, eleven, twelve, thirteen, fourteen, that get away with that."

"Yeah."

"And that are protected at the highest levels, either through the modeling industry, politics, big business, whatever it is. Absolutely. And there's a world out there. You're aware of the world; the internet's fueled it. You're aware of that world. And that's a dangerous world. And that's something that I want to protect my children from. I think all children need to be protected from that. And your industry, the space that you're in, I hope isn't a window into that, isn't fueling that, isn't being taken advantage of through that. And I want you to open your eyes a little bit wider to that, because that's a very powerful and dangerous world out there."

"Yeah," he admits, "there are pro-contact pedophiles or pro-contact MAPs, who do have an agenda to liberalize, as they would say, the law regarding sex between adults and children. And I totally oppose that. I don't want to be associated with any of those people. We need to expose those groups, the ones that actually are trying to cover up or to reduce the age of consent or to make excuses for the child sexual abuse. And I have done everything that I can to make sure that the work that I do is not a part of that, and that we are just driven by prevention and by expert guidance. But do those forces exist? Yes. I don't necessarily talk about them in the same conspiratorial way, but I do concede that there probably is a shadowy realm of people who want to make things easier for child abusers, and I'm not part of that."

"I understand. I just don't want your group to be a vehicle for any of that. And because you're very well-spoken, the group's involved with academia, and the way you kind of couch this in research studies and the language of statistics. I just wanted to be careful there. Okay. Be really careful. All right, Steven."

This was a warning. I've said my piece.

He says, "All right."

This is as close as we'll get to the darkness.

"How was that Fox News–esque interview?

"I don't know," he says. "This is probably about what I expected."

9

The Homeless Addict

Ray (not his real name) was bleeding. But now the blood was dry. It was on the back of his hand and forearm. His hair was a hive of thick brown matted waves . . . bedhead meets rock star. Cadbury cream eyes in another world. Shabby clothes. Loose. There was a smell. Thick and unwholesome. I'd found him slouching through Port Authority, the main bus hub terminal on the west side of midtown Manhattan. It's not a great scene here. Commuters, workers, runaways, tourists, addicts, and hustlers bustling around at different speeds and angles. I'd come here to interview a homeless guy—and found Ray. A white male, thirty-four, medium height, slim build, and strung out. I'm calling him Ray to protect him, but who knows if the name he gave me was real anyway. I shake his hand and get started (I have gloves on).

Ray sees homelessness as a game. "It's different every day," he says. "When I came out here, I came out here with pretty much nothing. I came out here with the idea that I wanted to do a few different things." He "wanted to kind of film it, but in the beginning, when I kept getting phones—I kept losing my phone. So I really couldn't keep recording it. But I pretty much make it a game—where am I going to stay? How am I going to eat?" He makes it a "trick" on how he "gets by."

When you interview homeless people, other street people always want to get in on the action. Interested in why someone wants to talk to this homeless guy, and not them. They want attention too. It's already started. My security guy and I politely, but firmly, shoo an aggressive dude away. He's asking questions and interrupting, showing off. "It's for a book project, buddy, just step away and give me a minute." It works, but he's lurking. And Ray's breath isn't wonderful. This is going to be a short interview.

Ray is from Long Island, originally, but he "came out here at the start of Covid" a few years back. He doesn't seem that upset he's homeless either. "Little entrepreneurial things" is how he hustles and gets money, food, and places to stay. "But I like the city because the city's different than Long Island." There's "opportunity out here," he says. "You can always find a place to stay." And "the more interesting or the more creative you are with how you're going to do things, you can really make anything happen." In a weird way, the New York homelessness shtick was a way for him to just find something to do. Ray "had no job" when Covid started, and he'd broken up with his girlfriend, so he "just came over here to just make something different."

At first, Ray says, he had bigger plans. "I wanted to do stand-up comedy, I wanted to do certain things, but everything was closed. So I kind of got stuck into the whole Covid thing, and I kind of got steered away from what I originally wanted to do, and I kind of got wrapped up in my whole thing." Now Ray lives life "day by day." There isn't any long-term planning, or even medium-term planning, you know, the kind of planning most people do to prosper. But delusions remain embedded. "I still have the same idea that the city always had unlimited possibilities and opportunities that you really can't get anywhere else. So I still believe that, but I have things on my shoulder that's holding me back." Success is just around the corner. Ray just needs to break free from what's holding him back.

He has his GED and some college education, but school wasn't really his thing. As a kid, "I was using drugs a little bit," he says. "I kind of got into trouble." That ended with "some charges" and "a little bit of jail time." He was either sentenced to "two to four" years or caught "two to four" charges. Hard to decipher everything Ray says. Senator John Fetterman is easier to understand. Ray's speech is slurred, his phrases are vague, and there is constant shifting and fidgeting. He's a mess.

"What originally did you get convicted of when you were in high school?" I ask.

"It was a burglary."

"What'd you take?"

"It was like a tit-for-tat thing or whatever. Someone got over on me, and then I went back and went in there and tried to make up for what I lost by taking some stuff. I took some bullshit like video games, and just whatever I could grab and stuff. But I got a burglary charge because I went in the house with the intent to commit a crime. But I was just young and stupid."

Felony charges. "Intent" is key. Just ask Hillary Clinton.

Ray's father was in construction but then got into "video production and stuff" with his mom. "They do music. They record independent artists, independent bands . . . music videos . . . or if you were doing a commercial or filming your podcast."

What's the mom's role?

"My mother, she's a singer. She does a Cher impersonation."

"Was there anything in your childhood that happened to you that was traumatic?" Besides his mom being a Cher impersonator.

"No. Well, no, that's why I say I had the good childhood, and got progressively worse with adulthood. I don't think the good childhood has nothing to do with why I do drugs."

"When you first did heroin, how old were you then? And how did you get there?"

"Fourteen was weed. Sixteen was like opiates. And twenty-one I think it was heroin."

I ask Ray if his parents know his situation. "Do you have a relationship?"

"Yeah, I got a good relationship with them. They want me to come back and see them more, but it gets hard going back and forth. . . . They know my situation. They're kind of dealing with their things, so when I'm there I kind of just brought extra stuff. So kind of just give them a break from their things. Because they got my sister's kids now, and they got a whole full household. So I would just be probably another thing that they got to deal with."

"You don't want to be a burden on the parents."

"Yeah."

Ray's sister had children. She couldn't care for them. So her parents stepped in. I don't have time to explore each family avenue with Ray. Keeping the momentum of the conversation going is more important. He's scattered and mumbling. The clock is ticking.

He came to the city without a real plan. Originally, "I first came out here because I started on a program" for drug addicts, he says. "It was like methadone." Then Ray started meeting people and stopped going back and forth from his Long Island home to the program in the city. He just stayed in the city because "it was easier." Ray just set out into the city without a place to live. And he's been homeless in the city for over three years. I empathize with him. Commuting daily on the Long Island Rail Road is soul-draining. I spent a decade taking that train into Manhattan. It makes choosing life on the streets seem like a logical option.

But Ray didn't have the discipline to stick to rehab. He wasn't—and isn't—consistent. "I get into little spurts where I miss it for a couple days," he says of the program. "I miss it, and then I get back on track. . . . When everything starts falling apart, I got to pick myself up, focus on getting back in and getting into the program, start getting back into something. Not just letting everything fall apart. I have to kind of have focus and get disciplined enough to go in the morning and actually keep up."

John Steinbeck supposedly once remarked that the reason socialism never came to America is that poor people in this country don't see themselves as poor—they see themselves as future rich people. That's Ray. He sees his homelessness as an opportunity—and eventually, that will make him someone. "Sometimes I'll get different things and just find little opportunities, find stuff to sell." He claims he has a podcast too—"I pretty much just talk to entrepreneurs and what they see about success, how they got success, and what they would tell aspiring entrepreneurs. But out here, I wanted to go for the street vendors, the street musicians, the people that play on the subways, because I love listening to the drummers, the violin. I'll say I have different characters that I make for acting or writing."

Do I believe Ray has a podcast? No. Like most people on the streets (and from Long Island), he embellishes.

Ray wants to be a writer. And on the street, "I see a lot of the characters that I'll be writing about," he says. "This is a good place for a writer to be if you're trying to write a project." He says he sees himself as a "Method actor," like Robert Downey Jr.—"an actor that doesn't break character" while they're filming a movie, even off-set. "I'm trying to do that thing, Method writing, where if you're writing a book or a movie, you'll go, and you'll actually live that character's life, and you actually live out the movie, kind of like in a Borat kind of way."

"Do you have any of your writing on you now?"

"I don't," Ray says. "I got a lot of my stuff at home."

Sure you do.

"I've been writing multiple stories at once, and a lot of it I'll be writing in my head. But with the Method writing thing, I'd be writing it in my head until I actually get things on paper . . . getting the idea down and then the transfer from paper to computer is actually when most of the work gets done."

You don't say.

Ray romanticizes his vagrancy. His brain is zonked. Pretending he's a starving artist to justify his descent into oblivion. The kind of making-yourself-the-character approach to writing that Ray's describing is a real thing—Hunter S. Thompson's "gonzo journalism," of course, is a famous example. Writers like Jack Kerouac too wrote semiautobiographical, semifictional accounts of their own exploits. Kerouac's *On the Road*, most famously, was an account of his own semi-homeless, vagrant exploits, traipsing all across the country with the characters he encountered on the way. Kerouac's was a restless, longing style— "Nothing behind me, everything ahead of me, as is ever so on the road." It was a fascination with the world, and particularly with America—a desire to cram as much experience into one's life as possible: "The only people for me are the mad ones, the ones who are mad to live, mad to talk, mad to be saved, desirous of everything at the same time, the ones who never yawn or say a commonplace thing, but burn, burn, burn like fabulous yellow roman candles exploding like spiders across the stars. . . ."

There's nothing artistic about Ray's experience at all. He doesn't even carry a pen. No journal. No tape recorder. Lost his iPhone years ago. Lost his mind too.

"What is your day-to-day like?" I ask.

"So sometimes I try to live off my means . . . you find warm places to go, especially when it's cold. I like the train. Sometimes I feel like I'm on a little roller coaster at night or whatever, it lulls you to sleep."

Ray maintains he has a poetic fascination with his own world. But it's not clear how much of it is voluntary—like Kerouac, who made a conscious decision to live the life he lived—versus how much of it is an attempt to make an otherwise bleak life something that's worthy of enchantment.

Ray is restless—looking for something he hasn't found: "Sometimes I look at the things that I was originally trying to do, and I'm almost feeling like the things that used to make me happy, it's not the same anymore," he says. It gets to the point where "everything has gotten so bad that maybe I need to change up and find new things that are going to keep me interested, and wanting to progress and get better rather than just give up and pull back into not caring. And so it's kind of hard, especially because I'm by myself out here." There's "a lot of help in the city," he says. "But still, you're alone, you're still by yourself. You know what I'm saying?"

Not really.

"You said you were selling stuff for money. What kind of stuff?"

"I get things like peanuts or candy and stuff, and I find it funny because I usually sell to the food guys on the street. I'll sell it to the food guys. So the food guys sell food to people that are hungry on the street, and I sell food to the food guys. And that's an inside joke I had."

Translation: Ray buys food from street vendors and sells the food back to different food vendors. He pockets the markup.

It's a depressing life. He knows it.

"I'll be trying to get myself together, and sometimes when my depression gets worse, I get worse with it and I'll not care. I won't go to my program and stuff, but then it won't be working until I get back on track and try to . . . It's difficult because I try not to go overboard. I don't want to get back into a place where it's just all negative. So I try to keep it under wraps, but then I'm also trying to deal with my own stuff and try to figure out what it is that I'm actually doing."

He's completely untethered from society, from himself too.

"What's the program that you're in right now, and how often do you go?"

The program Ray's in is called Greenwich House. It has a methadone maintenance treatment program. It's a legit nonprofit that's been around for over a century. But you can't help someone if they don't want help. Ray doesn't really want it.

"So you inject the heroin . . ."

"Yeah," he says. "Inject."

"How does that make you feel?"

"I mean, obviously . . . Well, how it's been getting, just the drugs in general, has been progressively getting worse. Well, a little bit. Sometimes I get better, but right now, since . . ."

I have no idea what he's saying. Ray's a rambling man.

"That first time you shot up, what was that like?"

"I was using [opioids] for a little bit, and then I think I was going through withdrawal. I think I was going through withdrawals, and I remember I couldn't get it. I was really sick, and I was selling at the time, and I remember I was really sick, and I kind of got it in my head, forget it. I'm going to shoot this. And I called one of my friends that did that because I had a couple opportunities to do it. And I let impulse and emotion . . . I was getting mad. Let me kind of facilitate the bad decision, and then I'll let the anger and adrenaline just take over and then you can just put it on that."

"Do you have any regrets that you did that?"

"Yeah, no. Obviously, yeah. And then obviously no because I always needed the chaos in my life. . . . But obviously I have regrets because things happen on the way that you don't plan and shit."

Ray spirals.

"In my life of all the years that I've been using, this has been the worst, where you would think I would just quit and just stop completely, but then it gets so frustrating that where I actually feel like I'm using out of spite sometimes. Like, I'm not even using, but I'm using out of spite because I feel like I'm being pushed into recovery when it's not. Recovery's fine, but when I'm being pushed into recovery then it feels like then I got to push back. Because I got to think if the only reason to ever get clean and the only reason to ever get sober would be to feel better for happiness or success, and there's no reason to do that if you're going to be miserable. And I mean, it goes back and forth because if I have the idea and I want to do it, then it's fine or whatever, but if I'm been pushed into it . . . Anytime I was on a court-mandated thing there was always a pushback."

Sobriety is miserable. Addiction is miserable. Ray uses heroin out of spite. Don't try to help Ray get clean. That'll only make him use more. Get it?

"Why do you think that's part of your personality? To push back against people that are trying to help you?"

"It's an identity thing," he explains. "One of the things I liked about out here was, I don't know, I guess the chaos and the problems and having to have that. I guess when it goes pleasure, pain, pleasure, pain."

Having problems means Ray exists. His life is that meaningless. The chaos proves he's alive.

"The worst part about drugs is withdrawals and the pain, but the more pain you go in, when you get the pleasure, the pleasure feels that much better."

That's junkie poetry.

"So if you were always high, it would get boring. Same thing when you only do heroin. It'll get boring. So you switch over to another drug, you do an upper. I call it a vacation drug. But it's the push-pull of the pain, pleasure, pain, the up-down."

"So you kind of like the chaos," I say. "You like the pain and the pleasure, the extreme back-and-forth of it."

"Yeah, I don't like . . . When you're in pain, you obviously are not like, oh this pain's just so good. You don't like the pain, but you need both. You need the push-pull because just like what I was saying, without sadness you won't have happiness. Without pain, you won't have pleasure. Without hate, you won't have love. I used to have a thought: What was created first, good or evil? You need evil first to create good because there'd be no reason for good, if there wasn't evil. There wouldn't be no bad. If there wasn't conflict, there wouldn't be no way to have the good to overcome the conflict."

The philosophy of self-destruction. It's just a shallow rationalization. It's not deep. Trust me, if Jesse Watters can understand it, it's not deep.

Ray is the Evel Knievel of heroin addicts. Crack open death's door for a peek. Who's that curious? Sounds like an excuse. Injecting black tar isn't an extreme sport. You're not a mystical frontiersman. You're slowly killing yourself and rebranding it as "research."

"So you've kind of opened up that wormhole. What does that look like? Tell us about that."

"It's interesting, but it's messed up because it could put you in. Talking about going as far as you come into insanity without going insane, you're opening up a door, most people aren't going to do that because it's dangerous. And there's really very limited room for success. And also, it puts you in a really depressive state, and that's why I use drugs to self-medicate."

So Ray self-medicates with heroin because he's depressed from doing so much heroin.

"If I had unlimited resources and I could do it with a scientist, I think if I can do it like that, I could do it in the safest way. Think about how crazy it'd be . . . to where you would overdose and have people right there with you ready to bring you back to life to kind of see if . . . And I'm sure they probably do studies like that to see what happens in those three minutes of death, in that minute of death to see what happens, and you bring them back. And if you actually had the medical resources to have that happen and then in a safe or scientific way, actually bring them back, what it would be like and actually document it."

"So you're experimenting with death, you're experimenting on yourself, and you're trying to get as close as you possibly can like a scientist?"

"Yeah," he says. But Ray claims it's not really him doing this. "It's a character, so I kind of toy with it myself. So that's a character that I'm writing about, but it's also something I think about, and I think about it so much, or play with. So it feels like I do it, but I don't have any of the resources to really do it the way I would want to. But I'm talking about how I would do it if I had those resources."

Fact check: Ray isn't writing anything. This isn't a character. This is who he is. Ray has disassociated himself from Ray to make killing Ray easier.

"Why do you think you like that chaotic lifestyle?"

"It isn't that I like it," he says. "I don't know. I'm just kind of drawn to it. It's like a need, it's needing that problem. Needing the problem to solve. If you don't have the problem then you kind of go seeking it. Like self-sabotage. I'm talking about it because it's something I've been thinking about. It's not like I go, Oh, I need a problem. It's not like I go consciously looking for a problem. It's like a subconscious thing."

"The self-sabotage, why do you think you feel that instinct?"

"I think it's just with depression and not living up to what you want. I don't know. It's hard to really . . . I don't know."

"Do you want to not be homeless anymore? Are you trying to get out of this state or you're enjoying this kind of life?"

"Yes and no. I'm not enjoying it. The homelessness itself isn't the problem. . . . I can go to my mother's, I can maybe get a place to live. The homelessness itself isn't really the problem. The things I'm trying to work on, my depression or a job or things like finding purpose and stuff, that's way more important than just having a home. The homelessness, that's nomadic and I like to move and find where I'm going and stuff. And I kind of stopped here."

Chronic homelessness is a choice for most people. Nearly all of them you talk to tell you that. The problem is the government doesn't want to listen. Liberals keep spending money on the homeless and homelessness goes up. Liberals then demand higher taxes to pay for more homeless "services." Nobody tells you this, but the homeless "problem" creates a lot of good-paying jobs and titles for liberals who "help" the homeless. Homelessness goes down and those jobs and titles go away. Liberals would rather feel compassionate helping the homeless stay comfortable on the streets than address the main drivers of homelessness: drug addiction, mental illness, and permissive city laws that allow camping out on public property.

"So the nomadic lifestyle, that's something you enjoy?"

"Yeah. And I go nomadic, I kind of stay around here a little bit, and I kind of get stuck in one place because of comfortability, or just the comfortability where I know people and stuff. But yeah, the actual homelessness itself isn't the big problem. That's actually the easy part."

Ray claims people envy him because "I have freedom that people don't. That's kind of easy being homeless; you don't really have that many responsibilities and stuff. There's a lot of stresses that come along with them, but that part, that's not even the part that bothers me."

"Do you worry about your safety or your comfort at all? Are you scared ever?"

"Yeah. Scared of where I'm at or something happening."

"You're vulnerable out here. You don't really have a permanent residence. You don't have a lot of resources. It's winter coming around the corner."

"I was always adapt," Ray assures me. "I just adapt to it."

"How does the city government or the police treat you? Do you have any interactions with them?"

"One of the things I like about here, I used to get arrested a lot more in Suffolk County [on Long Island]. Out here, I don't know, I kind of just blend in. I just do my own thing, be let alone, and I'm trying not to, I don't know. I just do what I need to do to survive and just try to do me."

Ray is still a child. Everyone is forced to take care of him. So he can prove he exists.

"It's like parents waking you up for school. The five more minutes or whatever I'm in the subway and they try to kick me out. So I feel like the raccoon in their garbage."

Vivid. Maybe Ray is a writer after all.

10

The No-Boundaries Parent

Child-rearing. It's challenging. Not every culture does it the same way. In Japan, "it isn't uncommon for seven-year-olds and even four-year-olds to ride the subway by themselves," NPR reports. In the Tibetan plateau, many communities continue to practice what is known as "fraternal polyandry," which is "the marriage of all brothers in a family to the same wife." This allows "families in areas of scarce farmable land to hold agricultural estates together," as a 2013 *Atlantic* piece detailed.

In the West, we've traditionally treated the two-parent model as a source of hierarchical authority. The parents impart their standards and wisdom to their children—and their children are expected to listen. It doesn't always work out perfectly. Look around. Some parents have "different" styles.

I discovered Kaytlynn online. "My kids don't go to school or doctors—people call my parenting 'abusive,' 'dangerous,'" the *New York Post* headline declared breathlessly. A *Daily Mail* write-up carried a similar title: "My children pick their own bedtimes, have a vegan diet and go barefoot—people accuse me of 'abuse' but I'm confident in my decisions." The tabloids report Kaytlynn "does not allow" her children "to go to school, see the doctor or eat meat, animal products or processed sugars," nor does she "require her kids to have a bedtime, sleep in their own bed or even wear shoes." The twenty-three-year-old "Missouri mommy blogger," as the *New York Post* piece put it, often treats her young children—the three-year-old Olive and the one-year-old Felix—as coequal peers: "Basically my philosophy is respectful parenting, just showing kids the same respect that adults get," she tells me. Part of what that means, in practice, is that if she tells her children "no," they don't have to obey. They can negotiate.

Along with her thirty-one-year-old husband, Jesse—whom she met while they were both working "at a health food store in Wisconsin"—Kaytlynn is intent on raising homeschooled, barefoot, vegan babies.

She's skinny, fit, and pale with nice large eyes and straight, thin, auburn hair. The woman is crunchy. Not liberal crunchy. Just crunchy.

"We try to go barefoot as much as we can because it's good for grounding and stuff like that."

Walking barefoot is "connecting you to the earth. The earth has charging properties, and so it's good for you to be exposing as much skin as you can to be getting the sun, and then also getting your feet on the ground, specifically on grass."

She's probably right. But do it privately. I don't love looking at strangers' feet.

Kaytlynn has been vegan herself "for six years," she says. "When I was around sixteen, I watched a documentary—*Vegucated*—and I wanted to go vegan, but my parents would not let me. The day I turned eighteen, I went fully vegan, and I have been since then."

She emancipated her stomach and emancipated herself from her parents. Growing up, she was the oldest of eight kids, but she "didn't like the way that my parents did things," she tells me. When it came to her mother and father's parenting style, she says, "There was a lot of shaming and guilt. I don't talk to my mom. I haven't talked to my mom in three years, because I wanted to keep my kids from that."

She still talks to her dad—"He's changed a lot, he knows that he screwed up," she says—but "my mom, she keeps saying she'll change, but she never did. So I was like, you know what? We're done."

In Kaytlynn's upbringing, "there was a lot of verbal abuse, and spankings and things like that, and I didn't agree with that growing up," she tells me. "I took a lot of notes growing up, being like, all right, I'm not going to do that to my kids because it makes me feel bad, and I don't want to make my kids feel bad."

For example, "as a little kid, if you spilled something, you were made to feel really shameful for that, even though accidents happen. So it's hard to rewire your brain that it's okay to make a mess."

This is where I have to cut her off. "It is not okay to make a mess. It is not okay. It happens, sure. But we need to be careful. We need to be careful and aware."

I feel a boiling rage ready to erupt. I'm a chill guy, but nothing makes me angrier than spilling. I'm very careful not to spill, and when someone else spills, I don't care how old they are. It drives me crazy. Be aware of your surroundings. Watch what you're doing. When new-age gurus talk about "being mindful," they're probably talking about not spilling. Spilling is something we can control. So why not control it? I'm constantly surveying the scene for potential spills. Glass on the edge of the table, a child's wingspan, a dog's trot path. Carelessness cannot be acceptable. I don't believe in clumsiness. I believe people are careless. If you raise your children to think spilling is no big deal, then they will spill more often. A stern admonishment with a disgusted scowl will send the right message. I want my children to "feel bad" for spilling. Not only is spilling wasteful, but it's going to stain. I detest stains. My eye is drawn to them. Stains are never able to be removed 100 percent. They linger and haunt me. My daughter Sofie once spilled an entire can of white paint onto my new kitchen floor. It took hours to clean, but I never could get all the white paint removed from the dark wood plank crevices. Every time I walked through the kitchen, I was reminded of "the accident." It's become family folklore. Both my daughters know how incensed I become when they spill, and they both sense how disappointed I can get. They immediately clean whatever is spilled, and we don't talk about it. Even if it doesn't stain, spilling is straight-up sloppy. It's rude. It's a party foul that should bring great shame to the spiller. It's downright inconsiderate and, obviously, uncoordinated. If, on extremely rare occasions, I spill coffee in my car, I immediately do breathing exercises to calm down. But I take full responsibility. Normalizing spilling normalizes carelessness, and a careless life is not worth living.

Kaytlynn reveals she got pregnant "about six months" before she got married. Right under the wire.

"Was your mom upset that you were pregnant during the ceremony?" I asked.

"She definitely wasn't pleased," said Kaytlynn. "She had me out of wedlock, and so I feel like she couldn't hate too much. And she finally got over it." But that wasn't it. Kaytlynn did the second thing parents hate at their children's weddings. "We did not have a pastor officiate the wedding. That she was not happy about."

Just make your parents happy for your wedding. It's not that hard. Wait to get pregnant and have a pastor officiate. The rest of your life, go nuts.

Kaytlynn's first pregnancy was a home birth. Her daughter. She used a midwife. But the delivery was rotten. When her water broke, her labor started, but her midwife was late. She barely made it in time. "I wasn't super-comfortable with them, and so I didn't want to be completely naked. And so they're like, 'Do you want to take your bra off?' And I said, 'No.' And so, as I'm pushing my baby out, they just ripped my bra off of me after I told them no. So that was upsetting. And then afterward, they pulled the placenta out of me." Apparently, you aren't supposed to pull. "My daughter was born twelve fifteen a.m. on Christmas Eve, and so they wanted to get home . . . and so they left my house a disaster. It was a waste of five thousand dollars. It was a waste of time."

With her son, Kaytlynn did things differently. She only got one ultrasound, just to find out the gender. "I got no prenatal care with him. I never saw a doctor, never got any tests done. And then I had him at home with just my husband and a birthkeeper, which is kind of similar to a doula. It's nonmedical; she's just kind of there to support. And then she did all the cleanup, so that was nice."

"You hired an Oath Keeper to deliver your baby?" I asked.

"No. A birthkeeper."

"Got it."

A "free birth" is when you have a baby at home with no medical professionals. The birthkeeper isn't trained, just there for support. All I hear is "Oath Keepers" and "birthers," and imagine people storming the capitol in Kenya looking for the long form. And there's no way my wife's delivering our baby at home. I'm not getting under center yelling, "Hike!" Plus, stains.

"What if this baby's breech? That didn't cross your mind?"

"You can feel a baby's breech," she says. "If I am forty weeks pregnant and I feel kicks on my rib cage, I know he's head down, where if I feel kicks down in my pelvic area, I know he's breech, and so I could do things to flip him. You can do maneuvers to flip the baby around."

Like a belly dancer who rolls her abs, I'm imagining.

"So you had a water birth?"

"We blew up a big tub and filled it up in our kitchen, and that's where I had them."

"Like the ones you see in the backyard?"

"It's similar to that."

"And you are underwater?"

"The baby is," she explains. "From my stomach down, I'm underwater. I've had both my kids in the water."

What's the point of that?

"Mostly comfort. When you're in water, you're lighter, and so it makes you feel better. Water is a natural pain reliever, and so it makes everything more comfortable. It's also said to be a smoother transition for the baby, because they lived in water for nine months."

I still don't understand how that works. Babies are born fish?

I read that Kaytlynn doesn't let her infants touch the ground. "You're carrying them around everywhere?"

"Yeah, we do. I baby-wear them pretty much all the time. We didn't really put them in strollers. But yeah, they preferred to be held. I held them for most of their naps."

"You hold them for naps?" I can't process this. "Don't you want a little free time for yourself to put them down in the crib or the bedroom?"

"Yeah, sometimes, but at the same time, I don't know. I'm that person that's like, 'Oh, I want a break. I need a break.' And then I don't have my babies with me, and then I'm like, 'Oh, actually I want them back.'"

We're looking at serious attachment issues here.

"You want your babies on you all the time?"

"Yeah. It's what's most natural. They just spent nine months in you, and then they're told to be separated from you for twelve hours at night. And then for every nap, which babies nap a lot, and I don't know, that's not natural. They want to be close to their mom. It's called the fourth trimester. The next three months after birth is the fourth trimester, which means that babies should still be on you a majority of the time."

The "fourth trimester" sounds like summer school. Not ideal.

"Did you get them vaccinated?" I think I know the answer.

"No, they are not."

"Not even the polio vaccine? Are they allowed to go to school without certain vaccinations?"

"We do plan to homeschool them, so that's not going to be a concern. Since ten, I've never gotten a flu vaccine or anything like that. I was homeschooled, but I wanted to try out high school for a semester, so I did have to get the tetanus shot. But besides that, I've never had vaccines since I was ten."

"And you're not worried about stepping on rusty nails?"

"No. We're aware of our surroundings, and we don't really go where rusty nails are, and so it's not too big of a concern."

They're obviously not that aware of their surroundings by the amount of spilling going on.

"But you're a barefoot person . . . ?"

"We do go barefoot a lot at the park. Where we live, I don't know, people throw glass everywhere, and I don't know why. So there's always glass on the ground. We have to wear shoes. And so there's always dog poop everywhere. Obviously, if you're on the concrete, you're not really getting the same benefit. There's a barrier between the ground and your feet there."

She's right about that. Not about the birthkeepers. But about bare feet on the grass being good for the soul. Of course, you don't just get tetanus from rusty nails. You can get the bacterial infection from any cut that gets dirty outside. She may want to look up herbal remedies for lockjaw, just in case.

"You have these two babies, and you're breastfeeding, obviously, and are you giving them the vegan diet?"

"Yeah. My kids have never had animal products."

"A succulent bite of a dry-aged rib eye, heavily marbleized, has never slipped down their gullet?"

"No," she says, not enticed by my mouthwatering steak description. "Our kids are great eaters. They eat so many fruits and vegetables, and their favorite food is quinoa and beans."

"I wish I could get my son to eat quinoa. Nice break from the sausage and the chicken fingers."

"We go to a chiropractor pretty regularly," she adds.

"Your one-year-old goes to a chiropractor?"

"My daughter's been seeing a chiropractor since she was two days old. My son's been seeing a chiropractor since he was a month old. They're very healthy. They're never sick. They're never constipated like a lot of kids. They don't get ear infections. They're very healthy."

"Wow. Okay. No vaccines. They're going to the chiropractor. They're not going to school. They're barefoot in the park, and they're vegans. Have they ever watched television?"

"We don't have a TV."

Worst part of these kids' lives is not the quinoa breakfasts and rusty nails through the feet. It's not having the pleasure of seeing me on Fox. Denying children access to Fox is like denying them access to clean drinking water. I'm this close to calling child protective services.

"And do you have set bedtimes?" I ask. "Or is it more of a free-for-all?"

"Technically, no," says Kaytlynn, "there's no set bedtime, but that doesn't mean that they don't sleep."

Well, when would they start sleeping?

"But yeah, that could be anywhere from as early as five p.m. or ten p.m. There was a good stretch where my kids were waking up between two thirty and three a.m. That was their wake-up time. I don't know why, it sucked, I'm not a morning person."

"That's crazy," I tell her. "Do you guys all sleep in the same bed together?"

"Yes, we always have. After having my son, we got two queen mattresses. We pushed them up together."

"Does that affect your sex life with your husband?"

"Not really," she says. "That's because my husband goes to bed at six p.m. because he has to wake up at two a.m. for work, and so I wouldn't be going to bed with him anyways, and he'd be waking up long before I do." Kaytlynn works around these challenges. "I guess you just have to get creative and use other opportunities and stuff like that."

"Are you worried that your sleeping arrangements and your sleep philosophy might be instilling some bad sleep habits?"

"I don't think so. The United States is one of the only countries that doesn't promote and actually talks against bed-sharing and co-sleeping. Most other cultures and countries all sleep together."

Fact check: no cultures are bed-sharing by pushing two queen mattresses together to fit the whole family.

"All the way up until age ten, most kids are sleeping with their parents, because biologically that's what we would be doing because you needed to sleep together to stay together in case there was an outside threat. And so if we're talking biologically, that's what we were designed to do, as well as the fact that there's a big push to get kids and babies to be independent and doing things by themselves so quickly."

Biologically, men for many years needed to impregnate as many women as possible, but we don't do that anymore. Well, most of us.

"I don't like sleeping alone," Kaytlynn finally explains, which is the real reason two queen mattresses are pushed together. "I like sleeping with my husband and having somebody in bed with me as a comfort. . . . And so I only can imagine how a young kid who is very little and very vulnerable and doesn't really understand that nothing's going to come and hurt them or anything like that. And so I think it's normal to establish a good attachment and bond. And then when they're ready, they'll sleep on their own."

Or when Kaytlynn is ready to sleep on her own. Which could be never.

"So tell me a little bit about your husband. He gets up pretty early for work. What does he do?"

"He's a morning stocker and forklift driver at Costco. And so he works from four a.m. to twelve thirty."

Is Kaytlynn's husband down with radical parenting? She says he very much was like, "You know more about this, and so I'll let you come up with this stuff, and then we'll talk about it. And then he's always just agreed with what I've said that we should do."

Nothing says "healthy relationship" like a spouse who never expresses opinions or makes decisions.

"Do the kids ever disrespect you? Do you have a hard time disciplining them?"

"They definitely have a personality and like to push buttons and do things that they're not supposed to. And it's definitely a learning curve." Kaytlynn says she "tries" to discipline them "but it's really hard." She resists "yelling" at them, or "raising [her] voice." Her parenting style is referred to as "gentle parenting." "Basically, my philosophy is respectful parenting, just showing kids the same respect that adults get."

"Do you think children should be treated equally with adults? And children should be treated with the same level of respect and authority?"

"Absolutely," she says, "if not more."

Why?

"Because as adults, we have a mature brain, we know how to act, and we know how to talk to people. We know what's right and wrong, whereas a kid does not, so kids deserve more leniency because they don't have a mature brain like adults do."

Adults who know how to act weren't raised by "gentle parents." Kaytlynn hasn't grasped that yet. Cause and effect.

"Do your children ever boss you around a little?"

"Yeah," Kaytlynn admits.

"When your daughter does talk back to you, how do you handle that?"

Kaytlynn says she just laughs. "She is just trying to be silly. We know she's not trying to disrespect us. She's three. She really doesn't know how to do that. She doesn't really know the difference between respect and disrespect."

Usually, parents teach the difference.

"A lot of times, she is just trying to be playful, and so I think parents are a little too serious. They think everything that their kid is doing is an attack on them. The kid is trying to upset them, and that's not the case. A lot of times kids are just kind of being funny. And so a lot of times when my daughter talks back, she has a big smile on her face. She's playing around."

Kaytlynn says if her kids disobey her, she lets them tell her why she's wrong. "If we say no to something or we tell them they have to do something, they can try and persuade us otherwise, if they come back with something good."

If you think America needs more lawyers, raise your children like Kaytlynn.

"Here's the scenario. Your three-year-old calls you a poopy face . . ."

"She is very into talking like that right now," says Kaytlynn. "Poop and butt are her favorite thing. I mean, honestly, it is funny."

It is.

"If they're hitting us, we tell them that's not okay. If you want to hit, you can go hit your stuffed animal or something like that."

"So they hit you."

"My one-year-old is kind of getting in the phase where he wants to hit and throw things at you. Yeah."

I don't let my kids hit me. Only if we're playing "hitting games." And I don't permit roughhousing. Only in the playroom or outside. If my kids climb on the coffee table or couch, I tell them, "This isn't a jungle gym." Kaytlynn, on the other hand, turned her house into a jungle gym.

"My husband built a big jungle gym. Our apartment is set up weird. We don't really have a living room. Our living room is the playroom, and they have a bedroom, our bedroom, it's really large. And so it has two recliners in it. And so our house is set up very much for our kids so that they can play. We do own really used things that were cheap. And so it's not the end of the world if it were to break or get damaged. And honestly, within reason, getting hurt is a natural consequence. If we tell them to stop jumping off something because they're going to get hurt, and they do it, and they get hurt, they learn from that."

"So you've redesigned your apartment, putting them first. You don't have the living room. You have a big playroom. In your bedroom, you've got people sleeping all over the place."

"Yeah," says Kaytlynn.

"A lot of parents don't do that," I tell her.

"No, and that's fine. I think everyone should make their home fit for their needs. For us, it just makes things easier. Honestly, there's less power struggle. There's less 'Get off that. Stop doing that.' If where we are a majority of the time is safe for the kids and is good for them, it makes it so much easier to just let them play and do what they want."

Kaytlynn refuses to parent, so she's arranged her house and habits so she doesn't have to parent. She's blurred the line between parent and child. Between parent and kid bedrooms, between playroom and living room. Avoidance is the parenting strategy, or "nonparenting." As a result, Kaytlynn is losing her identity as a mom, wife, and frankly, as an adult. I feel bad for her, and tell her she's sacrificing all of her adult needs to mollify her children.

She understands. "Yeah. I get told that a lot [online], the bags under my eyes and how tired I look. And that is because I am tired. I kind of have sacrificed my sleep in order to make my kids more comfortable and help them sleep better. And I don't get a lot of time to myself and things like that. And there are definitely days when it's hard."

She's opening up to me. I can see the sadness in her face. "Are you exhausted?"

"Most of the time I am, yes."

"Does that ever upset you?"

"Sometimes."

I ask if she drinks to handle stress. She doesn't. She uses medical marijuana.

"What was the ailment that you were able to obtain the medical marijuana card for?"

"Lower back pain. Since having my daughter, I've definitely had pretty bad lower back pain. Actually, my back just went out yesterday. And my husband had to come home from work early. Six months ago, I just leaned over to pick [my daughter] up, and my back went out, and I couldn't walk for an entire day. And since then, I've struggled with that back pain."

I know everything there is to know about back pain. After ten minutes of telling her about planking and stretching, I realize sleeping in bed with four people can't be helping. Then I realize something else. Should I get a medical marijuana card too?

Kaytlynn's stressed, her back went out, she's smoking to ease the pain, she's not sleeping well, bags under her eyes, not eating meat, not meshing with her husband at night, her kids are hitting her, calling her poopy face, and she doesn't watch Fox. What else could possibly go wrong? Well, Kaytlynn tells me she struggles with her mental health. "I struggled with depression and anxiety, and PTSD through most of my teenage years, and still as an adult. And that comes from the verbal and physical abuse that I had as a kid. And that hinders things that I can do as an adult. Even interacting with other adults is hard. Interacting with my kids can be hard because of that."

"What do you mean you have a hard time interacting with other adults?"

"I have a hard time communicating well with them. That's something that is hard, even in my relationship with my husband. Communicating, just being able to talk in general. It is hard just because growing up, I didn't really get to talk much. As kids, a lot of times you're told to be quiet and stop talking. And basically, what you say doesn't matter. And so I take that into adulthood. I have a hard time talking, thinking that what I say doesn't matter. Thinking that everything I say is wrong. And so I think that's what makes it hard for me to really want to talk to other adults. Just for fear of just not sounding like I'm saying the right thing."

"And you have trouble communicating with your husband too?"

"Yeah, it can still be a challenge. Also, it's hard communicating needs because I grew up being told that anytime you take time for yourself or you express a need, that's selfish. God tells you to always put everyone before yourself, and so if you don't, you're selfish. You're going to hell, whatever. And so yeah, I have a hard time communicating needs that I have. And so that kind of makes me suppress things or push my needs to the side until it's to the point where you kind of explode because you've just kind of built all this stuff up."

It's unlocking.

"That might be one of the things you brought with you to your parenting style. The 'Let's put everybody else first. If I do something for myself, I'm considered selfish.'"

"Yeah," she says, "it's definitely something I'm still working on. I went and got my hair done six months ago, and that's the very first time I had gone out and done something for myself since having my daughter. So almost three years. And that was definitely a hard thing to do."

She must think I'm the biggest narcissist. Haircuts, massage, sauna. But if the mom (or dad) doesn't take care of themselves, the children will grow up to not take care of themselves. You have to model behavior for your children.

Kaytlynn must have anger issues. How deep?

"I was getting frustrated with my son. I can't remember. I think he's pulling my hair or something. And my three-year-old told me, 'Mom, it's okay. He's a baby. You just have to breathe.' And so I was like, 'Okay, thank you. I do need to breathe. He is just a baby. He doesn't know what he's doing is wrong.'"

My three-year-old has never told me to calm down. Ever. Who's the parent here?

"Do you have road rage?" I ask. "You never just yell and scream in the car?"

"Yeah. Yeah, I sometimes do," she says. "My daughter will be like, 'What's wrong?' And I'm like, 'Oh, sometimes there's bad drivers out there.'"

This lady is STRESSED.

I tell her what her husband should be saying to her. "'Kaytlynn, go have a spa day. Spend the entire day at the spa. Nails, hair, feet, massage, wax. Whatever you want. Relax. I'll take the kids. You know what? Maybe hit the mall up. Go get yourself something. I'm taking you out to dinner tonight. We're going to relax. We're going to have a babysitter watch the kids, my parents will watch the kids,' whatever. Don't you think your husband should do that? It seems like you would really appreciate that."

"Yeah," says Kaytlynn, "I definitely would. We are a one-income household. We just don't have a lot of extra money, so that's a big reason I don't do things. We don't have family around, and I don't trust anyone to watch our kids. There's way too many horror stories out there. We don't have sitters."

"You seem to have attachment issues," I tell her. "Are you worried about passing those attachment issues along to [your kids]?"

"No. I think having a healthy attachment is good."

Kaytlynn isn't budging. Her style of parenting is "gentle parenting" or "respectful parenting." Kaytlynn needs an intervention. I tell her I'm a traditional parent. "Kids are thirsty for boundaries. They're kind of looking for the adults to tell them, 'This is the line, this is the proper way, don't cross this line.' And that kind of gives them a sense of identity and gives them a sense of where they fit into the world. And those kind of boundaries increase as they get older. And that's part of the growth process. It's sort of training wheels on a bike, right? You can't go as fast when you have training wheels on a bike. But if you first start riding a bike and you don't have training wheels, you're going to eat it. And then slowly you can take the training wheels off, you can ride a bike faster, et cetera, et cetera."

She just stares at me.

"Listen," I say. "I think you should be a little more selfish."

"I'll work on that," she says genuinely.

Jesse Watters is telling someone to be selfish. In this case, it's good advice.

"Kaytlynn, I'm a little worried about you." This is a tender moment. "I'm not going to lie. I want you to rest up."

"Yeah." Kaytlynn knows she's wearing herself down at a crazy clip.

"I want you to let the rage out when you feel rageful, but direct it appropriately. I want your husband to start taking you out and treating you special. The sleeping arrangements are a concern for me. The diet seems fine, I guess. And the barefoot through the park sounds like a good thing. I just want you to be happy. I'm worried that you're putting way too much pressure on yourself to do the opposite of what your mother did. There is a healthy balance, and I think you're going to be able to strike it. And again, get the MRI, because you could have a disc problem."

"Sure," she says. "Yeah, that's not a bad idea. Definitely."

That was the best pep talk I could deliver. Some of it sank in. But

Kaytlynn's husband has to take charge. After our interview, I asked to interview them together. Some good ol' marriage counseling courtesy of *Jesse Watters Primetime*. He declined. A bad sign of things to come.

Kaytlynn is a part of a self-described "crunchy community." She wears secondhand clothes, doesn't have internet, doesn't sleep well, and lets her kids call her "poopy head." They hit her and pull her hair. She's raised them vegan and takes them to chiropractors instead of school. She's stopped taking care of herself, doesn't use babysitters, and has back problems so severe she treats it with cannabis. She lacks confidence, has trust issues and trouble communicating. Plus, road rage. Her mother did a number on her. But she has the self-awareness to know this, and to know this lifestyle can't continue. But it will continue until Kaytlynn realizes that extreme attachment is unhealthy. And that children require parents, not peers. And that discipline is an expression of love, not anger. Parents can mess you up. And the messing up continues for generations until someone breaks the cycle. Break the cycle, Kaytlynn. And watch out for rusty nails.

11

The Toad Smoker

Everyone has their vices—booze, tobacco, prostitutes, chocolate, gambling, online shopping. When you need to take the edge off. It's only human.

Then there's Hector. He smokes toad venom and comes face-to-face with death itself.

To be fair, Hector doesn't consider smoking it a "vice." Yeah, he smokes toad, but he also serves as a spiritual guide for others who want to try it. You don't actually smoke the toad itself. You smoke the toad's psychedelic secretion. The indigenous tribes call it "bufo," and they're the guardians of the substance. "The keepers of the toad" have used it ritualistically for ages.

This drug isn't "chill." It can be terrifying: the small fishing tribes in Mexico who cultivate the "medicine" consider the toad the "God of the underworld."

"It sounds pretty hefty when you say it like that, but the reason they say that is when you pray with the toad, when you take the toad, you're briefly allowed to experience the afterlife for a few brief moments, and you come back," Hector says. The whole process lasts just fifteen to twenty minutes, but it can feel like an eternity. "Scientifically, when you take the 5-MeO-DMT"—that's the federally pro-hibited psychoactive chemical in the toad venom—"it turns off your prefrontal cortex," Hector says. "It stops your ego from thinking. It literally stops your neurons from firing. So, it's like your brain's not working correctly. Your consciousness leaves your body. And then once the effects start to wear off and your brain starts to fire again, that's when you come back."

"What's the trip like?" I ask.

"You're going into the universe, the great void. It's a beautiful place. You don't really get quite a lot of visuals. It's just more of a feeling. Sometimes, if you stare at the sun, the sun's really important. It's our biggest portal. So, if you take the medicine and you look at the sun and close your eyes, you can see different colors, and those colors are the way to the afterlife."

This is not intended to be medical advice. You should ask your doctor if staring directly into the sun is right for you.

"When you take the medicine, you go into a space that for some is quite scary, but for some is the most euphoric, beautiful place you could ever be."

Smoking toad venom is like an extreme sport. Volcano surfing, paraskiing, ice-climbing, free diving. Ridiculous risk. Not everyone makes it.

Hector's handsome. A half-white, half-indigenous Mexican kid. Late twenties, trim and healthy, alert. Well-groomed facial hair. He's light-skinned with dark features, white bandana wrapped around his head, rocking a bright yellow linen Native American–style spread-collar shirt. In his virtual background lurks an enormous toad, peering behind his head, its bulbous glassy eye looming in the Zoom. It's trippy, man.

He speaks about the toad with a religious reverence: The psychedelic venom is "sacred medicine," and ingesting it is "praying with the toad." "The Bible talks about a baptism when you go down, and you're resur-rected. Working with this toad is the true baptism." The first time he took it, "it changed my life profoundly. So yeah, I devoted my life to the medicine, and now I travel around and help people the way that I was helped."

Before finding the toad, Hector says he was a mess. He grew up poor in Texas. Was "molested by a guy in a trailer park." Pervert spent time in prison for it. Stepfather was a vet who struggled with PTSD. His real father was MIA.

He was "using cocaine on and off for about ten years since high school," down in South Texas, "real close to the border. It was a lot of drugs down there." He "could never quit for more than a couple months." And he "was in a very toxic marriage," with a young son in tow. After a life like this, Hector was desperate for a sense of meaning and spiritual purpose—and he found it in an unusual place.

Bufo was the remedy. Today, Hector is "almost four years sober"— after the first psychedelic-toad ceremony, he "quit cold turkey." Well, not exactly. After the toad ceremony, he "went into a real bad depression, and then I started microdosing mushrooms that my mom bought me. It brought me out of my depression, and I've been doing really good since."

Thank God for Mom's mushrooms. Now bufo is his only drug.

He quit cigarettes too: "At the time, I was smoking one and a half to two packs of cigarettes a day." During the ceremony "I put a blindfold on, and I put in earplugs. . . . Man, it was scary." There was "this voice in my head that told me, 'Hey, you can't breathe because you've been smoking too many cigarettes' . . . I could feel all the holes and the damage in my nasal cavity from all the cocaine. I was like, 'Man.' The back of my teeth were horrible. I was like, 'This is bad.' So yeah, I remember the voice of God or whatever it was. It sounded like my own voice, but it wasn't me. I was like, 'You got to stop doing the cocaine. It's rotting the inside of your nasal cavity. It's rotting your teeth.'"

The voice of God rang down from the heavens. "Stop snorting blow!!"

"How did you find yourself down in this tribal scene?" I ask Hector. "How did you come across these people?"

"I was at this church in Texas, and I was paying a lot of money every time I wanted a ceremony," he says. "I went to the owners of the place, and I was like, 'I feel called to work with this medicine on a bigger level.' They said, 'Well, we're having trouble sourcing medicine. If you can find some medicine, bring it back, and I'll teach you.'" So Hector drove south a couple of miles into Mexico and "was just hanging out."

Until a guy was like, "Hey, I know the Seri tribe. Do you want to go meet the elders?" "I was like, 'Holy shit, no way.' So, we got in the car, and we drove down there. That's when I met Luis. Luis is the head shaman of the Comcaac [tribe]. He's the one who served Mike Tyson."

Mike Tyson must've wanted to know what a near-death experience felt like—to know what his opponents experienced.

Hector spent two weeks with a foreign tribe in Mexico. "That first time going through a shamanic initiation, basically a vision quest, I was put on an island with no food and no water for four days, and just myself, and that's it. I made it through, and made a really strong connection to the spirit world. They put me through an initiation ceremony at the end of that."

It wasn't an easy experience, by any means. Hector talks about his vision quest as if it were a test: bufo "pushes you into psychosis from deprivation of sleep and food and water," he tells me. "If you can manage your way through that psychosis and come out and be okay, you're basically a shaman. You have the ability to handle yourself in an altered state of consciousness. It was one of the hardest and most scary things I've ever done in my life, [but also] one of the most beneficial. I found out that I can survive with nothing. It was amazing. I ended up getting a stomach ulcer from not eating for so long, and they gave me root water to drink for a few days. Yeah, it was pretty intense."

During the experience, "you're supposed to sing songs," he says. That's "the way of the shaman." Now, "when I serve somebody medicine," Hector sings to participants: "When you start to sing that song, the language and the vibration of your voice literally walks their soul up and out of their body. It helps separate their consciousness from their body, and it walks it through the portal, through the sun."

I ask him to give me a demonstration—without missing a beat, he breaks out into a kind of guttural but melodic chant, in a language I don't understand. I don't feel my consciousness separating from my body—but maybe that's because I haven't smoked anything. Yet.

Soon after his initiation, Hector traveled to a Mexican courthouse, filed the proper paperwork, returned to Texas, and legally established a legitimate toad-smoking religious organization called Yoosh Quii Yakoo. "It means house of God in the Seri language."

The indigenous tribe in Mexico that cultivates the toad lives on a "legitimate reservation" in Baja California, "where the Sonora Desert meets the sea." It is a tribe. The tribe is the Comcaac or the Seri tribe. Hector describes them as "a fishing community" who peacefully inhabited La Isla Tiburón (Shark Island). They're the keepers of the toad. To them, the toad is a deity. "The God of the underworld is what they say." The tribe lives in "family caves." Before I ask Hector about the divorce rate, he insists, "It's a beautiful place." If fish was the only thing on the menu, and I slept in a cave—with my wife *and* my sister, *and* my parents, *and* my wife's parents—I love everyone but please pass the toad. Still, Hector wants me to know, "It's quite profound." You'll find "random travelers" from across the world visiting, but "it takes guts to show up there by yourself," he says, and those who arrive solo "get treated with the most respect." The crazier you are, the more respect you get. It's just like the media.

The tribe "don't live for tomorrow." They plan nothing, he tells me. "They're really horrible with money." They just "live in the moment." What do they do all day? "They wake up, they go fish, they bring it home, they cook it, they go to bed. That's the life." Hector just described what millions of American men dream about their retirement.

There's a secret to catching fish. They serenade the sea. "There's songs that they sing to bring the fish in . . . you can pick up a fish with your hands, singing the song."

If I had to fish with my singing voice, I'd starve. You don't want to hear me sing.

The tribe has moved from family caves to "little cinder-block houses." No electricity, no running water. "It looks, to be quite honest," says Hector, "like a dump." There's a lot of trash everywhere.

The guy who owns the toad sanctuary is about three hours north of the actual tribe. He used to work for the cartel. After training with the tribe, the owner asked Hector for help getting some people off cocaine.

"So, there's three guys and one girl. The girl was about twenty-six years old. I served all of them medicine. The three guys, they ran drugs for the cartel, but I wasn't told until afterwards. But the girl that I served was one of the biggest hit men for the cartel. She had supposedly killed a couple hundred people. Yeah, it was intense."

"What was the woman's experience in the afterlife like, after killing all those people?"

"I felt sick. Going in and helping and singing for her, I physically started puking. It was horrible. I felt bad. She was throwing up and crying, and one of the toughest experiences that I've put somebody through."

If a hit man (or hit woman) goes into the afterlife for a second, they're not going to like what they see.

"She did not have a good time. I can tell you that much. It was really, really tough."

"Did she describe her experience to you?" I ask.

"No," he says. "She got up, and she left in a haste."

"The next day, one of the guys brought back a big old trash bag just full of weed. He was like, 'Here, I don't have any money, but here's this bag full of weed.' I was like, 'No, I can't take this across the border.'"

This was before Joe Biden became president.

On the heels of his first visit with the toad, Hector ended his marriage with his now ex-wife, Chloe: "After that first ceremony, on the way home, I told my mom, 'I'm divorcing Chloe. There's no way about it. I'm going to divorce her.' She's like, 'Well, just take your time.' About three months later, I divorced her."

He doesn't get to see his son, now five years old, as much as he'd like. "His mother is really quite bitter of who I've become and what I do now. So, I'm in a legal battle. As a matter of fact, I go to court in a few days to enforce my rights."

Would Hector smoke toad with his son? Yes, "if he feels called and it's something that he wants to do," Hector would give him the toad medicine too—even at a young age. Thirteen is the traditional age that the indigenous tribe Hector works with gives the venom to its young men: "At thirteen years old, they take the young men in the tribe who feel called, and they put them on the island for four days with no food or water. On the fifth day, they serve them medicine. So, thirteen is the rite of passage. I've served young friends of my family, fourteen, fifteen years old." That's appropriate, Hector argues: "If I would've had this medicine when I was that age, my whole life would be so much better. It taught me emotional stability, responsibility, compassion. The list just goes on."

The toad experience throttles lives: "This is the most serotonin substance known to man," he tells me. "You're going to be walking around feeling really, really, really good afterward. You'll want to make really hard decisions. Some people sell all their belongings and just go. So yeah, I've had a couple of people that weren't quite ready. They thought they were ready for the experience, but afterward, they didn't quite do so good because of a lack of daily structure of meditation and a spiritual practice, I would say. So, if you're going to do this, you have to have a plan for the few days afterward where you can really just hone in and sit with yourself and think and let the medicine work."

That doesn't mean that praying with the toad is for the faint of heart. Bufo isn't a party drug. The hallucinations are "basically like a near-death experience, but you really don't die," Hector says. "I mean, I've worked with hundreds and hundreds and hundreds of people, and I've never had any deaths." But he has seen some bad trips—and not the kind that you always come back from unscathed. "I have had people who have trouble integrating afterward," he says. "This medicine is one of the most powerful things on the face of this planet."

One man that Hector left "with a nice little bit of medicine—because I have access to an infinite amount"—went too far. "I got a phone call from his wife about nine months later, and he had been smoking the bufo every day. He had been taking it every day, and he had a psychotic break. To this day, he's still in a psychotic institution. So, you really got to be careful with these medications." Taking this drug is like Russian roulette.

The process from live toad in the wild to tripping your face off is gnarly. The toads are nocturnal. You peel them off the road after they've been run over while staring at streetlights (streetlights attract bugs, and toads eat bugs). "They take them to the ranch. We clean them off. We wash them off. We get them to urinate. So, that way, there's no urine in the medicine. There's no blood. There's no dirt or anything like that. We start a ceremony where we sing songs, we raise the vibration, and we collect medicine."

"How do you collect the medicine from the toad?"

"You pick it up, and you got to calm them down a little bit. You got to hum, and you got to sing a little bit and just give it a little bit of love.

It sounds weird, but if your energy's calm and everything's right, it'll just be there. You dunk it in water after it urinates to wash it off, and then you put a piece of glass or a tub or something, and you just pop the glands on there."

Apparently you can get it from them alive or dead. You pop the glands and collect the secretion—then what?

"It's dried off into little sheets, or sometimes you let it sit under the sun for twenty-four hours. Then I keep it in a jar in my purse. I don't let anybody touch it or handle it. Nobody touches that medicine but me. It's one of my most sacred items. I do a lot of weird rituals with it."

"And then do you put it in a pipe?"

"Exactly, yeah, you put it in a pipe. Yeah, it looks pretty bad, but you put it in a little meth pipe, and you vaporize it."

Hector's campaign to spread the drug far and wide—he's founded a "legitimate religious organization here in the United States" that can serve the medicine in indigenous churches, similar to how the psychedelic cactus peyote is protected by religious liberty in specific, circumscribed Native American rituals—is far less reckless than 1960s-era Timothy Leary–style experiments with LSD, and motivated by a far less hedonistic, "if it feels good, it is good" philosophy than many of the arguments one hears for drug legalization. He's seen the toad heal people, he insists. It may not be your cup of tea or mine. I'm doing just fine without any amphibious, slippery, pond-dwelling gods of the underworld in my life. But this is, at the end of the day, a free country—even if freedom means smoking a little psychedelic toad venom from time to time. That may not be what the Founding Fathers were thinking of when they wrote the Constitution. But then again: Had they ever tried bufo?

Hector himself has had some weird experiences serving the medicine as well as taking it. "I put a woman through an exorcism, and whatever demonic entity she had attached to her was now basically, long story short, inside of me," he recounts. "After I got done serving her, I left that ceremony. I felt horrible. I was fucked-up, man. I felt drunk. I had to have my girlfriend at the time drive the car. I couldn't drive. I was confused. I was lethargic. When I got home, I laid down and I went into a sleep paralysis. So, I was awake, but I was paralyzed.

I couldn't move. There was this big-ass being standing next to my bed, just scary as hell."

Hector's friend "brought up a little old woman from Colombia" who "takes care of the shamans." "She's the person who helps the shamans get rid of things that they can't get rid of," he says. "I kid you not, man, this woman with water and olive oil and salt and a long green onion, she restored my faith in Jesus Christ. She started praying with a silver crucifix. I took a little bit of salt that I got from the grocery store and drank some water with some olive oil. She told me to stick that onion down my throat and into a bucket, and I threw up a lizard."

Wait—what?

"Yeah, there's a lizard that came out of my body," Hector says. "It was this long." He holds out his hands to show me. "It was black. It had toes and shit, man. It freaked me out. I had to pick it up out of the bucket with a stick and walk it to a fire, and I had to burn it in the fire." Oh yeah, and Hector's son was with him throughout the whole ordeal. "He had my phone, so I didn't get pictures of it," Hector says. "I got rid of that demon."

"So there's a whole world of demons that circle around humanity and then can enter and exit throughout our souls?"

"Basically, yeah," he says. "One hundred percent."

Hector later tells me his mom used to have trouble sleeping. She saw a shaman. His mom "threw up a scorpion." Now she sleeps like a baby. No more sleep aids. Sounds normal.

"When you were growing up, was there any fascination with the spiritual world?" I ask.

"I actually had to go to therapy when I was younger because I would see things that weren't there," says Hector. "I remember one time when I was little, I was riding bikes with my little brother, and I could feel a really strong feeling. I remember feeling that jolt of fear, and I was like, 'Oh, fuck. Something's not right.' I look around, and I see this entity in a tree. I stopped riding my bike, and my brother, he kept going. I was screaming, 'Jordan, stop, stop, stop!' This thing came down out of the tree and knocked my brother off of the bike and was sitting there attacking him basically. That experience is what I had to go with therapy for. It was pretty hard-core. As I got a little bit older, that went away. Honestly, I was using cocaine and stuff at a very young age to deal with these feelings that I wasn't quite aware of at that time. So yeah, I've basically had some acute intuition my entire life."

It appears as though Hector's been dealing with demons his whole life. Also LSD. And "a little bit of heroin." "I just went on this whole thing and just trying to alter my conscience to where I didn't have to quite feel everything." Probably because he was molested by a guy in a trailer park when he was younger. Hector was born premature. "I wasn't supposed to live. I was hooked up in an incubator for months and months and months. I've gone through a lot of trouble. When I was eighteen, doing a lot of those drugs, man, I had my ass beaten. I almost died. I got a titanium plate in my face. My cheek is titanium, and I've been through a lot of stuff."

"Who hit you?"

"I was passed out drunk on a porch after a house party, and one of [my friends] came through and slapped me and then they left. Well, I sobered up and I used to fight a lot. I was like, 'Whoever hit me, come back. We're going to fight.' Four of them showed up and I got my ass beaten."

"Never fair."

"Yeah," he says. "I don't talk crap to anybody anymore. Also, I don't know my dad at all. He abandoned me. He has children with other women after me, and they're present in his life, but I found out that his whole family's from indigenous Mexico right around the same area where these toads are from. So, it's basically my blood." You get the sense Hector's interest in bufo is driven, partly, by his father's absence.

"Have you reached out to him since?" I ask.

"Yeah," Hector says. "I've talked to him. He doesn't really want quite much to do with me."

"Have you ever seen him in person?"

"I've seen him in person once in my adult life that I can remember. He came to my high school graduation and gave me a watch. He told me to watch my credit."

"How's your credit score right now?"

"Not too good."

"Do you still have the watch?" I ask.

"No."

Hector has been searching to connect with a father who never wanted to be found. Hector, bound by indigenous blood, strived to connect through a mystical practice that his father didn't practice. His father lives a straight life, with a family and a good credit score. His father's one meaningful effort was to tell him "watch your credit," but Hector missed the meaning and lost the watch. His mother is a drug addict. He was molested as a child and addicted to narcotics, and now lives with a metal plate in his face. That trauma and family dysfunction propelled Hector into the spirit world. He's escaped reality. It's too painful. He purposefully brings himself inches to death. He wants to leave the earth. Call it therapeutic, escapism, spiritualism—Hector exists in a different dimension. But he's not crazy. He's extremely genuine, even centered. There's a calm, peacefully present aura around him. His posture is perfect, eyes bright, connecting, laughing, listening. He obviously has put incredible time and thought into his process. I respect him. Not many people are cut out for being a bufo shaman. But if you want to smoke toad and cheat death, Hector is your guy.

12

The Eco-Sexual
Influencer

"I love sex," Hannah tells me.

But not like normal people.

"People talk about taking the showerhead and pleasuring themselves, but what if you just did the same thing with your legs open under a waterfall?"

Um. Okay. Sure, I guess.

Hannah is an eco-sexual. She defines it as "somebody who engages with the earth or nature looking for pleasure." She's also an herbalist, a wilderness guide, and a sex educator.

Eco-sexuality isn't "just about people having sex with trees," she explains. "I see it as an acknowledgment of the intersectionality of social justice issues. It can be art. It can be a deep expression of what it means to be wild in our own bodies in society. It's kind of like this radical reclamation of who we are, and it's also an offering back into this world that we live in, that we pull so much from and we benefit from so much, so calling back in reciprocity. And I think when you look at it on this expanded perspective, yes, we can laugh and say, 'Oh, haha, we're just out here fucking around with these flowers.' But really, there's just so much more involved."

Hannah grew up in "very rural" Indian Land, South Carolina, and spent "hours and hours" of her childhood "running around in creeks, in the forests, playing with rocks and building forts."

"I just always loved nature," she says wistfully. Her family loved to go camping. Her parents were white-water canoers, and her brother was a nature boy. "It really instilled in me a deep love for all things wild."

Hannah lives in Charleston, South Carolina, now. She's in her thirties, big blue eyes, healthy natural glow, wavy brown hair with glasses. She's tan and fit like a yoga instructor. Earnest yet relaxed, she has a soft and pleasant aura in a crunchy granola way. But obviously a freaky side too.

This is her eco-sexuality journey.

"I was a wilderness guide for many years," she says, "and as a naturalist, you're guiding people through these ecosystems, and you're explaining the wildlife and what's happening. I really started to see how interconnected humans are with nature and how we are reflected in the natural world. It's really interesting that we have a lot of little poems about the earth and how it relates to sexuality. For instance, the birds and the bees if you're having that talk. The earth is constantly creating and dying and creating again. And we as humans have this natural creativity. At the prime, we are animals at the very base. But we've been given gifts that a lot of animals don't necessarily have. We are still so pulled by our instinctive nature to create a new generation to build and also feel something deeper. That's where human sexuality becomes really interesting. A lot of what we feel is just for pleasure. Whereas a lot of the animal kingdom is solely having sex to make new babies, we get to have it and experience it just for the joy of doing so. So in explaining all of this to the people who were on my guided trips, I was like, I think there's something here."

"Don't dolphins and porcupines have sex for pleasure?" Don't ask me how I know that.

"Yeah, you're right, Jesse. There's a few that do. Bonobos are another one. Bonobos are one of our closest relatives, chimps and bonobos.

Bonobos are a species that will have sex to solve any issue. So if there's a border war, they're just like, 'Okay, y'all, just have sex, we're going to be good.'"

"We should send some bonobos to Ukraine," I offer. Should have been a diplomat.

"Chimps are kind of a very different breed," she says, smirking. "They're going to fight if there's a conflict. So we have two species that are most closely related to humans, and we only really mention the chimps and not bonobos."

Get in touch with your inner bonobos. "Make Love, Not War." China, what are you doing later?

Hannah enrolled at the Institute of Sexuality Education and Enlightenment. "I started with the reproductive system because I love sex, and it just seems like a good place to start . . . at the base of the seat of our spine." After wrapping up a two-year program studying human sexuality, her work shifted into "specializing in sex education with this lens of Earth-based holistic incorporated into it." She now claims the title "eco-sexual."

To Hannah, being an eco-sexual is "an identity and an orientation." What does that mean? "So just like you could be heterosexual, you could be eco-sexual. . . . It has this almost polyamorous aspect to it of, well, if I'm an eco-sexual and I'm taking Earth as my lover, and it also has allowed me to take myself as my lover and then to see who else I want to bring into that relationship. But keeping the earth and myself at the forefront."

"So you are in a relationship with the earth?" I ask.

"I think we're all in a relationship to the earth. It just depends on what relationship you want to think about it in. But yes, I would say that I am in a relationship with the earth."

"A sexual relationship?"

"Yes."

Hannah is in a sexual relationship with Earth.

"Since Earth is Mother Earth, would that make you a lesbian?" I'm fresh.

"I actually don't like to think of Earth as mother . . . but as lover."

Lover Earth.

"So you are really, by connecting with the animal kingdom and Earth, using that to expand the boundaries of human sexuality?"

"Yeah," she says. "I think sexuality has been limited to what we say is penis-in-vagina sex, and now we're thinking of other orifices and things going in other places, and that's really cool. But when we limit it down to just penetration, you're missing out on whole expansive experiences that could bring pleasure in very nuanced ways. And again, I think would probably lend to a more rich and happy relationship to yourself and to whoever you're relating with."

What does eco-sexuality look like in practice?

Hannah explains. "Something as simple as sitting on your porch in a rocking chair and feeling a cool summer breeze come by and the hairs on your skin standing up, that is eco-sexuality."

I've never been sexually aroused by a breeze . . . but I'm listening.

"Just noticing how, what elicits a response from your body, lying in the sun on a beach and just feeling the warmth on your skin. That's eco-sexuality. And these things are temperature play. So, if you're looking at kink and fetishes, the temperature play is a big part of that. So some people might put ice in a glass pleasure wand and use that if you really like the cold sensations. Other people might drip hot wax on them. And so you could see how just taking it into a different perspective gets you to those same places or similar places with just different tools. So using the sun or the wind opposed to a frozen dildo or wax."

"If you're out at the beach with the hot sun baking you, you're getting a little bit turned on by that?"

"Oh, I am so turned on." Hannah giggles. "I wouldn't necessarily pleasure myself right there on the beach. That's not a good thing to do here in the States. But it really, to me, is more about thinking about how can we expand the idea of our own pleasure. And when you begin to tap into these smaller aspects of what feels really good in your body, then you can take that into the bedroom and even into life. It's almost like a mindful meditation in a way. Mindfulness is all the rage right now. So it's just really being present.

"I have a ceremony coming up for my birthday. I'm going to get buried into the ground. And if you've ever been buried at the beach or had a weighted blanket on you, to me, it's like having somebody's body pressed up against you. So just the weight of something feeling on my body."

"Are you getting turned on by the weight of the soil?"

"Yeah," she says excitedly. "I love weight. I love feeling a heaviness to me. Even though I don't necessarily love suffocation, I do like weight sensations. So yeah, the ceremony is going to be like a rite of passage as well as a ceremony with Earth and a commitment to Earth.

"So also kinky is being flogged or whipped, and I do the same thing but with plants. So there's different plants that feel differently on my skin. Something that we see in bedrooms all the time are roses. People love giving roses to one another as an offering of intimacy and love. But if you thought about what a rose is, a rose not only has this beautiful, sweet smell, but the petals are so soft. If you've ever sprinkled them over a bed, it feels so good to roll around in. But if you touch the stem, they're spiny and thorny, and there's a kink tool that you roll on your skin that elicits a similar thorny feeling. So you could just take the stem of a rose and gently press it into the skin of your lover or into your own skin. And that would be eco-sexuality. I think anybody who enjoys being in nature and spending time in nature and slowing down for a little bit outside is probably an eco-sexual, and they just don't know it yet."

"So stop and smell the roses, and then hit me with the rose."

"A little bit of both," says Hannah.

"I think I get it now," I say. "Let me just see if I can recap this. So it's an acute awareness of the sensations that are derived from Mother Earth, whether it's water, whether it's wind, whether it's heat from the sun, whether it's coolness, or whether it's the traction from a branch or a rose stem. You're trying to capture those feelings, the awareness, the mindfulness of those feelings translates into a sexual pleasure. And then you take that into the bedroom, where you just experience it solo. Is that it?"

"Yeah, Jesse, you're catching on."

I've always been a fast learner.

I'm getting Native American vibes from Hannah. "The Wind God, the Sun God? Is that where you're going towards?" I ask.

"Yeah, I would say my eco-sexuality has roots in paganism and Earth-based religions. Even though I am not necessarily those things, and nor do I have an expansive knowledge on these different religions, I think it can be a really connecting aspect. Because this was, even in Christianity, the Father, the Son, the Holy Ghost, the Son could be the sun. If you really want to get into religion, I think nature is just a part of every religion. Earth is like a heaven on Earth to me. It is our heaven. We get to walk around in it every day. It's so beautiful."

Does Hannah hallucinate?

"I mostly engage with mushrooms. Yes . . . maybe that's partly where the exploration of sensation has come in for myself, is like going into these altered mind states and just being so enamored with how wet my hands were or the glistening of the dew. Just spending thirty minutes oohing and aahing over these little things. So, I think that's kind of a fun bridge into sex. And sex being an altered state, I mean most people are, not every time, but often I feel like I can reach these states where I don't know what's happening around me. I feel just completely, almost out of body. My mind even feels over-oxygenated, kind of from heavy breathing, and that changes the composition of where my mind and state is at. So yeah, I'm very curious about what the intersection of those are."

Hannah "came out online" as an eco-sexual. She allowed her "traditional" and "politically conservative" parents to take it as it is. "My dad just does his thing. He's like, 'All right, I'm not even going to pay attention to this too much, but I love you and support you.' And Mom is my biggest fan. She likes everything and comments on everything."

Hannah's Instagram reveals her drinking dandelion tea with a female friend in a backyard bathtub, being gently flogged with branches, topless in a wheat field, and engaged in various other earthy pursuits. I call her an "eco-sexual influencer," and she accepts the title.

She's very happy with where she is now, but admits, "It was tough growing up in the Bible Belt of the South in a small town where I'm obviously very different than what people want me to be.

"Like many women," says Hannah, "there was a lot of suppression of my own wild nature. A lot of people-pleasing, a lot of just trying to fit in with the social crowds in middle school and high school. And I think there was a large portion of my life I didn't stop to think, why am I doing this? Do I even like this? I had just poured so much of my soul out to others. And then, when I started wilderness guiding, I began to really see the beauty in everything around me. I was really depressed for a long time, and nature really brought me back to my body and to this realm to Earth. When I saw the beauty in the world that was around me, I had some recognition that I am made of bone, which is made of soil and stardust. I am just another part of this earth. And if I can see the beauty in this earth and I can see the beauty in my own self, and that called me back into my body, into my sexuality, into my wildness, into my own freedom and what I really wanted."

I feel a powerful urge to go on a hike, reconnect with my stardust.

"I found myself trying to make my family happy, trying to make my peers happy, trying to make my teachers happy. Always making good grades, always wanting to not say anything wrong so I didn't offend people, but I really wasn't being authentic. I felt like I was dulling myself down to be so bland because I was afraid that if I really said what I was thinking, that people would not want to be my friend. And that's like the middle school version of it. But it began to just expand into all these aspects of my life. And even when I started dating, taking on whatever my partner's hobbies were and just giving myself away and then returning back to myself asking, what do I like?

"I think I was just a rebel in my heart through and through. I didn't like the church. I grew up Southern Baptist. The people were nice but weren't kind. I think there's a difference. In the South, I think there's this southern hospitality thing that we have going on, but it seems really fake and we can all put on a good face and a good smile. And it's really not. We're gossiping as soon as you walk by. This doesn't make any sense. Can we not just say what we feel with respect? Can we not just be honest about it?"

Bless your heart, Hannah.

She drove her parents crazy sometimes. Never fitting into any box. "I was calling tables 'chairs,' and I was calling cats 'dogs,' and my parents were so annoyed. I remember them saying, 'Hannah, stop! Just call it what it is!'" Hannah was always questioning everything from a very young age, never wanting to color within the lines. But she was always very feminine.

"I've always loved my femininity. I feel like a woman in so many ways. So I love getting dressed up for the dances. I love being on this feminine spectrum." But then Hannah would break the mold somehow, bust out "the worm" at a dance or stand up in the middle of class and catch side-eyes. Hannah diagnoses this as "wildness" or "hyperactivity." She was constantly told, "Calm down and be pretty." "I remember getting told that a lot. Like, 'You're so much prettier when you smile.' So, teaching me not to have emotions. I'm a very expressive person. And that felt shut down a lot of the times."

Hannah's rebellion against Southern Baptist morality finds room to roam not just in the bedroom, but all around her, since Earth is her bedroom. The untamed wild is an opportunity to take on animalistic sexual roles. Evolutionary biology points to the peacocking aspect of male sexuality: men compete and perform to attract mates. For some time, it was with as many mates as possible, and women choose to mate with one man, the highest-value man. The female is the one who really gets the choice, and the males are the ones who have to put on all of the charades. Hannah argues that "there's a lot of examples throughout the animal kingdom that say otherwise. Women or females in a lot of species are actually seeking multiple partners quite often, and it just doesn't fit into the same script. So when you bring in all of the examples, it actually allows us to expand our own human sexuality to see that, oh, there's not just this binary system, but there is this wider range of different ways to interact with people and with Earth."

By adopting jungle law, Hannah has expanded human sexuality into radical new territory. This governing philosophy allows her to challenge not just traditional human sexuality, but everything traditional. She spoke about eco-sexuality as a threat to "colonialism," "patriarchy," etc. . . . but I could tell her heart wasn't in it. Hannah is not a ranting political progressive. She's just really into sex. The more wild the kink, the better. She's intriguing, and quite harmless. Unless you're a shrubbery branch broken off for a flogging.

Guys, Hannah the wild child is taken, but there's an opening.

"Yeah, I do have a partner right now."

"Was this a relationship that developed through eco-sexuality? Is he into eco-sexuality too?"

"Definitely not as much as I am, but he understands where I'm coming from, and he understands that for me, it's more than just a lifestyle. Yeah, he's super-accepting, and I'm really appreciative of that. It just was something that we talked about and became just a base-level understanding of where I'm at. And I think he loves that it's quirky and different." It's probably tough to get too jealous about your girlfriend's relationship with a tree.

"Do you ever plan to get married or be in a long-term monogamous relationship?"

"Yeah, I would love to be married one day, and yeah, I have the deep desire to be loved and in love with a partner in human form. But I don't like to put too many rules on my relationships if I can help it."

Hannah says she's open to inviting others into her relationship.

"Are you bisexual?"

"I am fluid."

"What does that mean?"

"I am just attracted to whomever I'm attracted to. I feel most attracted to certain types of males. I have my types, you know. But I have been attracted to many people who identify as women or somewhere in between."

"What is your type?"

"I tend to like a kind of someone who's tall, bigger set, I like them wide, I guess, very kindhearted. I really can feel their heart. Loves to spend time outside. Funny."

"Do you see children in your future?"

"Yeah," she says. "I would love some children at some point. No time soon. There's no rush. I really love the life I live right now, so I'm just going to keep doing that. But yeah, I would love a family and a little piece of land with a cow." Specifically, a "Highland cow—they're really furry. They're supercute. I want one of those."

Where would the cow fit into Hannah's relationship? I'm afraid to ask.

13

The Emotional Support Squirrel Caretaker

"I am not computer-savvy. So I'm kind of in stupid mode."

That was Cindy explaining why I couldn't hear her for the last ten minutes on Zoom. She was muted. A big woman, Cindy is in her sixties with gray hair, wearing what looks like a tank top.

"So, how are we doing this morning?" I ask.

Cindy is "doing really good, just waiting for a hurricane to come in."

She lives in Florida. Hurricane Ian is barreling toward her. She's not evacuating. It's a category 5. "We're just going to hunker down." She sighs. Cindy has too many animals. Riding it out is her only option, she tells me.

Her trailer resembles a petting zoo. She lives with two crested geckos, two turtles, two dogs, and two bearded dragons. The crested geckos (lizards) are named Fire and Ice. The two turtles are Dean and Stevie. Cindy refers to Stevie as a "she" but "isn't sure" Stevie is actually a girl.

"I believe so, but she's blind. She has no eyes, and her shell is distorted. I guess when she was developing, it just didn't work out right for her."

"A blind turtle named Stevie," I say, smiling.

"As in Stevie Wonder," Cindy explains.

"Yes, Cindy, that's good."

"Because Stevie Wonder was blind."

Thank you, Cindy. Yes, he still is.

The names of the bearded dragons are Taco and Tangerine. The latter "because when he was little, his color was tangerine color."

"Why Taco?" I wonder. "Is it a Hispanic bearded dragon?"

"No," says Cindy, "he's just my baby."

The dogs are Onyx and Samson. This time, I avoid inquiring into the names' origins.

Cindy grew up with dogs, cats, rabbits, pheasants, and ducks. "You name it, we had it." But the animal I'm interested in is Cindy's squirrel.

"And you have an emotional support squirrel?"

"I did," she says with a heavy heart. "She passed away a year ago."

"I'm sorry," I say, as if the squirrel were a family member.

Cindy's friend gave her a squirrel as a gift when it was just five weeks old. "She was fully haired when we got her. Her tail hadn't sprouted out yet, but she would fit in the palm of my hand like this."

Cindy demonstrates how a baby squirrel would appear in the palm of her hand. She leaves her palm extended out for a while. The friend had called and announced, "I have a baby for you," and when Cindy picked her up "she was all wrapped up in a towel, and I uncovered her and just fell in love with her immediately. And I picked her up and stuck her against my face and cuddled her, and I said, 'Okay, you're going home with me.'"

"Are you married, Cindy?"

"Yes, I'm married. I have my husband, Mike, at forty-one years coming up."

"What does he think of the emotional support squirrel?"

"Oh," said Cindy, "he didn't care. He just didn't want to touch her is all, because she would bite him. Only him. She just didn't like him."

"Your emotional support squirrel only bit your husband?"

"Yes."

"Were you secretly happy that the squirrel bit your husband?"

"Yeah, kind of."

Cindy is semifamous. Not just for having an emotional support squirrel, but for getting kicked out of an airport for boarding a plane with her emotional support squirrel. It's a tale of injustice, corruption, and tragedy, the way Cindy tells it.

"I had to get paperwork from my doctor, my psychologist, psychiatrist, whatever you want to call her," she explains, clearly not falling into the trap of credentialism that has consumed the country of late.

Then Cindy called Frontier Airlines. "I said, 'Listen, she's in a case. It's a cat carrier. She's twelve weeks old. I do have to feed her once in a while, maybe on a plane because she's little. She nurses on a bottle. I feed her birdseed too.'" Frontier asked if the squirrel was an emotional support animal. "I said, 'Yes, she is. She's my baby, and I have documents stating that she is my support.' Anytime I felt bad or was in a bad mood, I'd pick her up, and I'd just cuddle her." Frontier gave her permission to bring the squirrel on board the flight from Florida to Ohio.

"So we went to the airport, went through check-in, and they said, 'What do you have in the bag?' And I showed them. I said, 'My baby squirrel.' 'Okay, as long as she's in a case,' they said. Got all the way through the corridor, went through security, and I asked them, I said, 'Since I'm being radiated or my bags are being x-rayed,' I said, 'can I take my baby out of the case and carry her through?'" Cindy was cleared through, "baby in hand with the tail sticking out right here."

Cindy says she showed security the squirrel in her hands and showed it again to "the girls at the gate." "The stewardess even asked me, 'What do you have?' And again, I told them, 'I have a baby squirrel. She's my support squirrel. I have documentation stating that she is.'" Cindy said the stewardess responded "fine" and told her to take her seat.

"Well, the next thing I knew was there was a woman that came from the back of the plane, and she leans over the seat at me and she said, 'You are a liar.' I said, 'What?' 'You're a liar. What do you have in that bag?' I said, 'A support squirrel.' 'You have to get off this plane right now.' 'What are you talking about? I'm in my seat. I've been all through the airport with her, and I got permission from your headquarters.' 'I don't care. Get off.' I said, 'No, my ticket is paid for and I'm already here.' I mean, I'm disabled anyway, and was pushed down to the gate in a wheelchair.

"Well, she brought another couple of stewardesses around, and they said, 'You have to get off this plane. We don't allow rodents on our plane.' I said, 'She's not a rodent, she's twelve weeks old, she's a baby. She fits in the palm of my hand. That's how big she is. She's in a case.' 'You have to get off, or I'll take your luggage.' I said, 'Don't you take my luggage.' I said, 'I have medication in my luggage, in the overhead. I have medication in there, and don't you touch my medicine.'

"So then I see the pilot come through, and the pilot's standing there, and he says, 'We don't allow squirrels on our planes.' I said, 'But I have documentation.' 'I don't want to see it. Just, please, get off the plane.' And the first woman that came at me and called me a liar, I said, 'That woman,' and I pointed at her, I said, 'needs to be fired.' I said, 'She came up here as rude as all could be, and she told me I was a liar. I am not a liar. I had permission from everybody. Here's my letter.' 'Nope, put it away, I don't want to see it . . . if you don't get off the plane, then we're going to have to unload the entire plane.'

"I said, 'Well, since I'm such a liar and such a bad person for having a rodent on your plane,' I said, 'unload everybody.' I'm watching people go by, and some snide comments come out of it."

"What did people say to you?" I asked.

"You're making us get off the f'in plane," and a few other rude comments.

"One of the stewardesses says, 'Then we're going to have to bring the police on.' I said, 'Bring them on. I don't care.' Here come five Orlando police officers on the plane. And as I was being wheeled out, everybody that had been on the plane was all standing around, and well, I sort of flipped them off."

What a sight to behold. After all the passengers were forced to disembark, Cindy gave them the middle finger while being pushed out of the gate in a wheelchair, her caged squirrel resting on her lap. The moment was captured on camera. Cindy's extraction appeared in the local news that night.

"Passengers were yelling, 'Yeah, yeah, get her out of here. Get her off.' And needless to say, they walked me out, well, pushed me out in a wheelchair, opened the front doors. I said, 'It's hot here.' I said, 'Can I stay in air-conditioning?' 'No, you are to go out of the airport.' So they pushed me out onto the concrete, and I had to call my husband back. He was already out of Orlando. Had to call him back to come and get me. And by this time, I'm bawling, I'm just so upset, sitting on the concrete."

Once home, "needless to say, Frontier and I got into it." According to Cindy, Frontier denied they gave her permission to bring her emotional support squirrel on their plane. "In fact, I even had the name of the woman that I talked to. 'She doesn't work here,' said Frontier. What do you mean, she doesn't work here? We just talked to her a few days ago. 'She doesn't work here. There's nobody by that name here.'"

I listen intently, trying not to take sides. It's a he-said, she-said.

The next day, Cindy was given a new ticket, departing at 6 a.m., without Daisy, the squirrel. "It was devastating." Her daughter picked her up in Ohio, and on the way home they stopped at a local news studio for an interview. "And, of course, the videos went crazy," said Cindy. "I was seen in, I don't know how many thousands of cities and rural areas. I made it completely through to, where was it? Japan, China, somewhere over that way. And all of these comments coming in, and it was like, oh my God. I just turned it off. I didn't want to hear it. I didn't want to see it. My video with me flipping this crowd off was on there, and me being escorted out with these five cops. And one of the cops made a comment, and I said, 'Listen here, mister.' I said, 'I don't know who you think you are.' I said, 'But I'm married to a retired cop.' And he lipped off something else. I don't remember what it was. And I said, 'You ought to know. You ought to know.'"

Cindy spent two weeks in Ohio without Daisy. The separation had a serious impact on Daisy's emotional well-being. "I came home, and my squirrel wouldn't even come to me. In that short period of time, because my daughter and my husband took care of her, she had forgotten who I was."

"Wow."

"It took me about a month before she would finally let me hold her, inside of her cage, but she wouldn't come outside of the cage. I could hold her just in one hand, and her hanging on to the bars of the cage that we had her in, and it . . . Excuse me."

Cindy's verklempt, then settles back down.

"It devastated me, because I couldn't hold her, I couldn't cuddle her,

I couldn't do anything with her. But I loved her anyway. I kept her. She didn't bite. She would play tetherball with me."

"Tetherball?"

"Tetherball. Yeah. It was an eight-ball key chain, and I put fuzz around it, so that if it bumped her in the head, it wouldn't hurt her. I hung it from the top of her cage, and she could reach it standing up on her back feet, and she would take that tetherball, or that eight ball, and she would just bat it back and forth with her hands. I would wiggle it, and I'd say, 'Get it, Daisy, get it. Get it, Daisy.' And she would grab a hold of it with all four claws and hang upside down, and oh, you name it, she was a little clown. But I couldn't take her out of the cage at all."

But why just have one emotional support squirrel when you could have two?

"It was a year or so later I got another call from this lady. She says, 'I have a little boy for you.' And I went and got him, and he only had one eye open. He was just five weeks. I named him Dandy. Daisy and Dandy.

"He would climb up my arm onto my shoulder. I could walk completely through the house with him, and it even got to the point where I trusted him enough that I would take him outside."

Imagine what the wild squirrels thought, seeing Dandy the house squirrel enjoying captivity. Must have made them reconsider their options. Maybe burying acorns and dodging cars carried too much risk. Perhaps pet ownership could provide just enough freedom in exchange for reliable food and shelter. Dandy had totally changed the game.

This is the lifestyle that Cindy envisioned for Daisy. But alas, "I wasn't allowed to do that because rodents don't belong on airplanes. Which I could see if it was a rat, a mouse, or some other kind of rodent. But a squirrel, they are so sweet and so delicate, especially down here. They're not like the squirrels up north. Squirrels up north are big, and they weigh a couple of pounds apiece, full grown."

Cindy is right. Northern squirrels aren't to be messed with. They're savagely territorial. Some will scratch your eyeballs out for no reason, just for clout. The fish and wildlife commissions up north have been trying to penetrate the squirrel populations for years, but the species are tightly knit and highly loyal. Once a task force takes down a squirrel family in New York, another one, even more ruthless, will just pop up across the river in New Jersey. It's like playing Whac-A-Mole. But with squirrels. Local authorities have been demoralized and defunded since 2020. Squirrels now run entire towns. It's sad, because a lot of innocent people are being hurt.

Cindy reminisced about Daisy's brown fur, petite build, and "fluffy tail."

"She jabbered like squirrels did. And every time I would get up out of bed, she would see me, because she would be standing there watching for me. And I'd get up, and I'd say, 'Good morning, beautiful.' And she would start acting up and running all around the cage and talking to me, chattering."

"What does it sound like when Daisy jabbers?" I ask, hoping to hear a dead-on squirrel jabber impression.

"Well, it varied. They have very different chatters, but she would just chirp at me. Chirp, chirp, chirp, like so."

I give the impression a C. I guess I was just expecting more passion. And range.

"But if she felt danger, there was a different call for a danger sign. And if she was mad, she'd let you know it. She definitely flipped her tail and chattered at you. She did that mainly to my husband because she just didn't like him."

Was Daisy the squirrel a lesbian? I hadn't ruled it out. Maybe she just didn't like men. Further investigation was needed.

Squirrels are, in fact, relatively clever animals—they're ranked among the most intelligent rodents. They're one of only a handful of wild animal species that will eat out of a human's hand. So, the idea of an emotional support squirrel might not be as crazy as it seems. But again: at the end of the day, they're still squirrels. They might be smarter than humans when it comes to retrieving nuts, but other than that, we're grading on a curve when it comes to their "intelligence."

"What are you seeing the psychiatrist for?" I asked Cindy.

"Depression, mainly."

"Does that run in your family?"

"Yes. I mean, my mom was very depressed at one time, but we always had dogs around.

"In fact, when I was about eighteen years old I cared for a little chipmunk in my home with my parents."

"What was the chipmunk's name?"

"Chipper, of course." Of course.

"I thought you were going to say Alvin."

"No," says Cindy. "Chipper, because he was a chipmunk."

Never mind.

Cindy has "a few other mental things going on as well," she confesses. We'll get to those in a moment. For now, I learn more about Chipper and Cindy's physical relationship.

"I could pick her up or mess with her. I'd sit beside her for hours with my hand in the cage, or my head in the cage."

For me, sticking your head in a cage with any animal is tempting fate. Not for Cindy. This is when the fun begins.

"She would come up, and she would give me kisses."

Apparently, Chipper is female.

"Oh, yeah. She would touch her nose against my lip or on my nose, or she would take a hold of my skin with her teeth, and she just barely nibbled, never see a mark there. I don't know if she was playing, but she was showing me affection. Yeah."

"Was it romantic affection or just friendly affection?"

"Probably just friendly," says Cindy, "because she had never been with a male before."

Cindy's deductive reasoning seems flawed, but what's important is this: she's deriving deep enjoyment from a chipmunk chewing on her chin. Clearly, real human affection was lacking. Nevertheless, it was thoughtful of Chipper not to leave a mark. Discretion is key. You wouldn't want people gossiping.

But back to Daisy the squirrel, who Cindy agreed was better than any medication a doctor could prescribe. Twenty milligrams of squirrel twice a day balanced her mood. In Cindy's eloquently evocative telling, Daisy made her "feel much better" because she "could mess with her."

"She gave me kisses," she says. Would that make Dandy the male squirrel jealous? And who would he be jealous of, Cindy or Daisy?

"I would take Dandy over to Daisy's cage, and they would sniff each other. I didn't let him in. I didn't want babies. Well, I did, but my husband wouldn't let me put them together."

Mike ran a tight ship. Dogs, lizards, blind turtles living in a trailer. You obviously can't have more than two squirrels. That would be crazy.

"I just lost Dandy about a year ago," says Cindy, still in some state of mourning.

"When you say lost, do you mean he passed away? Or you literally lost him?"

"No, he passed away."

RIP, Dandy.

It was the dang hurricane. "We were in the middle of a move from Hurricane Irma. Well, now we have another hurricane coming in. His name is Ethan. Ian. Ian, I'm sorry. I think that's his name. Anyway, my husband had him with him. He put them up in a hotel until they could get our new mobile home set up, because we had rats in the other mobile home and couldn't get rid of them. Only because Hurricane Irma just rattled our trailer to pieces, and it broke boards underneath, we didn't know it. It rattled everything loose. Well, then the rats started coming in. Well, it ended up being a little over six months before we could move back into our new home, and my husband had taken him out of the hotel because we didn't want the hotel to know that they had a squirrel there. It was bad enough that we had a dog there. He put him in his cage, his little, tiny cage, birdcage, and took him out in the truck to do something. I don't remember what it was. He let him sit in the truck for a little bit, and he passed away with heat exhaustion."

"I'm so sorry," I say. "Do you harbor any suspicions that because of all of the biting incidents, and the threat of potential procreation, that your husband may have played a hand in the unfortunate death of Dandy?"

"Oh," says Cindy, "absolutely not."

"You're ruling your husband out as a suspect?"

"Oh, definitely."

I'm inclined to request an interview with Mike (without a lawyer present), but my instincts tell me to hold off until I gather more evidence. What I'm most interested in is why Cindy is so depressed that she self-medicates with squirrel.

"Did you have a traumatic childhood experience?" I ask.

"Yes," she says. "I grew up as the baby of the family. My dad was an abusive alcoholic, and that burns a memory in your brain that'll never go away. He would take the abuse out on my mom. So yeah, that leaves scars."

Thankfully, Cindy's dad quit drinking. "He joined AA and was a completely different person—him and I were best buds."

"That must have just been a wonderful transition," I add.

"It took a while for that to happen, because of course I didn't quite trust him much. He had earned my trust, and he was a whoremonger."

Whoremonger isn't a word you hear much anymore. Yet it rolled out of Cindy's mouth so matter-of-factly. I wonder what qualifies someone as a "whoremonger." I imagine it's more than a few whores here and there. It's probably an unsatiable need for whores after each payday or whenever you're inebriated, or both. One whore per week? Two whores? When does just being a "john" end and being a full-blown "whoremonger" begin? It's like obscenity. You know it when you see it.

"So he was out with other women, and that didn't settle well after I turned eighteen. He was mad at Mom, went out. I thought he was going to a bar and I never did find him. I said, 'Mom, I hope you have some bail money.' She says, 'Why?' I said, 'Because if I find him and I find he's in a bar and he's with another woman,' I said, 'Mom, I'm going to beat the tar out of him.' I said, 'I might tear this bar apart.' I said, 'But he's not getting away with it anymore.'"

The whoremonger warmonger. Tearing up bars, beating out the tar, pocket full of bail money, tonight's the final straw.

"Because at that point, I was not afraid of him. At that point, I had muscles that no girl should ever have. All right. I worked in a restaurant in the kitchen. It was nothing for me to pick up a hundred, hundred and fifty, two hundred pounds of meat after I had just cut it and put it in a cooler. Just on a big tray over my shoulder and put it away. So I knew that I could take him at that point."

That's a lot of meat. Was this a restaurant or a slaughterhouse?

"Luckily for him, I never found him. I checked all of his original watering holes, and he wasn't there. He came home. He heard words from me, got words from Mom, and never did it again. Never again."

I can't help but think how the whores reacted. Suddenly no more whoremonger. Had they budgeted for this? Steady, reliable income immediately dries up. No explanation. Not even as a professional courtesy. As a whore, you have to anticipate volatile market conditions. Married blue-collar alcoholics with four children can't whoremonger in perpetuity. The family or the law will soon put a stop to it.

"But even still, Christmas was always an argument, fistfight, whatever with my brothers or my mom or whatever. I don't care for Christmas at all. What else? Camping became a bore because at four years old I remember being huddled up in the corner of our camper with him fist-beating my mom on the bed beside me. So yeah, the depression is still there, but it's not as bad as it used to be."

Cindy has lived a hard life. It's heartbreaking. If Frontier Airlines had only known the whole story, Daisy would have gotten an upgrade.

The tragedy continued.

"Probably about ten years ago I had major surgery. My colon perforated, and I had a colostomy bag on. Well, I went back to work, and it would melt. I swear the bag was wax, and it would melt from the heat. I worked in a lightbulb factory where we actually made lightbulbs."

Overweight, working in a lightbulb factory in the Florida heat is one thing. But with a melting colostomy bag? Poor thing.

"I felt dirty all the time. It's like nobody wants to be close to me. Nobody wants . . . because every once in a while, that would crack open the colostomy wound. And I would have to excuse myself and take care of things and everything else."

Oh dear.

"That was a major depression, major, because I felt dirty all the time, which I wasn't dirty, I was showering. I was doing everything I had to do. And that really set me back. Now, at that point, I was to the point where I didn't trust my family, my kids, my husband. I thought that they were conspiring against me for one reason or another."

Ugh.

"I had four surgeries in three years. Major surgeries on my stomach. My kids had to take care of me, and my husband would too. He would bring me something to eat and talk to me or whatever. It was horrible. I would never wish that on anybody. Not even my biggest enemy if I had one. That's how horrible that experience was for me."

Cindy is a kind soul.

"Now I got this big old scar. They took out my belly button. It's gone. I don't have a belly button anymore because they had to cut me so many times they just took it out."

"Oh boy." I contemplate asking Cindy to lift her shirt and show me where her belly button once was. Is that inappropriate?

"I was going to have a tattoo put there of a belly button, but I couldn't find one that I liked."

If it were me, I'd get a tattoo of a belly button. Either that or a leprechaun. And I'd name my leprechaun tattoo "Lucky." Why? Because he's a leprechaun.

"And did Daisy come along right at the right time?"

"Yes, she did. I was still trying to work my way out of a depression, and she came into my life, and it's like, 'Oh my God, how could you ever love anything more than your children? As much as I love this squirrel.' Will I get another one? In a heartbeat. You better believe it. I will have another squirrel."

Cindy is determined to take her next squirrel on an airplane. "I mean a support animal is a support animal no matter what it is."

"Do you understand where people are coming from?" I ask. "Maybe someone doesn't feel comfortable flying on a plane next to a squirrel or one of your other more exotic pets?"

"I fully understand where they're coming from. Because if somebody came on and sat down beside me with a spider in their hand, they would have a new door in the plane. I do not like spiders at all. So yes, I totally understand."

Cindy still doesn't understand. The way she feels about spiders is how some people feel about squirrels. "But with a tiny little squirrel, I mean a baby twelve weeks old, she's not very big, come on. And she's in a container where she can't get out. I didn't have to tell anybody what I had in there. Could have told them it was a dog. But no, I told them the truth."

If she had lied, Daisy would still be alive. Wrestle those ethics around in your head.

"Do you think there should be any limitations on emotional support animals on airplanes?"

"Within reason, yes," she says, depending on who's doing the reasoning. "I mean, I really wouldn't want to get on a plane with an alligator on it, seated next to me or in my row." Maybe if the spider was in first class. Maybe.

What about an emotional support bird on a plane?

"We had a bird at one time . . . was an Amazon parrot, a blue-front Amazon, and he was probably about ten inches tall. I know what kind of damage birds can do. I mean, they tear up everything. If you let them. Mine grabbed hold of a light cord one day, and I hear this little buzz, and he had bit through the power cord and got shocked."

Wow.

"Yeah, but he was okay. We immediately picked him up, and I said, 'I told you not to bite that.' He went in his cage. He stayed there for a while. Didn't want to come back out."

"Did you call the bird Sparky?"

"Nope. Name was Pete. Why?"

I'm worried for Cindy. Hurricane Ian is bearing down on her, and she's wasting precious time on Zoom. "I hope the winds don't rattle you and everyone stays safe. With all your animals, you're going to have to find Noah's Ark if you have to get out of Dodge."

Cindy assures me the dogs have collars with their name tags on them. As for the squirrels and dragons and "the other critters," "they'll go in the truck . . . and do what we have to do."

We say our goodbyes. But Cindy forgets to leave the Zoom. I hear her deep in conversation with her sister or her husband. Not sure which one, but whoever it is, they're getting reamed out by Cindy.

"It doesn't matter. We have a fucking hurricane coming in, and I don't have enough dog food to last that long!"

She doesn't let up.

"I'm not yelling at you. This is goddamn bullshit. Get the fuck out of here, I don't want to get in touch with you. Son of a bitch."

More controversy.

"What kind of dog food do we have . . . Nutrena? How do you spell that?"

"Pedigree."

"Pedigree, never mind."

For millions of people, life is pain. Chaos, dysfunction, and pain. Raised on heavy doses of pain and betrayal, some flock to solitude. Others erase their memories with intoxicants. Cindy surrounded herself with animals to love her. She keeps them in cages so they can never leave the house and whoremonger. She loves them on her own terms, and they love her back, provided she keeps providing them food. The zoo trailer is Cindy's world. She's in total control. It's where she's happy. No drunk fistfights, ripped colostomy bags, or emergency stomach surgeries. Only a hurricane can disrupt her. Or Frontier Airlines. But Frontier Airlines is just symbolic of most realms outside Cindy's trailer. Sometimes a doctor's note and verbal permission from a customer service representative isn't valid enough to fly a caged baby squirrel from Florida to Ohio. The unflexible intersection of corporate policy, mental health exemptions, and federal aviation guidelines can be unforgiving. Some might call this "the real world." Cindy calls it "horseshit." If only the pilot, stewardesses, passengers, and Frontier's corporate compliance executives would have been able to stop for two hours and hear Cindy's traumatic story, our beloved Daisy would have been airborne, quietly nursing a bottle from a cage in coach. Maybe even gobbling up the free peanuts. Cindy, I hear you. You're welcome on my plane anytime. And I hate squirrels.

14

The Stalinist

"You were looking for communists, and you found them. You found the real thing here."

I've hit pay dirt. Chris is an actual communist. A living, breathing, straight-up commie. . . . (Actually he's several commies. I interviewed Chris and a friend, and they were so interchangeable I can't tell which was which in the recording. You'll see what I mean.) He makes me feel like I've been trekking through jungles and finally came in contact with a mythical tribe. But Chris isn't wearing a loincloth, wide-eyed, hoisting a spear.

"I work for Frito-Lay," he says nonchalantly. "I do the gas stations, all the supermarkets, all that stuff. We sell the chips."

What's the newest flavor?

"We've got Mexican Street Corn Cheetos."

Brilliant. It's a California thing.

Chris lives in San Diego, by the border.

"I see you're wearing military fatigues. Does that have any symbolic meaning?" I ask.

"No. Well, I like hunting. We support many things. We are Americans, I guess." He guesses.

Chris is a clean-cut, thirty, white, normal-looking guy. Not what I expected.

"We typically have a timekeeper," he says. I'm not sure why.

"If it's okay, I guess we can keep time every five minutes. We could just say like, it's now eleven thirty-five a.m."

I've cleared my schedule, so I don't need to hear an announcement of what time it is every five minutes. Plus, I have a watch. And an iPhone. Must be a communist thing.

"It's really cool that you reached out to us, Jesse."

Chris is genuinely excited to hear from me. He's a member of the "Party of Communist USA."

(This is not to be confused with "Communist Party USA." That group is "subversive" and only "exists to subvert the communist movement in this country.")

Chris says he'd like us to work together "because of the Ukraine issue." "Obviously, with Fox News, it seems like there's kind of a spectrum of people. You have Tucker Carlson." (Had.) "We support Tulsi Gabbard very much. She is not a communist. But she's against the US expansion of NATO and against all these wars. And she's a real veteran. And the fact that you converse with her and that Tucker has her on the show is a part of why we're having this interview."

"Do I have some sort of honorary acceptance into the communist movement in the United States?"

"No," says Chris. "This would be considered mass work."

(Mass work is the communist version of community organizing.)

"Who's the guy that Greg Gutfeld always makes fun of?"

"Kilmeade?"

"Yes. So this guy, and I'm sorry if I just say this stuff, but obviously we know there's many CIA agents [at Fox]. You have to understand US intelligence is omnipotent."

So Kilmeade is CIA. Figures.

"This is why we want to meet with you because we're creating an electoral front with Democrats and Republicans around our country in an anti-NATO electoral front. And it's more than just Ukraine. So I'll go very brief now. It's now eleven fifty a.m. Pacific."

Every time American presidents meet with Russian leaders, we hear how the Russian leader gives the American president a history lesson, whether our president wants one or not. In this case, I was Biden, and Chris was Putin. I let the aggrieved fire hose of Russian history blast me head-on. It's the polar opposite of everything we've been taught in the West. Listening to another country's propaganda (excuse me, historical perspective) is refreshing.

"If you were to look at Europe in World War II, Americans are taught that it was all like one big Nazi flag. But didn't look like that on the map. It would've looked just like the EU, a bunch of little, tiny countries. Each country had its own fascism. But what happened was all these little countries, they collaborated with the Germans. So, in Ukraine in particular, you had Bandera [a Nazi collaborator]. Local collaborators trained with the SS [the Waffen-SS]. And when people think of all these Nazi crimes, the gas chambers, the shooting people, burning villages, it wasn't just Germans who did it. It was the local people. They did it to their own neighbors, basically. But they were losing. They were losing really bad."

Fact check: true (so far).

Chris continues. "And it was much like the conflict today."

Hmmm.

Chris is fluent in postwar European history. It pours earnestly from his mouth. After the Germans surrendered to General George S. Patton, he recounts, we brought Hitler's spymaster, General Reinhard Gehlen, back to the United States to debrief him because he possessed the preeminent intelligence docket on the Soviet Union, our new geopolitical enemy. Relying on former fascist intelligence networks, the United States orchestrated uprisings in Eastern Europe during the Cold War to thwart communist entrenchment.

Fact check: true.

Here's where it gets fuzzy.

Chris claims "real fascism" is back. "What the Ukraine people are doing" is "the resurgence of fascism." Here's how the story goes. The offspring of Nazi collaborators have now reemerged to integrate themselves into leadership positions at NATO and the European Commission. "Their grandparents wore the Nazi uniforms." He rattles off some names that my preliminary research shows are indirect descendants, but not what I'd consider a Nazi family tree. The difference between Europeans and Americans, as Chris tells it, is that Europeans never rebelled against their kings, so poor Europeans have been living under European nobility since Roman times. "These inbred nobles" with their "Habsburg chins" were defeated by Russian communists, "we [America] rebuilt them" with the Marshall Plan, and now they're back.

The United States, together with these hereditary fascist forces, staged a coup in Ukraine in 2014 ("the Maidan Revolution"). Paramilitary forces were unleashed, trade unionists were beaten, union halls were burned, and Soviet monuments and burial grounds were desecrated. "Many people died liberating these countries from fascism," but Chris says Russian monuments are being "destroyed." The fascists are staging a counterrevolution. "Fascism was never actually exterminated. It was defeated, but it was not gotten rid of."

Ukrainian president Volodymyr Zelenskyy has suspended elections, suspended major opposition parties, and banished Orthodox churches, and is considering abolishing collective bargaining. Flexing wartime powers to root out Russian influence is how Zelenskyy justifies this. Chris sees the return of fascism. He sees it all over Europe, even in America, "although not in the Republican Party."

"Everybody says Trump is a fascist. But it's the Democrats who are supporting the resurgence of fascism. It's Joe Biden. That was why we wanted to meet with you."

Am I forging an antifascist global alliance with American communists? I need to hear more.

Did Joe Biden initiate the war in Ukraine?

"Yes," by expanding NATO and keeping "the Nazi collaborator group alive" in Europe. "The special military operation" was advocated for by the Communist Party in the Duma (Russia's version of the Senate), "not Putin." "If anything, people say Putin's half-assed it. Putin could have done a better job. But at least he did it. The point is that they finally did something, and it's going to be a new world now. There's going to be de-globalization." Chris is adamant that Russia isn't going to lose. "They're just going to keep fighting," and as it gets colder and Europeans freeze and suffer inflation, "are they really going to keep sending weapons to Zelenskyy?"

So what's the advantage for the United States?

"Three main points," says Chris, excitedly, as if he knows Washington, DC, better than it knows itself. "Number one, it's geopolitical. It'll be the final destruction of this black spot on the map that we don't own [Russia]." The goal is to "carve it up" and "balkanize Russia into a bunch of little countries so they can be controlled." Number two is to "weaken" the European Union's economy. The war has already ripped apart Germany's supply chains, especially the continent's oil and gas pipelines. Chris is smart for a communist. "We want to be masters" of Europe. The third reason is "money laundering." Since "we don't manufacture anything in America anymore, the financial district will feast on Ukraine." Chris doesn't believe in globalism. He wants to make things in America again. "The globalists don't believe in America. That's why it's our task as communists to uphold our American revolution. And to say that we are the real Americans. That these people like Zelenskyy or Hunter Biden, they're not the real Americans."

I ask Chris what his plans are for America. "All of our ancestors came to this country for a reason. It's a positive thing. The American Revolution. We actually support it. We carry the flag."

Phew. A revolution would mess up my commute.

Chris doesn't want to overthrow our government. Yet. "Revolution happens when there's class conflicts within certain countries. And when there's interfighting between the ruling class, and this gives the broad masses of people an opportunity. But there is no such force to do such a thing now. And we are not in a revolutionary period, but we're in an antifascist period.

"And it's really dangerous for us. The reason why we, in particular, the communists have to be vocal about this is because fascism kills communists. They kill us. They want to kill me. They want to kill all of us. That's the first thing they do. They just kill all the communists."

This alliance thing now sounds risky.

"Communists should align with people who want to protect bourgeois democratic rights, meaning the civil liberties that we have in our Constitution, against fascists. We want to do the same thing. That is the position of the political forces that we represent, is that we should align with all forces who are against fascism, both international fascism and domestic. So we would see the creation of an electoral front that is populous, wants to reindustrialize the country, wants to pull out of NATO, and is anti-imperialist. Our focus now is building an antimonopoly coalition and an antimonopoly front to fight against influences such as Bezos, Klaus Schwab, Bill Gates, and others, the Ford Foundation, and various other billionaires and capitalists who are destroying this country and destroying our constitutional rights."

"And so you are reaching out informally to the Teddy Roosevelt of Fox News, Jesse Watters, whose trust-busting instincts you find somewhat appealing. I'm honored."

So where did we go wrong?

"During the post–Cold War environment, the American government came into a kind of a social contract with Americans. American workers would have good-paying industrial jobs that were backed by unions, and in exchange, American workers would implicitly support the status quo and support the Democrats or Republicans in the Cold War. That contract has eroded, and it has been violated by the American government. If you look at NAFTA, Bill Clinton, or what happened under Jimmy Carter with basically the beginning of the Green New Deal, so to speak. We do not support the Green New Deal. It is our position that we don't want the lives of American workers to get worse. We want them to get better. We want Americans to live comfortably; we want them to have good jobs; we want them to raise families. And we see the forces that currently control the government, control the Democratic Party, and control sections of the Republican Party as hostile toward the American working class."

Do you see the populist wing of the Republican Party as a potential ally?

"We see the populist wing of the Republican Party, in a sense, as not populist enough. Trump during 2016 was actually promising to give every American health care. He was promising better wages. He was promising ending these regime-change wars. I mean, in a sense, we really want a populist movement to develop in America that is able to unite people on both the political left and the political right, and fight against the monopolies and the imperialists."

I have to bring Chris to Mar-a-Lago. He could be onto something.

"Can you have socialized, government-run health care and higher wages? Is that possible?"

"As Henry Ford said, 'We don't make cars so people can drive them. We make cars so we can make money.' We would like to see an America where production is resumed for social use, meaning we want to make cars so American families can drive them."

Henry Ford never said that, but he did say the opposite, which Chris would probably agree with: "The highest use of capital is not to make more money, but to make money do more for the betterment of life."

"Why is it that America doesn't have high-speed rail? Why is it that we have a higher infant mortality rate than most of Europe? Why is it that we don't have good health care in this country? We need to re-industrialize. We need to have nuclear power. There's so much that we can do with all the money that's being wasted on all these foreign policy adventures and also in our generally mind-boggling financial system, which is coming apart as we speak, as it has nothing to do with actual material conditions to the American people and more has to do with stock buybacks and the kind of casino capitalism that we now live under."

I ask, "Can you have both? A motor company selling cars at a profit, but also having American consumers enjoy those automobiles?"

"The contradiction is that who controls that company? The CEOs do, the capitalists do, the shareholders. Why is it that we have to buy a new iPhone every one or two years, and it comes apart? Why is it that we don't make good appliances anymore that break down in a year? We want to organize production."

"You want to go back to the early twentieth century, where the idea of quality craftsmanship was critical? When things were built to last?"

"It's not that we want to go back. It's that we want to build a future that combines science and technology with production organized for social use. So we want to use the automation that we have with computers and with new factories. We want higher-quality products, but it's not that we have to go back to basically just one man working on a single thing. We can do so much with modern technology, such as nuclear power and fusion energy."

These communists are starting to make sense. Did I just say that?

What about the workers in this new communist economy . . . are communists for open borders?

"Every commonsense country has borders. It's not that we are anti-immigrant, this country was made up of immigrants, but what you see in terms of our border right now, the reason why there are millions of people trying to come into America from Central and South America is because the USA, through its foreign policy, has destabilized these entire regions to perpetuate this kind of crisis. I mean, George H. W. Bush, when he was director of the CIA, he was funding narcoterrorists who were killing and butchering nuns and Christians in Nicaragua and this destabilized the entire region. And this type of policy was, is a product of the Cold War. It resulted in the kind of wreckage we're seeing at the border right now. So our solution would be, we need to end US imperialism, enter into a positive relationship with Latin America, in which we encourage economic development through win-win trade and cooperation. While at the same time we need to maintain a stable border."

"Do you blame Uncle Sam for what's going on in Venezuela? Or do you blame the twenty years of social dictatorship there?"

"Hugo Chavez transformed the country. Venezuela, before the Bolivar Revolution, was far worse off compared to what it is now. What happened with Venezuela is that Obama conspired with Saudi Arabia and other Gulf states and through OPEC to destabilize oil prices, and this basically devastated their economy. The US still technically doesn't recognize Venezuela. We still recognize Juan Guaido, who's this clown who's living on a yacht somewhere. The people of Venezuela do not hate the United States, nor do any other people within the world who are under socialist governments. They just want to be left alone. They want to be allowed to economically develop. The US by implementing sanctions policy, by attempting regime change in all these measures against socialist countries, this doesn't make America popular. This actually hurts our foreign relations with the world. And if you want the lives of Venezuelans and Cubans, for that matter, to get better, I would say drop the embargo and drop the sanctions and let the free market of ideas sort things out. If the Cuban economy is so bad, and if the Venezuelan economy is so bad, then why does every single capitalist country on Earth have to sanction and try and destabilize every social-ist economy?"

"Do you describe yourselves as Stalinists?"

"Yes. We support Stalin."

You support what happened in Eastern Europe?

"Eastern Europe was the house that Stalin built. It wasn't done by coups. It was actually progressive forces which won elections in those countries. Mass movements. Stalin actually didn't impose communism on Eastern Europe. The uniting factor in Germany, Poland, Bulgaria, Romania, and Czechoslovakia is that these were united fronts. These were all antifascists. People who were sent to the concentration camps, people who were part of the partisan units who fought against the Nazis. That is where Eastern Europe came out of during this period."

There were a few coups in there, but he's sort of right. Mostly they turned communist through elections where only the communists were allowed to run for office. What about the famous famines under communism?

"The Soviet Union during this period was industrializing. Western Europe and the United States, they had the advantage of being able to industrialize over a period of hundreds of years. The Soviets industrial-ized within a period of ten years. And it is a very rough transformation from a backward agricultural economy to modern industry. It's why you saw famines and serious political instability in the Soviet Union during the 1930s. But this wasn't a man-made famine. In 1933 and 1934, there was a drought that occurred in Ukraine, southern Russia, and Kazakh-stan, and this caused production to be overestimated. And there was a famine, just like there was for hundreds of years prior during the Rus-sian Empire. This was a cyclical thing that happened every time there was a drought. And it was a Soviet Union, by implementing collectiv-ization, modernizing agriculture, and implementing mechanization, that stopped the famine. If you note, there were no more famines in the Soviet Union after the period of collectivization ended, and after World War II, pretty much; food security was achieved."

Chris should be head of marketing for Russian communism. But what about the purges?

"The Stalin period is the most lied about period in terms of Soviet history. There is nothing that Stalin did that Lenin didn't also do. The gulags existed for hundreds of years under the Russian Empire, and the Soviet Union inherited this penal system. What the Soviets did, however, is that they made it a lot more humane. Most people in the gulags were not in there for political purposes; most of them were regular criminals."

Humane gulags. Great name for a band. Stalin did inherit forced labor camps with an estimated hundred thousand criminals in them. He cranked that number up to about five million with prisoners who committed crimes against the state. Sometimes I think Chris might not be telling the whole story.

"The purges happened when the Soviet Union was under attack during the thirties. If you think about it, the British spied on America, the French spied on the British, all countries spy on each other. But the capitalist countries of the world are going to spy more on the only socialist country around. There were plots. There were people within the Soviet state security agencies themselves who were also not loyal to the Soviet government. And it was because these people were plotting to kill Soviet leaders."

Chris explains the show trials weren't for show. "The trials were not staged at all. The witnesses were allowed to defend themselves. The witnesses were unharmed. There was no evidence of torture.

"All the liberals talk about in terms of our country are the problems. And yes, we have problems. America started with the genocide of Native Americans. That happened. Japanese internment camps, that was awful. Jim Crow segregation, slavery. These were all awful things. But at the same time, would it be fair to just describe US history as just all of those events?"

It seems to me there's a difference between celebrating America despite injustices that violate our core beliefs and celebrating Russia for injustices necessary to their core beliefs, but Chris is on a roll.

"There has never been a socialist or a communist country that has been allowed to individually trade with nations, act on their own, or just have any autonomy from the global system. They've constantly been invaded, undermined, and under attack. I mean, the CIA tried to kill Fidel Castro six hundred times. Imagine if another foreign power, say Saddam tried to kill George Bush six hundred times? There's a reason why everyone says, 'Oh, communism has a death toll of increasingly large numbers.' They come up with these numbers that aren't historically based in anything. But what would happen if communists said, 'Okay, well, let's count the deaths of capitalism and colonialism.' If you did a fair assessment, how would those numbers turn out?"

We pivot to Chinese communism. The Cultural Revolution, the Great Leap Forward, always a rationalization. Chris admits it was "a rough period," but says the famines occurred because the British made them grow opium, China wasn't a politically or geographically unified country, and the Japanese invaded. Chris points to America. The pioneers "cleared" Native Americans from their land, and now Bill Gates is buying small farmers out of their land. "Modernity is a very brutal process."

Then why hasn't communism been able to flourish in America as a reaction against "brutality"?

"This was not allowed during the Cold War. You had the cross-dressing degenerate J. Edgar Hoover. I will call him that because he lived with his mother in a basement, and he was this disgusting guy. Him, along with Roy Cohn, who is also a disgusting creature. And [Senator Joseph] McCarthy, who was a drunk and drank himself to death. They decided, along with sections of the US capitalist class, to destroy the most progressive party that was around, which was the Communist Party. They acted against our constitutional rights. It doesn't say anywhere in the Constitution that I can't be a communist. I'm an American, and I respect my Constitution. I have the First Amendment.

"America right now operates under a system of monopoly capitalism. Cars are not produced because families and workers need them. They're produced because some fat cat wants profit so you can go to Jeffrey Epstein's island and engage in debauchery.

"When socialism does come to America, and I could imagine they would take the form of lots of worker cooperatives, but you'd also see independent entrepreneurs, mom-and-pop shops. The difference would be both the financial and the large centers of production, meaning oil or natural resources, gas mineral extractions. All of that would, of course should, be under public ownership along with elements of the military-industrial complex being nationalized so we could still have an army."

"What do you mean by public ownership?"

"Basically, a state organization that would receive public funding and that would basically be under state control and state production."

"Nationalized energy companies?" He's losing me.

"Yes, and use the profits from those companies to put them into the public budget to help pay for schools, expanded roads, high-speed energy, and reduce taxes. Communists do not like taxation."

He's reeling me back in.

Chris says rent in Cuba is very affordable. "Young Americans are sometimes spending half their paychecks, if not more, on a shitty apartment, while also living with two other people. Communism, of course, in America, it's going to be implemented with an American flag, and it's going to be as American as apple pie."

But if you do nationalize the energy sector in this country, and it's run by public employees, and it's not profit-driven, do you think it's going to be as efficient and effective?

Chris points to Enron. Then pensions that get wiped out in fraudulent markets. He wants a return to the gold standard. He wants public banking so only the government can issue lines of credit, not private banks.

But it doesn't stack. Chris wants to put the people in government, who got us into $33 trillion in debt, in charge of the *entire* banking system. "God no," he says. "We want a new government. A people's government." I'm confused because people always run the government. I guess he just wants different people?

"We support the federal government, for example. Think about the 1960s. They call it the Great Society. You didn't even have to lock your car. You can leave your keys in your car, leave your door open. One guy worked. His wife was a homemaker. He raised a whole family. Just working at the post office. Now you got to work two or three jobs."

Chris wants to make America great again.

"Right now in America, economic planning is carried out by Amazon and a lot of these megacorporations exclusively for short-term profit at the neglect of the worker, at the neglect of the overall economy. It's the difference of planning. That's what we want to do. We want to build a new America. We are not anti-work."

How 'bout a five-year plan. Stalin would be proud.

"When people first interact with me, I sound like a conservative, but I'm a communist. All I want is to improve this country. Critical race theory has nothing to do with Marxism or communism. That was part of the 1960s and the CIA perpetuating a cultural Cold War against the left."

"I think we've gone so far left. We've gone full circle back to the right," I said.

"The Nazis were really into paganism. They were into the occult. They were into veganism. They were all about animal rights. Think of Hitler in the twenties. He was an art student. He was very sensitive. He sounds like a modern leftist. It's gone full circle.

"The capitalists have always been funding fascism. It was the communists who were the first antifascists. We do not mean modern Antifa. Modern Antifa shamed the name of antifascism. They beat up our people in San Francisco. Modern Antifa are anarchists.

"When the FBI went after Trump supporters and hurt people you'll notice that all these so-called antifascists cheer that on. We don't like the FBI. The first victims of the FBI were communists."

Do communists support the Green New Deal?

"It's going to be green capitalism. So basically, you're going to have to buy a new car. You're going to be using new infrastructure. Someone is going to profit from that. It's not going to be us. The problem I have with the Green New Deal is the green part. The left has this de-growth policy where it's like they want to have people use cars less, have people use trains less, bike more, whatever. But honestly, part of socialism is growth. We want to continue building on our economy. But we're not against growth.

"The whole point of socialism is to advance to a higher stage of economic living, a higher state of production where we are able to produce more, but we're also able to live more comfortably. And have you ever noticed that a lot of these green groups never push nuclear power? They never push fusion energy or higher forms of energy. So there's nothing wrong with having a clean environment. But this idea that we should punish working-class Americans, we should force them to buy new cars. We should take away what they already have. Climate change does exist. No one's denying that. But the way to solve it is to move to higher forms of energy."

"What are your opinions on the stock market?"

"It's a derivatives market, and it's a casino. It doesn't reflect the American economy. It's a bubble. And it's going to burst eventually."

Chris tells me Communist Party USA (a false flag front group propped up to destroy "real" communists) invested in the stock market in the 1990s and now has $10 million. "We have nothing. But we are building so much, and we don't have any of this. We don't have that money."

The irony goes right over Chris's head.

What about artificial intelligence (AI) and automation?

"Automation under capitalism is a nightmare. Robots driving cars. That means millions of cabdrivers are unemployed. Under capitalism, there has to be unemployment. If there's no unemployment, then there's no reserve army of labor that bosses can threaten you with to cause you to accept lower pay and lower wages. Under capitalism, you need that. Under socialism, automation would be a very good thing. Automation means better production. And under socialism, you have universal employment. You have a state system where you are allowed to choose your own career."

When we say seizing the means of production, what does that mean?

"What is the most fundamental means of production? It's land. It's the ability to grow your own. The ability to grow your own food. In America, a bunch of big agriculture and a bunch of billionaires control almost all of our land. So in America, we want a return of small farmers, people having their own plots of land, people being able to grow their own food, and people having control over their own lives.

"Going back to a more agrarian-attuned system, wouldn't that be de-growth?"

"Megacorporations are producing a lot of food en masse that ends up wasted. We do need sustainability, but that doesn't mean that we're going to take things away from the American people. We need to promote gardening and small farms. But we do need centralized production as well."

Chris flirted with conservatism growing up. "I've always been someone who's been looking for dissident and alternative ideas. I've always been someone who's been skeptical of mainstream narratives. One of the things I find special about the MAGA movement is that it's one of the few movements in this country that has a genuine political basis in favor of average people."

Chris also supported Bernie Sanders. "He was populistic, and that really spoke to me. Why don't we have health care? Why don't we have a productive economy? Why do we have so many problems? Why are we overseas everywhere? When I started out as a communist, I was part of the Hate America crowd." Then Chris started reading about the history of American communism. "I went from being an anti-American communist to being a normal American communist of the old left. We aren't new left. We do not identify with the new left. We are the old left.

"A lot of average people are stuck in this trap where it's like, oh, I don't like the Democrats, but the Republicans are so much worse. Or like, oh, I don't like the Republicans, but the Democrats are so much worse. The ruling class has us by the balls."

"Are you worried about growing up and not having material things, not having a certain lifestyle that makes you comfortable?"

"No one wants to be poor. I don't want to be wealthy, but I want to be able to live comfortably. And I generally fear that my entire generation also has fears around that. We don't want to live in a situation that a lot of millennials are in now, where we have to live in our parents' basements until we're thirty or forty. And we're stuck in these permanent teenage years instead of growing into full adults and being able to have families. In capitalist America, it's almost impossible for young people to have families. A lot of conservatives talk about, oh, young people aren't having babies or kids anymore. Well, it's because, economically, we're unable to. We don't have health care access. Housing is expensive. We don't live in a country that fosters communal living or family development.

"I don't want to be in some mansion. People need to be modest, in a sense. If you're just one or two people, you should have a house.

You don't need a mansion, unless you're living with a huge family of ten people. We just got to get our priorities right because the culture that is fostered here, it's like you've got to drive the latest BMW, some $350,000 Mercedes. German technology, it breaks down."

German cars break down? Really?

"That's all it does."

"My mother's car, she drives a Volkswagen, breaks down in the winter. It's consistent. It happened in the 1940s when they invaded the Soviet Union. Their tanks broke down in the winter. Same thing that happened today with their cars. They break down in the winter. There's something about the winter and Germans."

As we wind it down, Chris has a suggestion. "We can end the meeting with a song."

With a song?

"It's a song by a guy named Paul Robeson. It's called 'The House I Live In.' He sings about America. It's on YouTube, and then we could end the meeting with that song."

I ask if this is really important to him, and he says it is.

Now I have a suggestion. "Guys, can we call each other comrades now?"

"We use that word. Yeah, it's a thing of respect. But this song's very important."

"Am I going to get indoctrinated if I hear it?"

"Oh God, no. It's a normal American song. Sinatra sang it too, Jesse."

"I'm scared. Plus, I gotta run. Merry Christmas, Chris. Are we celebrating Christmas? Or is this not a thing?"

"We're normal people. We celebrate Christmas."

You are normal. Too normal. And that's what scares me.

15

The Statue-Toppling
American Indian

"What tribe are you from?" I ask Mike.

"You probably know it as Chippewa, but we call ourselves the Anishinabe," he says.

"Why don't you refer to yourself as Chippewa?"

"It's a white man's word. If someone is Italian, you can't call them Portuguese just because you named them Portuguese. They're Italian. Like the Dakota and the Lakota, they don't like being called Sioux."

And we're off!

Mike is a Native American who lives in Minneapolis. He's also part French. A French fur trader married his ancestor. Mike's married, has four kids, and is a leader in the American Indian Movement. And he hates America.

"I grew up in a household of drugs and alcohol, which still a lot of Native Americans are. When I was six years old, the Indian Relocation Program relocated us from the reservation to the city. We ended up in 1968 in Mount Airy projects over in St. Paul. And my dad got a job. They gave us furniture. It lasted maybe a year, and then we were back on the res."

For the next ten years, Mike and his family moved back and forth from the city to the reservation nine times, until he dropped out of high school and moved out on his own.

"When you have to move out and go to the city with the Indian Relocation Program, and supposedly pick yourself up by your bootstraps and become a hardworking American and assimilate. You know? That was the plan. And it failed miserably. Because right now, we have so many of our own people who don't know why they don't fit in, who don't know why they can't make it, who don't know why they're such a loser, and they're on drugs and alcohol. And from my point of view, what's happened to my family and my people, when they were removed."

Mike is bitter. "They ended up with the land, and we ended up with the Bible."

On the heels of the George Floyd riots, Mike toppled the Christopher Columbus statue in downtown Minneapolis. "I was sentenced to a hundred hours of community service to teach and educate in the schools on the genocide that happened here in order to create the United States and Minnesota. And the judge says, 'Once you complete those hundred hours, I'll drop all charges against you.' No fine, no restitution, no nothing. So, I handed in a hundred and fifty hours."

What exactly did Mike teach our youth?

"Those pilgrims, those pioneers, and those settlers, for the most part, were extreme white Christian terrorists. That's what I tell the kids in school. That's what I tell their parents and their teachers. But the first thing I always say to people is that, 'You did not do it.' I have a message for the white people or the non-Native people, whenever I give a speech: 'You did not do it because you were not here. We do not hold you responsible. Just like I wasn't here, and it did not happen to me. That happened a hundred years ago, two hundred years ago. But the animosity comes from the fact that you all are benefiting from what happened. And me and my family are still hurting from what happened.'"

Mike isn't charging eleven-year-olds with genocide. How thoughtful.

"They always tell us this. That happened a long time ago. Get over it. What if I said, 'The Holocaust happened a long time ago. Get over it'? Whenever I hear 9/11, the very next word is 'never forget.' If it's okay for them to never forget 9/11, how come I'm supposed to forget what happened to us?"

I make it a rule on TV to never compare anything to the Holocaust, 9/11, or slavery. Each event is so evil, so unique, and so emotionally tender, that making comparisons rarely serves the case you're trying to make. Mike is personally bearing the cultural weight of all American Indians decimated by disease, conquest, and federal abuse. Careful not to disrespect him. It's time to try another tack. I play devil's advocate and approach the issue from a different direction.

"Mike, do you think that some cultures are better than other cultures? Do you think a culture that values toleration and respect, has a basic view of women's rights, has a basic view of free speech, religious toleration, et cetera, is better than a culture that only responds to sectarian conflict with violence and persecution, that mutilates the genitalia of young women at an early age before they hit puberty, that tolerates pedophilia, et cetera, et cetera, that stones women to death?"

"Yes," he says. "I would absolutely agree one hundred percent. But this country sexually mutilates boys every single day. Every single day, these boys are sexually mutilated."

"How do we sexually mutilate little boys?" I ask.

"Well, when you cut their foreskin off, that was meant to be there."

So, Mike is against circumcision.

"If it's not okay to circumcise little girls every time they're born, why is it okay to circumcise little boys?"

Let's try this again.

"Mike, I'm playing devil's advocate. When you have a civilization that comes to a new land, and there's a collision with the civilization that is currently inhabiting that land, and whether through violence or disease, broken treaties, what have you, one civilization loses, technically. Then the new civilization comes in, dominates, politically, culturally, militarily. Other cultures have accepted losses. Have the Native Americans accepted the loss that they sustained from these European settlers?"

"Let me put it this way," he says. "I know Native Americans who are assimilated. They go to church all the time. A lot of Natives call them apples. Red on the outside, white on the inside. We say they're fully assimilated. Then, in the black community, they call them Oreos. The Oreo cookie: black on the outside, white on the inside. We do have that. We have Native Americans who are very successful, run businesses, but they are assimilated. The ones who are not assimilated, the ones who are pushing back, the ones who are trying to turn around and learn their songs and their dance and their ceremonies and their history, those are the ones who you see trying to save the wild rice beds from the pipelines. Those are the ones who will never accept. We have to accept it to some extent, because this is the world in which we live. We have to accept things. We have to get a driver's license. We have to get a Social Security card. We have to do all these things in order to live in this society."

"You seem to be still in the active-resistance mode."

"Yes, we want land back."

"What kind of land are we talking about, and how would that happen?"

Currently, Mike is working to obtain a six-acre park in Minneapolis. "I want to make a memorial garden and plant some of our medicines, our tobacco, our sage, our sweetgrass." In addition to other parks, which he says are on Indian burial ground, Mike wants Minnesota to "give back" Fort Snelling. "They have the American flag flying over Fort Snelling, which was a concentration camp. That would be the exact same thing as having a Nazi flag still flying over Auschwitz."

Mike says the "historical trauma" American Indians suffered has resulted in generational mental illness, which manifests in drug and alcohol addiction. "Those people, they don't know why they can't make it, why they can't fit in. It's because this is not a society that we were made for. We were made by the creator to live in creation. The only way they could tame us was to kill us.

"If you took a pack of wolves and you wanted to tame them, you take the puppies away, and you put them in a zoo. Then you feed them dog chow. Before they grow up and die, they have puppies. Then those puppies grow up, and they die, and they have puppies. Now, today, you go to the zoo, and you see the wolves there. They look like wolves. They sound like wolves. If I took them and put them back into the wilderness where their ancestors came from, they are going to die. In order to be a proper wolf, those pups needed to be with the pack seven days a week, twenty-four hours a day. Same thing with us. In order for me to be a proper Anishinabe, I needed to be with the pack, the tribe, seven days a week, twenty-four hours a day, so I could learn which medicines to pick, which food to eat, which trails to take. When they split us, and they took my parents and grandparents away, that's when it stopped. That's why I can no longer be a proper Anishinabe or a proper wolf. I'm neither wolf nor dog. I don't fit into this world. See, in order for me to fit into the white society, I have to cut all the Native parts off, and I can fit in that little circle perfectly. The ones who don't understand that say, 'Oh my God, I had a rough week. I'm going to have a couple of shots and a drink,' and it's because of the society. Humans were not created to live in this kind of society. We all got our Facebooks, we all got our hopping on planes to go places. And while this is all happening, the earth is burning. And all of that is because of commercialism, because of materialism, because of capitalism. We've got to keep taking and taking and taking and taking and taking."

"Are you saying that the Native peoples in North America were not designed by God to live in Westernized culture? They're not designed to assimilate to modern culture?"

"I think all people were created to live off the land. So, if the white people, when they showed up, if they would've adopted our ways, I believe right now today I would be able to walk down to the Mississippi River and take a drink of the water. But our elder brothers, the eagle, the owl, the bear, the rabbit, the squirrel, the deer, they have to go and drink that water every single day. But we won't. And every single day, there's an endangered species added to the extinction list. And once all that's gone, where are we going to get our food, our clothing, our housing, our medicine? That's where we get it all from. We were not created to live in an artificial world."

The Roman Empire reached as far as modern-day London. The Romans dominated, but also introduced civilized culture. But when the Romans left, London regressed. Architectural insight, commercial activity, logistical efficiency, and higher standards of living were lost. Does Mike see any benefit to the advancements European colonists introduced into North America?

"Oh, absolutely," says Mike. His son's life was saved at the Mayo Clinic. "White blood cells were attacking his brain stem. Western medicine, that Western knowledge helped save him." But now he's thirty-seven years old in a wheelchair. "Before, he was perfectly healthy. So, what caused it? Was it this environment?"

I'm not a doctor. I have no idea. But Mike claims all technological advancement is negative, even planes, trains, and automobiles.

"Anything that's going to cause harm to the planet" is a bad thing, Mike proclaims.

"But Mike, we have developed and benefited massively as a result of a distinctly European view of humanity's relationship to the earth, which is very different from the Native American one. The Native American one views humans as in sort of a symbiotic relationship with the earth. The European view, rooted in the Bible, sees Earth as a resource that was given to us to use for humanity. There is something beautiful about the Native American view, but it does not lend itself to modern medicine, modern transportation, all of the technologies that you enjoy, our ability to talk to each other right now."

"We are the cancer on this planet."

"Okay, Mike, I don't agree with that, but would you be open to consider maybe the possibility that we might be able to create harmonious balance with the earth?"

Mike believes the Indians have created the balance, not us. And what does that have to do with tearing down Christopher Columbus?

He'd known Minnesota's lieutenant governor, Peggy Flanagan, for twenty years—and had been speaking about "deporting" the Columbus statue. Originally, his idea was a gathering of Chinese, Palestinian, and Somali immigrants who would sing, dance, eat, and exchange histories at the State Capitol in a proper removal ceremony. "But then, after George Floyd happened, I saw on Facebook that someone was going to take him down in the middle of the night. And I understand why people do that. They don't want the law. They just want him down. But we've been protesting that statue for years. And so, I got ahold of one of my elders, and I told him about my plan to take him down with a big celebration. And he said, 'No, the time's over for that. That's Minnesota nice. Done playing Minnesota nice.' And so, the next day, I made a Facebook post about, 'Bring your drums. This piece of shit is coming down today.'

"I called the governor's office, and I invited them to be on the rope. And I told them, 'I know you're busy with the riots, but I just need you for five minutes. I'll put you on the front of the rope.' I knew that nobody would accept. But this was the way that I could make it public and let them know what was going to happen.

"And so around four o'clock, I went out, bought the rope, picked up a couple of my friends, went down to the capitol. I told my friend, 'At five o'clock, I need this rope at my feet.' I said, 'Before that, I was just a tourist. I'm just down there as a tourist.'

"A lieutenant tried to hand me the paperwork. I said, 'No. Your process is what's keeping him up there.' I said, 'We're not going to go through the process.' I said, 'We've got our own process today.'

"Five o'clock came, the rope landed at my feet. I made a noose. We ended up getting it over his head. We put two of them across. I asked all the women to step forward to be on the front of the rope as a symbol of our missing and murdered Indian women, and the legacy of Columbus, the raping. And then I told the men to stand behind the women and give them their strength. I said, 'And from this point on, you stand behind our women.' And they tugged, and within a minute, it came toppling over."

"How did that feel?"

"Oh, it felt wonderful. I just wish I would've been on the rope. But those women are my heroes. They're the ones who deserve the credit. I took the blame. I planned it. I organized it. I bought the rope, but I did not pull him down. I will not take credit for that. But I do wish I was on that rope that day."

"There's a photo of you with your leg on the statue as it's toppled, posing in victory."

"That was in reference to George Floyd. And we know George was not a hero, a saint, I guess you could say. And I don't know really anybody who's a saint. But because of what happened, because of the murder of him, they elevated him."

"Columbus was Italian," I say. "He sailed for the Spanish Crown. His destination was India. Can't you ever see Columbus through the lens of fifteenth-century humanity? Instead of looking at him through 2023, do you ever see 1492? What was that like, to get in that ship and go across an ocean? No one's ever done that before. You don't know where you're going to land. Riskiest thing that anyone's ever done up until that point. He lands. And he lands in a place where the civilization is outmatched. Technologically, but also in terms of the viral load too, he was far superior. Do you understand the time that he was in, or do you just see him as a bloodthirsty genocidal rapist?"

"Yeah, it was amazing," admits Mike. "When you're looking at it from a historical point of view, like Leif Erikson, when he popped over. Same thing. And so you can look at it through those eyes. But we live in 2023, so we also have to look at it from this point of view."

"How so?"

"Because when they say, 'Well, it was a different time back then. It was a different time.' Yep, you're right. So, if that's the case, well then now is a different time, and we know better. And since we know better, we should use that knowledge and spread that knowledge of what we know better. So, we know everybody was doing slavery back then. It's like, 'Well, it was no big deal.' Well, we know now it was a big deal. It wasn't the right thing to do. We know back then people were signing treaties and then throwing them in the garbage chute because they got the land. 'Well, that's the way they did things back then.' Well, 2023, we know better. We know better. So let's fix those mistakes that happened way back then. Not just forget about them. Not just say, 'Well, that just happened, and that's the way it was.' No, we know that it was wrong. Today, we look back because we know history. We know that was wrong. Let's try to rectify it. Let's try to even this out."

"You say 'even it out,'" I tell him. "And that's an interesting phrase. If you take that to its logical conclusion, then people living today would be constantly having to even things out for things that happened hundreds and thousands of years ago, all over the planet. The Japanese, the Tutsi, you know, the Ottoman Empire. Take your pick. Our lives would constantly be absorbed in apologizing and evening things out. You think that's the move here? Because then you have to apologize to other tribes your tribe wronged, and even things out."

Mike is listening intently. His eyes narrow. I continue.

"I want to acknowledge our history in graphic detail. There was vicious warfare on both sides. Indian raids, cutting open the white pioneer women's bellies, take the baby out, slit their throats, horrible."

Mike says he doesn't want the federal government to give *all* the land back. Thank goodness. I was worried I'd have to migrate to Mexico. "But they do have land that nobody is using. They have city parks. They have national forests. They have land that they could give back. They could make it a little more even. That's where America has to be honorable and honor those treaties, and if those treaties were honored, we may be as rich as some of the Saudis are now."

"We're going to have to give you guys back all the natural gas deposits in the Dakotas?"

"Well, look, they took it."

"Are you allowed to use the oil-drilling equipment that we invented? We'll give it back to you, but you can't use anything that we invented."

"They took the Black Hills, and then they gave it back, and then they found gold in Them Dar Hills. So, then they took it back again."

"But the only reason the gold was profitable is because of the financial system we invented. Gold didn't mean anything to Native Americans before we got there."

Mike wants nothing to do with our civilization, except he'll take the wealth our civilization created.

"You talk about monuments. Somebody had once said what? 'I suppose Mount Rushmore is next.' Well, no, it's not next, but it is on the list."

"Hold on. You want to tear down our statues and the testaments to the greatest figures in our civilization. You want to do away with Mount Rushmore?"

"Yeah, your greatest figures."

"Right, so why should we let you?"

"What do you mean let?"

"Why do we not have a right to defend ourselves? And by 'we,' I don't mean white people. I mean participants in Western civilization, which includes a vast variety of races, but you see yourself as an opponent of all of that and everything it's built. That's fine. It's your right that you enjoy living in a free country, but I'm not sure why we should indulge those requests."

"But the only reason why it's a free country is because it was never paid for."

"We conquered it and settled it."

"But was there a treaty signed saying we'll give you this for this land?"

"Some of the land, yes, and honoring treaties is generally a good thing. But the Columbus statue had nothing to do with the treaties. Tearing down Mount Rushmore has nothing to do with treaties, right? I'd like to keep Mount Rushmore. I'd like to keep that statue."

"Right, because you love those people, and you honor them."

"I do, and the majority of Americans do as well. So, why should Americans give our land back to people who are actively undermining the civilization that we love? You're committed to destroying the country that we actually live in and all of the sort of fruits and benefits that we enjoy."

"That would be the same thing as saying, 'Don't touch my Hitler statue.' Well, who wants a Hitler statue?"

"No, I'm talking about America."

"But we look at Columbus as Hitler."

"But I don't. You are opposed to American civilization. I understand where you're coming from."

"When I saw January Sixth, I loved it. I love seeing those people, and I thought, 'My God, this country's coming to an end, finally.' I loved it."

Let's get back on track.

"Mike, we're tearing down statues of Christopher Columbus, and we're putting up statues of George Floyd, who you yourself said was no saint."

"Compared to Columbus, he was a saint."

"What is wrong with putting up a beautiful statue near Columbus? I'll let you have it an inch higher than Columbus. A Native American of your choice. I don't think we should be tearing down statues. We should have an honest appreciation and understanding of our history, and statues are a part of what society at the time felt was worthy of that type of honor, but to tear them down seems immature."

"Didn't they recently take a statue down of a coach who got caught molesting all these young boys?"

"Penn State's [Joe] Paterno for having a coach that got caught. The difference is that Paterno was not a symbol of our great civilizational achievements. My fundamental objection to tearing down the statues of Columbus, Jefferson, Washington, and Lincoln is that it's not just about the statues. It's actually about tearing down the symbols of American civilization and undermining the nation's pride and confidence in its own achievements. Those statues symbolize American identity, what it means to be an American, the things that we've done, where we come from, what we've achieved, what we owe to one another. It's a symbolic representation of the ethos of the nation. Now, I think this is a great nation, the greatest nation in the history of the world, actually. So, I bristle at the suggestion that we should be taking down statues that represent that greatness. It's really about fundamentally an assault on American identity. That's actually the debate we're having. It's about much more than statues. It's about what we've achieved, and whether or not we should be proud of that and have confidence in ourselves."

"So, were you happy when Saddam Hussein's statue came down with the help of Americans by the way? That statue meant a lot to the Iraqi people."

Did it?

"Mike, if you don't think that losers should have statues put up, well then could you make the argument that there should be nothing honoring Native Americans? There should be no statue of a Native American because technically they lost."

Mike doesn't accept that American Indians lost. "For the most part, those treaties were signed amicably. There was no, 'Yeah, we beat you and we got this land.' It wasn't like that. You didn't honor the treaty and now we want the land back."

"Mike, if those treaties hadn't been signed, a lot of the Native Americans would've died in battle."

"There was an abundance of land. It wasn't like they were fighting over a small island, where one side had to be completely obliterated. I mean, we're talking about the continental United States of America here. You could win a few skirmishes, you could decisively defeat some of these tribes in these battles, and they were, but there's so much land. The treaty was just a way to say, all right, you guys are going to go over here, we're going to go over here now."

"You're making this sound like this was all one big peaceful negotiation in a boardroom. The treaties were the result of military victories, significant military victories over and over and over again. Do you feel like your people were outsmarted or outmaneuvered?"

"We didn't know we were going to get the knife in the back."

"I'm not speaking about you personally, but the tribes were naïve?"

"I guess you could say they were naïve to greed and capitalism and materialism at that time."

"So, they were not perceptive?"

"They weren't perceptive."

"Yeah, this was all new to them. It would be kind of like someone coming from five hundred years ago popping into the United States today, seeing skyscrapers and light-rail and Uber, all this stuff. It would be unimaginable.

"It was not a fair fight."

"No."

"Right. You said God ordained that these two cultures are unassimilable. So, it's almost like destiny, that this settler culture came in and dominated."

"Yeah, that seemed like that, and it seems like that's why we're heading off this cliff, because of that settler culture."

Actually, we're heading off this cliff because of cancel culture.

"What about Native American mascots?"

"I don't even think you should have to ask, because it's not just the mascots. They name their cars after us. The Pontiac, the Buick, the Comanche, the Cherokee, the Winnebago. Then they named their killing machines after us. I mean, they committed genocide against us, and they have the Tomahawk missile, the Apache, all these things, so it's not just the team names that we have to fight. Should we have the Kansas City N*ggers? Hey, go, N*ggers. The Los Angeles Wetbacks, hell yeah, let's have some Wetbacks, the New York Kikes, let's have the New York Kikes."

"Aren't you a fan of the Minnesota Vikings?"

"No, I don't like professional football at all because of how much money it's wasting."

"Mike, you missed my joke. The Vikings—a white European culture that also had a mascot named after them."

"Right, so are they telling the Vikings, go back to the reservation? Vikings don't have anything like the tomahawk chop or anything like that, so there's no comparison between the Vikings and the Redskins."

"Okay. What about the Trojans of USC? They have the Roman helmet. They go out there with the face mask and the red little hair. You've seen that. Proud warriors."

"How many Romans are upset that they were defeated and this happened to them? None, none. That's the point I'm trying to make: they name their cars after us, they name their war machines after us, they name their sports teams after us, why? Why would you do such a thing to a people that were defeated and then make fun of it on top of it?"

"Well, we just name things after lots of stuff. The Celtics. They're Irish. You, you don't want your name anywhere?"

"Not used like that, absolutely not."

"Where, if it's not a seventy-five-thousand-dollar car and if it's not a two-billion-dollar sports franchise that millions of fans go and cheer for and wear on their jerseys, where would you like your names to be recognized within the American culture, commercially?"

"Probably not on anything, commercially."

Okay then. "I don't want to leave on a sour note. You're very passionate. You've opened my eyes to a lot of things. I do understand and empathize with the fact that you do have a chip on your shoulder, and you're angry about what had happened. I hope this conversation has been helpful to you. It's been helpful to me as well. I have a lot of respect for your people, your tribe, your history, and what both of our cultures have gone through going back many, many generations. I hope we can live in more harmony and in more harmony with the earth."

"Thank you," says Mike. "And you know what? I had a good time. I don't look at any of this as animosity whatsoever because, like I said, you weren't here. You didn't do it. I learned things, always, whenever I'm speaking to people, because I can only learn while I'm listening. I've never learned anything while I was speaking, ever, ever. I appreciate listening to you. If there's anything you can do about helping us with getting our land back, I'd appreciate it."

If I grew up as Mike did, I'd hate this country too. His family ripped out of the reservation, placed in the projects, transient during his formative years, mother an alcoholic, destitute, his son crippled by disease. But Mike is a fighter. And that I respect. He's driven. His cause is futile. But his life has purpose, and that's more than you can say for most Americans. His worldview is 100 percent opposite of mine. But our conversation was civil. We both listened. Believing European civilization and American Indian civilization are, as ordained by God, incompatible was something I'd never contemplated. Are certain civilizations fundamentally incompatible? Mike says yes. I'm not so sure. Almost every culture on Earth has shown the ability to assimilate into American society. But when you combine a hostile history, an antagonistic ideology, modern versus premodern, and opposing conceptions of man's relationship to Earth, those civilizations will be at odds forever.

Mike admitted his culture was destined to be defeated, just as Americans believe in Manifest Destiny. But that doesn't mean we can't learn from each other. As America throttles into technological oblivion, it's critical we gather ourselves and absorb the wisdom of the Native tribes who nurtured this land before us. Generational knowledge from indigenous peoples must be tapped into in order for us to achieve balance. Past atrocities should be acknowledged. Tribes should be honored. But returning land, just like slavery reparations, isn't something American society will ever indulge. Demographic expansion, disease, technological prowess, and military superiority pushed American Indians off the land and into reservations. For them, it was a tragic loss. They fought bravely. Their spirit lives among us. It even lives within senators from Massachusetts.

16

The
Decriminalizing-Drugs
Guru

"All my heroes shot themselves in the head."

Doc—the name he goes by—has a mischievous gleam in his eyes, a defiant air punctuated with a faint grin that suggests none of this is completely serious. The specific hero in question he's referencing, the famous "gonzo journalism" pioneer Hunter S. Thompson, did, in fact, shoot himself in the head at the age of sixty-seven, sitting in the kitchen of his Aspen, Colorado, cabin. In the middle of a phone call with his wife. While his daughter-in-law and six-year-old grandson were in the house. ("I was on the phone with him, he set the receiver down, and he did it. I heard the clicking of the gun," his wife told the *Aspen Daily News* at the time. "He wanted to leave on top of his game. I wish I could have been more supportive of his decision.")

Doc is "just kidding" about the heroes-shooting-themselves-in-the-head line, he assures me. The real reason he likes Thompson, above all else, is the writer's almost superhuman drug habit. Thompson's most famous book, *Fear and Loathing in Las Vegas*, is a pseudobiographical account of a drug-fueled bender in the City of Sin, traipsing through a series of increasingly absurd situations armed with a laundry list of standard-issue psychoactive drugs—alcohol, weed, cocaine, LSD—plus some of the weirder ones—peyote, mushrooms, various unnamed inhalants—and some, like ether, that practically no one had ever heard of before. "We had two bags of grass, seventy-five pellets of mescaline, five sheets of high-powered blotter acid, a salt-shaker half full of cocaine, and a whole galaxy of multi-colored uppers, downers, screamers, laughers . . . and also a quart of tequila, a quart of rum, a case of Budweiser, a pint of raw ether and two dozen amyls. . . . The only thing that really worried me was the ether."

Thompson's daily routine, as legend has it, was outlined by regular lines of cocaine—beginning just forty-five minutes after he woke up—glasses of Cheval, weed, LSD, beer and wine, and . . . fried onion rings. The writer's drug use was at times an attempt to turn himself into a sort of mythical storybook character, to live a life insane enough to write books about. Norman Mailer called him "a legend in successful self-abuse." Doc's routine isn't quite as manic—very few human beings have lived the way Thompson did and lived to tell the tale—but he does share his hero's appetite for a near-constant IV drip of mind-altering substances, as well as his sort of vaguely surreal, tongue-in-cheek attitude about the purpose of using drugs.

Doc is a drug user's drug user. It's less about the drugs themselves, and more about the adventure of taking them. He appears on Zoom with the background from *Saturday Night Live*'s "Weekend Update." As Doc machine-gun fires his biography, I have to redirect him back to key details he glosses over.

"I live in Hollywood, California, right now but was born up in Big Bear, California, little snowboard resort town. But I bounced all around as a kid. My mom was just kind of wild and young when she had me. My whole elementary school, middle school, I went to a different school every year, sometimes two or three times a year. Just knew that everything's fleeting, so kind of have that attachment/commitment issue a little bit. Bob Dylan said something about, to him touring and traveling is like breathing. He needs it to feel alive. My mom had me till I was eight, and then my dad had me from nine to seventeen. I got taken by foster care in Big Bear and moved to Victorville. Every single year until college, I went to a different school. And then junior college in Humboldt was the best six years of my life."

"When were you in foster care?"

"The guy my mom was with punched some dude at the bar that turned out to be an off-duty officer, yada, yada, yada. My mom was just a wild child. My dad was pretty wild too. I was just a bad kid at that point. I got expelled and suspended and everything. Quit playing sports and started skateboarding and smoking pot and listening to Black Sabbath and stuff. I was seventeen. It was pretty shitty. No money, alcoholic at sixteen years old. I was just so mad at my dad. And I came home drunk off vodka and like a bat out of hell. And my cat's trying to escape out the window. And my dad called the cops on me. And then I was stupid and drunk, and I told the cops, 'I'm the leader.' They're like, 'You in a gang?' And I said, 'Yeah, I'm the leader of the KKK.' And so I get into the jail, the guard comes up to me, and he's like, 'Hey, man, I don't want you preaching none of the word.' And I go, 'What, the word?' And he goes, 'Yeah, man, you're in the KKK, right?' And I was like, 'No, no, no. I was just drunk, man.' I still think it's on my record too. But they would have you rainbow up, which is like a black guy, Mexican guy, white guy, black guy, and you stand there with your hands on your knees. It was a shit show. I was in there for twenty-eight days."

"You took a swing at your dad?"

"I threw a chair at him. I smoked a joint in the house, and he came home, and he was so livid at me. And he was like, 'You're eighteen years old. I can finally fight you as a man.' And we literally squared off. And he came at me with a walking stick, and I hit him with a baseball bat, the bottom end of the baseball bat. It just popped him a little bit, and it busted his eye. The cops came. They took me to my grandma's house. And then my dad got a restraining order against me. He actually passed away in 2012. I loved him to death. He was a construction worker, alcoholic but never wanted to admit it."

"What were you so angry with him about at that time?"

"I think he was just a bar-stool dad. Nothing I would do would ever be good enough for him. And it was just the vodka. And just being the poor kid, and having smelly feet and being embarrassed to take off my shoes, and just hating him for it."

"So you were resentful?"

"Yeah, I was really resentful. When my dad passed, I didn't really cry. It was hard to really feel anything about it. But his dad was an asshole to him too and abandoned him when he was a kid. He was shuffled around a bit too."

"You've been to prison a few times?"

"I was with my buddy Justin. We're drinking beers and we go into this little store, and this guy's just kind of being an asshole to us. And I said something along the lines of, 'Where's that girl that works here? She's a lot nicer to me than you are.' And he comes around the back of the thing with a cane, and he's coming to beat me up. He is swinging at me, and I kind of just back up and just rabbit-punch him a little bit just to get him off of me."

Doc was arrested. He did ten days and spent his twenty-third birthday staring "across the glass" at his girlfriend at the time. His life is filled with "movie moments." It all starts with his mother.

"I want to make a Netflix series about my mom because she's literally 'LA girl.' She was friends with 'What you talking about, Willis?'"

"Todd Bridges from *Diff'rent Strokes*?"

"Todd Bridges, she was really good friends with him. He was at my mom and dad's wedding, and it was a shotgun wedding. She was like six months pregnant with me. My grandpa tried to push her downstairs when she was pregnant with me, I guess. They didn't want her to have the baby. And so I was blessed to even be able to live this life in a lot of ways."

I want to interrupt him but figure it's best to let him keep going.

"My aunt dated Erik Estrada and would pick them up from school in high school. She lived this just far-out, spoiled-rotten lifestyle. And then just wanted to do whatever she wanted to do. She ended up shoveling frozen shit in Nebraska at a livestock auction. That's what she wanted to do. And then all of a sudden she had three boys by herself. We came back to California. And my grandma came and picked us all up one day after school and just took us all back down to Southern California, and we stayed with our aunts."

Suddenly Doc's pet turtle saunters into the picture behind the *SNL* "Weekend Update" backdrop. Then his cat appears.

"Did she have the three boys with three different guys?"

"Yeah, all different dads except she named the middle one my dad's last name, for some reason."

"She named the wrong child after your father?"

"Yeah."

"When did you start using drugs?" I ask.

"I think I smoked pot for the first time at twelve years old. And then, by the time I was thirteen, fourteen, I did cocaine. And I was like, I just did cocaine. And then it was funny because then fast-forward five years, and I'm actually watering cannabis plants for my mom, in Humboldt County, California. This is fucking bizarre. And then I became a pretty bad alcoholic at fifteen, sixteen. And then got taken by foster care, and then I kind of quit everything. And then I just experimented with a lot of stuff during Humboldt college years, like acid and mushrooms. And just anything I could try, PCP, synthetic mescaline, ketamine, ecstasy, anything I could really try. I'm a big fan of Hunter S. Thompson, and I think that kind of corrupted my mind a little bit to want to go over that edge."

In 2011, Doc pulled up to the Occupy Wall Street protests in San Francisco in a limo. "I felt like I was in the middle of something really happening. I'm like, this is my turn, I guess, or whatever." He picked his "buddy" up at Revolution Café. They parked in a "Masonic" parking garage and slept in the limo ("cheaper than a hotel and super funny"). When Doc arrived at the financial district, "there's dudes putting phone books and duct tape around them being like, 'They're coming tonight, man, it's happening tonight.' And I'm sitting in this tent, this guy's like, 'Oh, you can stay in this tent. It's empty.' All of a sudden, I hear someone outside, and the next thing I know, it was a big line of all these SWAT team guys coming out. And I'll never forget, I was walking up, and I see all these SWAT team guys coming out, and they were like, 'You got to leave Occupy San Francisco. We've given you your three-day notice. Blah, blah, blah.' And then it was just like, remember *Benny Hill* where they're just chasing each other through all the doors and stuff? It was like that. I just felt this gonzo Hunter Thompson moment where I'm just like, 'Oh my God, all these cops are coming down and just like . . .' Yeah, it was insanity. And I'm in a limo."

"Are you aligned with the Occupy Wall Street movement, or you just got caught up in the scene for a second?"

"I hate San Francisco, but I love San Francisco. I love the history of it, I love the city itself. But I've just had some of the shittiest experiences I've ever had in my life in a city there. What happened with Occupy was they got a lot of money, and then all these kids just got iPads. There was no real voice in the Occupy. It was just screaming into a well."

What side of the political aisle is Doc on?

"When I got money, I'm Republican, but when I'm broke, I'm Democrat."

Doc's first acid trip was at nineteen. "I went to Humboldt, and my buddy picked me up, and he was like, 'Yeah, you want to try acid or whatever?' I was like, 'Yeah, I really want to try it.' And I did it by myself." Doc's description of the trip was as follows: "It's dead babies in the cheese or something. So they take me back to their house, and I look up at the ceiling, and the stucco looks like a lizard orgy. And I'm just like, 'Oh God.' And I look over at my friend and his girlfriend, and she starts looking like a guy a little bit. And I look over, and I'm like, 'I'm not gay.' And they're like, 'What?' And I'm like, 'I'm not gay.' And they're like, 'What are you talking about?' And I'm like, 'Yeah, I'm not gay.' And I stand up, and I go to the door, and I look in the mirror, and I got bleach-blond hair and big framed glasses. And I go, 'I'm so fucking gay.'"

I'm now laughing.

"I've had a trip where I thought I was a million years old. I've had a trip where I thought I was in a painting, and everything that was around me was made up of people that were painted into this painting of chairs and tables and couches; it was pretty bizarre. But I stopped taking it because a lot of my heroes that did that stuff, by the time they were thirty-eight, they're burnt-out."

Doc claims he "invented microdosing," which is taking small amounts of psychedelics while working to enhance productivity. "I think mushrooms are one of the most powerful and greatest tools that we ever had. I think Jesus Christ was a mushroom, in that sense of Christ consciousness and that feeling of oneness. Have you ever read *Island* by Aldous Huxley? You realize you're not just a spit in the ocean. You're the entire ocean. If you're with a girl, you don't belong to her. She doesn't belong to you. You're just together. Mushrooms unlock in that sense of just what it is to be human."

Music that "sounds like two fucking Transformers having sex, hot, heavy sex." This is the festival Doc tells me about. "And my buddy was like, 'Yeah, we could get in for free at this festival, but we got to do trash pickup and stuff.' And I was like, 'Yeah, for sure, dude, that sounds awesome. Let's do it.' And we're doing trash pickup, this guy's like, 'Yo, bro, you want some K or whatever?' He's like, 'Put your thumb out, like this, so it's a shovel.' And he gives it to me. And it was a fucking big old part of it. And next thing I know I'm leaning up against the men's bathroom, and I was like, 'I'm not gay.'"

I'm dying laughing.

"But then I'm sitting down and all these people's feet, and I'm talking to their feet, and I'm like, 'Oh.' And I get up out of that, and it was just so hard, I felt like a zombie. And then I went, and I sat down, I somehow got down by the water, and I blew it all out of my nose. At the time, I was working this job selling Google ad space. So, I felt like they were rewiring my brain, and what the ketamine was doing was showing me how they were rewiring my brain."

I start going down the list. "What about the ecstasy?"

"Oh, ecstasy, that was a weird one. That was when I was dating Vanessa, and I was nineteen. I remember kissing my girlfriend, and our gum was all sticky, and so it was like that, 'I'll stop the world and melt with you.' But it was just gum coming through the lips. It was just a fucking weird time. I just remember that next morning having Kurt Cobain, Nirvana stuck in my head where it was like, 'I found my friends, they're in my head.' You know? And I couldn't pee either. Ecstasy, it's like you can't pee afterward. Man, I don't really like that stuff. And you never know what you're going to get with that shit."

The combinations of drugs. Doc's done PCP and mescaline. Or cocaine and ketamine. "They call it Calvin Klein."

"You're still doing all these drugs?"

"I'm still doing them all, but I just know my limits now. And I'm thirty-five, so. My grandpa always said, 'There's always tomorrow, no one to pull the reins.' You know what I mean?"

Not really. "What narcotics are you currently dabbling in?" I ask.

"It's the crystal methamphetamine," admits Doc. "It's stupid. I don't know. I'm just a fucking peanut head." He justifies that drug use. "A lot of it's my grandpa passing away. It's a lot of that grief, and I'm trying to just conceal my feelings from it."

Doc believes drugs should be decriminalized. Not just marijuana and cocaine. All drugs, including meth, crack, and even heroin. "I think it should just be decriminalized and that people should be treated like patients instead of criminals. Be able to get the right help that they need, from detox or a meeting, or a safe place that they could stay."

Decriminalizing drugs would look something like this. "Everybody who's arrested with a drug-related situation should go to rehab instead," he explains. "Instead of sending people to jail, send them to fail." This means drug users get assigned menial tasks and have to assimilate their way back into society. "They have to be underneath Betty the baker. Betty is their boss. They're getting a routine to where they can get more responsibility or feel like they're a productive part of the community."

If you're arrested for stealing a car high on crack, Doc would see to it that you work at a bakery. Even if you're selling crack, Doc wants to send you straight to Betty the baker.

"Doc, distributing hard-core narcotics is like giving people deadly poisons," I counter.

"We drink Coca-Cola too. There's a corner everywhere that you can buy Coca-Cola, and I mean that shit is not good for us either."

Typically, Coca-Cola drinkers don't stick up convenience stores for cash to feed their habit.

"What happens when you throw [drug addicts] in jail? They just get with more criminals and they learn more crime."

Doc claims people commit drug crimes to get a respite from family life.

"There's guys that literally just go into jail because they want to get away from their wife and their kids because they're screaming all the time. They get so fucked-up so they can go and spend ten, fifteen, twenty days in the clink and have a break from the woman. 'Oh I miss you baby, I miss you so much.' Then he goes to play spades."

Going to jail to take a break from your woman. Ultimate power move.

"Do you think that if you did decriminalize drugs federally, drugs would become so readily available, and so prevalent, it would strip the taboo out of it, and more people would then take drugs?"

"I think the taboo will always be there. I think that the only people that'll be pissed-off is probably the Mexican cartels and the CIA."

Here's the problem. Drug decriminalization has been tried before. Oregon tried it. It's been a disaster. "Less than one percent of the people ticketed have actually gone to treatment. They haven't sent any more funding to treatment. And fatal overdoses have gone up like sixty percent with a death count in the thousands."

Doc doesn't even take rehab seriously. "I'm hoping that I can just get famous, and then I go to Passages Malibu. I don't need no drugs. Just send me some good fresh orange juice, scrambled eggs in the morning, yoga. I'm into it. Let me heal, baby. I want to heal." He laughs.

"Do you think if you decriminalized drugs, schoolkids would get more into drugs than they are now?"

"Those kids are the most into it, and it's probably because they can't do it. It's the idea, 'Don't push the red button, kid,' and they go and they push the red button. You tell someone not to do something, they want to do it. It's just human nature. I think that they'll look back on us and be like, 'Yeah, just opium for the masses.' Just give them opiates and make them dependent on it and give the kids methamphetamines, which is basically what Ritalin and Adderall and all that stuff is, just amphetamine. And then those poor kids that had it since they were eleven, twelve years old, they end up thirty-three years old and wondering why they have this chemical dependency, because they've been on it all their lives and they don't know who they really are. And that's sad. It's existential crisis shit."

Doc flatlined once. From fentanyl. Narcan saved his life.

"It's like a drug where you have to buy another drug with it just in case you fucking almost die, which I almost died."

What happened?

"My girlfriend went and got cocaine, the ex-girlfriend. And I came back and I did two lines of it, and then all of a sudden I felt like I was on ketamine. I lost it. It was like ego death. I saw myself from a third-person view. And I was like, 'I don't think I'm good.' And in the back of my mind I was like, 'Tell her you're not good.' And in the front of my mind, I was like, 'No, I'm fine. I'm going to be fine.' But I had to be like, 'No, no, I don't think I'm good.' And she called the paramedics. And I don't even remember them giving me the Narcan, but they pulled me back up out of it. And yeah, so I just kept trying to do little bits of it to build my tolerance up."

"You're purposely trying to do fentanyl?"

"I'm not purposely. Well, I mean a couple times. It just depends on if I drink too much. Opiates are not my friend. I don't really like them. You can't shit. It's a downer drug, and you turn green and pasty."

"Wait. Just so I can understand, you're saying you don't want it, but you also sometimes actively seek out fentanyl so that you have more of a tolerance? Is that what you're saying?"

"And that's my excuse, for sure, is that 'Oh well, at least if I do little bits of it that if I ever get a bad batch or a coke from someone, it won't affect me as bad.'"

Doc makes a constitutional argument for decriminalization. "I think people should have the right to choose their own consciousness of what they want to put in their body." He doesn't make a judgment. "It's their body, their choice, just like abortions."

"But doesn't that harm the rest of society? Are you saying people should be able to drive stoned?"

"People drive slow when they're stoned, are almost more aware."

"They also have slower response times, right?"

"But I have a slower response time after I eat a couple Arby's sandwiches. You know what I mean?"

Not *that* slow.

"I think alcohol is literally the worst drug in the fucking world, and it's the one that's most socially acceptable to everyone. And I think it's the one that has destroyed more homes, more families, it's put more people behind bars, it's killed more people. It's made people do things that they would never fucking do in any kind of state of mind. I don't know anyone that gets superstoned and wants to fight somebody."

"Do you think people should be able to go to work on heroin?"

"I mean, good luck. What kind of job is it? Do they sit down a lot? You'd be surprised by how many functioning addicts that are out there. You'd have no idea."

But life doesn't always revolve around the sanctity of individual choice. You must balance that with policies that are in the interest of the common good of society. "If you let people do whatever they want to themselves, they might not be directly hurting other people in that moment, but that behavior is bad for society; it breaks down society. If everyone's on heroin, everyone's nodding off the whole time."

Doc says we're already there, so why not.

"I don't think it's a choice to be an addict. I think it's hereditary. But I think that life isn't fair, but I'm sure that it's a circus."

"But Doc, every culture does have some sort of boundary, whether it's African culture, whether it's Asian culture, every culture through-out the world as long as there have been societies have always said, 'You know what? We're going to allow this, but we're not going to allow that.' And that's kind of what defines those cultures, what's acceptable and what's unacceptable. Do you think you might lose the culture if all of a sudden you could do whatever you want, whenever you want it? Do you think that kind of libertarian anarchy, do you think you might lose the identity of America that way?"

I get Doc to agree that we do need limits. "It's like when you live in LA, there's so much shit to do, that you just don't do anything. You know what I mean? You have so many options that you're like, 'Ah, you know what? I'm just going to fucking stay in.'

"It's like Netflix. There's too many options. No one just watches any-thing anymore. They just scroll."

"Doc, why do people love taking drugs so much? Is it escapism?"

"I think psychology-wise, I think it's the need for acceptance. Think about when you were a kid like, 'Oh, man, we're drinking beers, man.' It was like, 'Cool, if I drink a beer, I'm going to be cool.' It's that social acceptance with alcoholism. With weed, it's more of it's that culture, so I smoke weed, and I listen to Bob Marley, man, I'm inside. I feel a part of something. You know what I mean? Or I grow weed, bro, so I'm a part of this farmer thing. Like I said, they give kids amphetamines and Grandma fucking opiates. It's like either way we're getting drugs somehow one way or another, whether it's a guy in a white coat or a guy on a street corner."

Years ago, there were different avenues for young people to go down for social acceptance. The military, Boy Scouts, church, sports, civic institutions. "Do you think we've lost that and now, people are seeking different social contexts to join because there aren't those traditional places to become a part of something anymore?"

"Yeah, my generation got blindsided by the cell phones. All my adult relationships and everything is all on Facebook. They didn't have that back in the day. You had to go cruising, find the thing to do. It was like you call your buddy from your mom's house landline and be like, 'All right, we're going to meet at the Pink Dot at six, man. If you're not there by six thirty, we're going somewhere. We don't know yet. We're going to figure it out.' I think that it's going into the world with curiosity rather than judgment is where you get the best of life. Because when you're curious about something, it's a mystery almost, and you want to go chase down the mystery, as opposed to when you're expecting things or you're sitting around in LA, instead of going to a concert you can watch a concert at home on video. I don't have to go because I can live vicariously through everybody else. Sharing experiences strips individualism and binds us all in together."

For a meth head, Doc gets it.

Doc has seen his friend in an open casket at fourteen years old. He lost his grandpa, his "best friend." He watched his parents fight. His dad spent most of the time at the bar, cheated on his mom. Doc never had a true parent. Never had guidance or discipline. This is why he strikes for an apprenticeship from Betty the baker.

"When I was a kid, that was all I wanted, man, a mom and dad, and to come home with the new dog and get dinner on the table. I wanted that sweet American life, and I didn't have that because my mom was just a wild child, a sex addict. She wasn't able to be a parent. And then I had to be the parent. So, she would leave the kids with me for two, three days, and then I'd have to figure out how to cook. I think at nine years old, I was like, 'I don't want to be a parent. I want to be a kid.'

"And then same thing with my dad, though. I still had to parent myself with him too. That's why I got a turtle and a cat, I think, at thirty-five years old, because it's something I wanted when I was eleven probably, and I'm just living it out. Oh, I got a turtle and a cat now. I got stickers on my window like a fucking child. It's a part of the art, though, too because I think as an artist you kind of have to stay in that child-like mindset where the imagination can run free, and there's nothing limiting you."

17

The Anti-Natalist

Alexandra Cuc is an anti-natalist.

"I will never have kids. And I don't think others should have children as well."

She runs an organization, Stop Having Kids, and passes out condoms on weekends.

Most anti-natalists are motivated by environmental concerns— ecological destruction caused by overpopulation, human contributions to climate change, and so on. But for Alexandra Cuc, it's deeper than that. "Even if the climate was in decent shape, I would still be an anti-natalist."

Alexandra isn't bad-looking. Most men would want to have kids with her. But they can't. Her tubes were removed. She even made her boyfriend get a vasectomy.

A blue jay is tattooed on her neck. She has a completely tattooed arm sleeve. One tattoo says "Humans Are Trash."

"I feel like there's going to be humans that are totally trashy, and then there's humans that are more higher-quality trash, but at the end of the day, I feel that one way or another, just as a species, we're pretty trashy in general."

"Should I be taking this personally, Alexandra?"

"I don't know. It's up to you. If it makes you feel better, I think I'm trash too."

It doesn't make me feel better.

"I never really had that kind of desire to be a parent growing up. And then I got pregnant when I was nineteen. I was on birth control. We had used a condom, but unfortunately it all failed. And that was my first experience with pregnancy and the reality of possibly becoming a parent. And it just scared me so much. It scared the crap out of me."

Naturally, unplanned pregnancies in college are scary.

"And so, at nineteen, being in college and everything, I got an abortion, and I felt a lot of relief."

Alexandra says she never felt an ounce of "grief" about the abortion. Ten years later, she discovered that some Chinese people dine on dogs. She became a vegan. Animal rights activism became a passion that informed her anti-natalism. "Just kind of realizing how apathetic the majority of humans are really kind of strengthened my anti-natalism. Because it felt like doing vegan advocacy, animal rights activism, it just felt a little futile. Because even if someone, let's say they did go vegan, and they had a child, you'll never be able to guarantee that child will remain vegan, that they'll continue on with your beliefs."

That would be like me not having children because I couldn't guarantee that child would remain a conservative. It's a risk. But if it happens, at least I cancel out their vote.

"Even if someone goes vegan and then they have a kid, that would undo all of the work that they've done if that child chooses to not be vegan for the rest of their life. So, for me, that was too much of a risk."

Yes, kids are risky. And they won't believe everything you believe. And they'll occasionally disappoint you. And maybe they even throw you in an old folks' home and forge your will. But who cares?! You'll be dead soon, and they were cute when they were little.

Even if her hypothetical offspring followed her ideology it still wouldn't be worth it. "It would be very traumatic for them to have to witness so much injustice of not just nonhumans, but humans as well. There's a lot of oppression around the world that most of us are pretty powerless to stop. And it's a very overwhelming feeling, being able to see what's happening and not be able to change it. So I wouldn't want to put that on someone else if they don't exist."

Since life is suffering, how very thoughtful to save them from such pain.

"Not being able to guarantee their safety, not being able to guarantee their well-being. And then also too, not being able to guarantee that they will be a good person. I mean, terrible people have existed throughout history, and I'm sure their parents thought that they did a pretty all-right job raising them. But it's never any kind of guarantee. So, for me personally, I would rather just not gamble with somebody else's life, which is that person that I would be bringing into existence."

It never crossed my mind when I was conceiving children: What if I'm creating a serial killer? Or someone who listens to Nirvana.

"You could give birth to Harvey Weinstein?"

"Yeah, totally. Or like the next Hitler, or the next Bill Gates or whoever, you know? Whether we do it willingly or not, we do harm each other. So, I feel like when you don't exist, you're not deprived of anything. You're not forced into anything."

I guess not existing is the ultimate freedom. The ultimate power. You can't destroy someone who doesn't exist. But then again, if you don't exist, you can't enjoy wine.

"Alexandra, how do you get pregnant if you are on birth control and someone's using a condom? I mean, that sounds so hard."

"Yeah, I mean, nothing is a hundred percent effective unless you sterilize. So unfortunately, I wasn't necessarily the best at always diligently taking the pill every single day. So there's that part. And then also too the condom came off, and we just didn't realize. Most people don't even get the right size or wear condoms properly. And that could be a huge issue. So I've given out free condoms, and people just in different sizes and—everyone grabs the really big condoms. And it's like, okay, I don't care what size your penis is, just please grab the right one. So it's effective. But yeah, that's how that happened."

If nobody's around, grab the right size. If a woman is there, you grab the extra-large. Since you're probably not having sex with the girl who's handing out the condoms, just do it to make an impression. You can always get condoms that fit at 7-Eleven. And if you do happen to have sex with the girl who's handing out the condoms, she'll notice that it doesn't fit. So you'll have to use a different condom. And then the girl who handed out the condoms is wondering what other girls you're sleeping with since you aren't using the condom she gave you. And then she'll think you're a player. And she'll want to date you, because deep down all girls like players, because girls like guys that other girls are sleeping with. Now you have options.

Alexandra says she belongs to a "small grassroots movement" called Stop Having Kids. She wants to "normalize 'child freedom,' normalize anti-natalism, get people to think critically about the implications of having kids and bringing another person into existence. And obviously, we would hope that after discussing it with us, people would want to opt out of procreation. And for those that do want to parent, we would encourage them to prioritize already existing life. So whether that's adoption or fostering."

"What is child freedom?"

"So that's just normalizing living without kids. Not every single person wants to be a parent. And that's totally fine. And that's what we want to validate as well, because there's still that big stigma around being a child-free person. People look at it, there's something wrong with you. Are you broken? They just assume the worst."

When I see a couple without children, I just assume they're neat freaks and want to keep their house spotless. I respect it. When I see a couple with lots of children, I just assume they're Mormon, or Catholic, or careless. Or wealthy.

Alexandra lives in Canada. She was born in Romania. She claims her mother did a number on her, and her grandmother did a number on her mother. "Living through communism, there was that scarcity mindset. My mom never felt like she could really get what she wanted." Her grandmother wouldn't even buy her mother a dress. "So with me, she basically gave me absolutely everything that I ever wanted." But her mom had "that coldness," which she got from her grandmother. Communication was lacking. "So when my grandma found out that my mom was pregnant, which my mom hid from her, my grandma just stopped talking to her. They lived in the same apartment building, but my grandma was furious. She didn't talk to my mom. Even when I was born, my grandma wasn't there. My grandma wanted nothing to do with my mom or me as a little baby for, I think, six or seven months of my life."

She was "really colicky." Still not an excuse. But this was tough on the family. Her parents were young, in college, working, not sleeping. "It was a huge struggle for them."

Alexandra's mom is "very cold." If she's angry, "you will know. You can literally feel the energy. She's very hard to talk to. She didn't address any of that stuff. And then, when it came to that scarcity mindset, she went the complete opposite. 'Have everything you want. This will make you happy. This will show you that I love you,' blah, blah, blah. When in reality, I just wanted to be able to talk to her."

Growing up, I wish I had a little less talking and a little more "have everything you want."

Her grandfather cheated on her grandmother, had two strokes, and "regressed into a child." Meaning her grandmother had to take care of him "until he passed away and stuff." Romania sounds lovely.

Alexandra's father is a Canadian truck driver, or as Justin Trudeau says, "a terrorist." He was "crushed" when his daughter told him she wasn't having kids. He didn't fully grasp the finality of it at first. Then she got sterilized and had her tubes removed, "and he got the point." Her mother is much more understanding and supports her. Mom said, "Why would you want to bring children into this world with all this suffering?"

The last couple of years have been tough. "The pandemic, there's always some sort of war going on somewhere. Life is just getting so expensive in general for everyone. Things just aren't that great." Alexandra bemoans the post-9/11 "surveillance state," "the propaganda," and, of course, the brainwashing. The Canadian lockdowns really irked her. "People were so capable of agreeing with mandating medical procedures that they didn't agree with. They were totally fine with ousting people out of society. I think just the social fabric of our current society is unraveling."

Tell me about it. However, that hasn't stopped me from having children. Four.

Alexandra moved from Romania to Canada at age five. Then from

Ontario to America last year. But she's not staying here. "I'm going to make my way down to Mexico, and live there for a little while. So, I just wanted to change up my lifestyle a little bit too. That was another thing that I realized. I just don't want to be stuck somewhere."

That's certainly an advantage of being childless. Live in Cancún for a while? Leave this weekend? Sure!

"I was just an average kid, I guess," she says, "an average student." Went to Catholic school even though she's "not religious at all." Started "smoking weed," when she was "pretty young." "Not something that I would recommend for people because I definitely feel like now, my short-term memory isn't as great as it probably could be. I forget stuff pretty easily."

I forget stuff pretty easily too. Luckily, my assistant remembers stuff for me. Still, don't do drugs, kids. Not everyone gets an assistant.

Alexandra was an accounting major in college. Then she dropped out. "I figured that I didn't really want a career as an accountant. I didn't want to have that added stress on myself. So, I was happy with just being a bookkeeper." She took courses elsewhere, got a diploma, moved to Calgary, and started working.

"I started working for Merry Maids, it's a home cleaning franchise. And so, I did that for twelve years, and worked my way up to manager. And then I was going to buy the business because I really enjoyed it. And so I started working towards buying it, and then the pandemic hit. I was really thankful that I didn't buy it. I almost bought a house twice too, and didn't. And I'm thankful I didn't do that either."

Owning a home and a business is most people's dream. For Alexandra, it was too much stress. "My stress was making sure our team members had jobs, and making sure they were safe. But then also, to have the added stress of having a huge loan payment, and then having to deal with all of the rent, and all of those other things. It was a lot. It was just really scary for me. So, I was like, 'I just don't want to put myself through this.'"

Is Alexandra avoiding stress or responsibility?

"You've mentioned a few times you want to avoid stress—"

"Unnecessary stress," she interrupts.

"Are you generally stressed-out on a baseline level?"

"I wouldn't say on a baseline level, but I can get stressed-out very easily, I feel like. You can't control everything. But yeah, things are stressful, it can be scary, and things happen all the time. You can get into a car accident. You can break your foot. There are so many things that can just randomly happen that if I can avoid unnecessary stress and self-inflicted stress, then why not?"

"I don't want to play armchair psychiatrist or anything like that," I say. (Actually, I do.) "But I'm interested in this as it relates to the anti-natalism campaign. I feel like you are stressed-out regularly, and you make big life decisions in order to limit potential stressful situations. And those things could possibly have an upside, but they could also possibly have a downside. You don't want to get a house, or buy a business, because something bad might happen. But good things could happen too."

"True," she admits.

"I feel like you might be one of those glass-half-empty type of people."

"Probably. Yeah. I would probably consider myself definitely more on the pessimistic side of things. But it comes from reality and experience. And all you have to do is just take a look around, whether it's in the US, or Canada, or in Europe, or in Iran, or in Saudi Arabia. Literally, all you have to do is look around, and there are a lot of things to be pessimistic about. There are a lot of things that do give me pleasure. I feel like you can have a meaningful life. I'm not a nihilist. I think that you can find joy in life. But for me personally, that's not enough to warrant bringing another person into existence. We live in a really ugly world."

I'm not going to let Alexandra slide into the darkness. I must save her.

"Go back to World War II when all these countries were fighting each other, and we had the Holocaust. People were still having children. They were buying houses, they were getting raises, there were happy moments. Yes, there were some really, really dark moments, but out of those dark moments came great joy, came great victories over totalitarianism, came great freedom. People returned to parades. They had babies, then those were the baby boomers. There are dark times in history, and people usually confront those as a society, and then they become more resilient, and they have happiness as a result of that. And they become better people. Do you see that as a possibility?"

"Yes. Sure, people can become better. I still don't think that is, for me personally, a justification to bring another person into existence. I always find it so bizarre that in the most dark times, you could be in the middle of a war zone, and people are still having kids. But it seems so cyclical to me that it's inevitable that we'll go through another superdark time again. And it just seems like we do this over and over and over. It's almost like *Groundhog Day* with the things that we do. Yeah, we may have defeated totalitarianism with the Nazis and stuff, but then look at what's happening today. We still have governments that are trying to be as authoritarian as possible. We still haven't eradicated slavery. There are open-air slave markets. It's happening right now."

"You would agree that things are getting better, or would you say that the world is getting worse?"

"I think technology has made it a lot easier for people to live. But I don't think things are necessarily getting better on a humanity level. I think we've just advanced technologically enough that things look better. But I don't think as a species, our consciousness has really changed that much. We're still imperialists. We still rape each other. We still kill each other. We still exploit each other. There's still a lot of really terrible things that happen that we do to each other."

"But just look at it statistically," I say. "We are a less violent society. If you look at what we used to do, go back one hundred years, go back two hundred, three hundred, and four hundred, we're continuing to rape less, to murder less, to exploit less. Those things statistically are true. So, there is improvement."

Give me something, Alexandra!!

"Okay, maybe there might be a little bit less rape but there are lots of places where rape is still just normal. Maybe statistically, it looks a little bit better. I don't know. I don't see it. And we just keep adding more people."

"You have a great life. You have a partner. You have a good-paying job. You're going to go to Mexico. It doesn't seem that bad. Those things might not have been possible for someone in your position a hundred years ago to just gallivant down to Mexico and have a drink and do your thing. This is a pretty nice, safe environment. You appreciate that, right? There are people who live in the projects that have absolutely nothing, and they're procreating because they're not thinking, 'Oh, I don't want to have a baby because I live in the projects, and bullets are flying, and people are getting arrested left and right.' They think, 'Hey, let's have a baby. Let's go for it.'"

"I know in China," says Alexandra, "they're making it incredibly challenging for men to get vasectomies. There are lots of women in African countries who don't want to be mothers, but unfortunately, they're forced into motherhood at fifteen years old. There are a lot of anti-natalists in India because of that cultural pressure to have kids and to have that status for the parents. Like, 'Oh, look at my kid, he's got these children, and they're going to take care of me when I'm older, and et cetera, et cetera.' So, I think there's a lot of pressure on all people across the world to procreate, and a lot of people don't want to do that, whether they're in a really good situation or whether they're in a really shitty situation."

Of all the problems in China, access to vasectomies doesn't seem that urgent.

Alexandra, if she had a baby, doesn't believe she could provide it with an equal or better lifestyle than she had. She doesn't even want to chance it. "I would rather not experiment with someone, you know? I'd rather not try and find that personal growth, or whatever someone wants to call it, by using another human being to do that."

"Do you think not existing is a better state than existing?"

"I think so. I know what existence is like, and I feel like not existing in the first place, so just not even being born, is the ideal state."

"But nonexistence, there is no 'You.'" I'm having a hard time contemplating no Jesse Watters.

"Exactly. If I was never born, I wouldn't know the difference."

"Do you wish you were never born?"

"Yeah, I think if I wasn't born, my mom and my dad would've had a completely different life. I almost wasn't born, actually. My mom didn't want to keep me. She just didn't have access to abortion."

Her mom actually told her this. Oof.

"I've met a lot of people," she tells me, "who wish they were never

born, but are okay with their existence and don't want to kill themselves or un-alive themselves. And then there are people who would
love to just get out of here. But unfortunately, they're just unable to
because un-aliving yourself isn't something that's very easy for a lot
of people, and it's not always effective. That's another scary thing. It's
like if you try and kill yourself and it doesn't work, and then you could
end up even more worse off than you were before. And even sometimes
just talking about killing yourself can land you in a psych ward or something like that."

Alexandra prefers "un-aliving" to "committing suicide." I think "un-
awakening" sounds better.

"I don't think that my existence has such a massive impact that
if I never existed in the first place, the world would be completely
different."

She feels replaceable. She feels all humans are replaceable. What if
the man who invented the wheel was never born because his mother
was an anti-natalist? Alexandra argues that the wheel is used for nefar-
ious things. "They used it to cart slaves and stuff like that."

Also, Alexandra was raped as a teenager. She was in high school and
knew the guy. He was a little older. He was her weed dealer. "I went
over there to pick up some weed and had a couple of drinks because we
were friends. And then I just remember starting to really pass out on
the couch, but I had only had a couple drinks, and then I just remember waking up with him being on top of me and stuff. I just couldn't do
anything. Yeah. Once that happened and I woke up, I was able to figure
out what just happened. I basically just walked myself home and left
and never talked about it."

"I'm sure you never went and bought weed from him again."

"No. And I blocked him on Facebook."

Alexandra doesn't want to burden a potential child with the trauma
of this rape that she "hasn't unpacked fully."

Taken to the logical conclusion, anti-natalism slowly collapses society. The safety net is reliant on a tax base that it can tax and provide
benefits for larger groups of people. The baby boomers are all about
to retire. The millennials will be taxed to take care of them. Thank-

fully, the millennial generation is a very large one. But in other countries, sometimes those replacement generations aren't large enough, and these safety nets crash. Then you have to raise taxes, and that depresses growth and that discourages more young people from having babies. This cycle destroys the economy, and the population descends into poverty.

Alexandra's answer to this? People need to "promote health and encourage people to really take care of their own bodies." But if the government can't take care of old Alexandra, and her children can't take care of her (because she doesn't have any), what will her retirement look like?

"I don't know if I'm going to live until I'm eighty. So, I'm hoping that by then, there's voluntary euthanasia."

Most retirees look forward to golf, warm weather, and spending time with their grandchildren. Alexandra looks forward to un-aliving herself.

It's interesting to see Alexandra on the screen. At times, she's effervescent, flashing a bright smile. Then she shuts down into a sad, depressed space.

"I feel like I'm not depressed in the clinical sense. I like to say I'm functionally depressed because I am sad. The world is a very sad place. I feel like I expose myself to a lot of sad things because I like to learn. I like to know what's going on in the world around me and not just locally, but globally as well. So, I think there are a lot of things to be really sad about. There's a lot of sad things happening all the time. But I consider myself a pretty humorous person. I like to laugh. I like to have fun and stuff. So, I guess I'm happily depressed."

Alexandra enjoys wallowing in sadness. Nothing I can say makes her see the bright side. I took her on as a challenge and failed. I feel sorry for her. Her mother screwed her up. Heavy teen marijuana use didn't help, not to mention the sexual assault at seventeen. Plus, living in Canada can't be invigorating. But people have suffered plenty more than she has. They've gone on to live fruitful lives. They've borne children who thrived. Happiness is a choice. Going through the stages of life, career, marriage, homeownership, and family creates momentum and growth. Striving through obstacles generates happiness. The process is critical for individual development. Also, critical for societal development. In a way, Alexandra isn't participating in society. That is a choice. Her choice. I also blame her stupid boyfriend.

The unfairness of the world is a permanent fact. But we've found a way to muddle through, together. We haven't found a way to escape the heart-wrenching cruelty of this world. But we have learned that suffering is only one side of the coin. We should spend the short time we've been given here seeking the light rather than mourning the darkness. If you can do that, you'll find that the human experience is a miraculous gift—not a burden to be avoided.

18

The Traffic-Blocking
Climate Extremist

Paul, sixty-one, from Kalamazoo, Michigan, sat and blocked traffic on the DC Beltway for hours on July Fourth. Horns honking, dads screaming, backing up both lanes in bumper-to-bumper traffic didn't rattle him. Police were called. Thirteen people were arrested. Why? To "raise awareness" of "the climate crisis."

I hate three things in life. Traffic, people who cause traffic, and most of all, people who cause traffic intentionally. Good thing this interview is over Zoom.

Paul is, ironically, a mobilizer. A "Climate Change Mobilizer." He helps run a group called "Declare Emergency." Whatever else you might say about Paul, you can't accuse him of understating his case.

"I was in finance for twenty-five years," says Paul. He was a vice president and loan officer at a variety of banks until he recently resigned. "I quit so I could focus full-time on climate change."

Quitting was a rash decision. "I don't have enough money to retire on. I don't know what I'm going to do. And it's frankly, that's the trade-off I made because the situation is so dire for the climate. I live here in a town house in DC. I'm going to have to sell it because I can't do this forever. And yeah, that's where I am."

"Wait a second, Paul, you strike me as a thoughtful planner. Obviously, if you were in the commercial loan space, you understand risk. What if you're wrong about the world ending, and you've not built up enough of a nest egg?"

"I don't say the world is necessarily going to end, first of all, but I do think there's going to be an enormous amount of suffering that we're going to see people going through not too far into the future. And I think that the acuity of the crisis is such that it makes sacrifices like I'm making here logical."

Quitting a successful career in banking without adequate savings to warn others about the end of the world doesn't seem logical. But Paul didn't graduate from college until he was thirty-six, so there's more to this story.

After watching former vice president Al Gore's documentary *An Inconvenient Truth*, Paul was alarmed. "I remember in particular the scene where there's the hockey stick, what they call the hockey stick graph, which is where he shows the progression of CO_2 in the atmosphere, and it just goes way up in recent years." He started devouring books about the climate. "That's when I came to Jesus, so to speak."

The difference between Al and Paul: Al made a career from climate change. Paul lost his career from climate change.

"Paul, I remember the hockey stick graph being juiced. Did you ever figure that out?"

"I have not heard that."

(Hacked emails revealed that climate scientists didn't agree that Michael Mann's hockey stick graph was the most accurate.)

"Gore has been proven wrong. He said the North Pole was not going to have any ice caps on it in the summer by 2013. The North Pole still has ice caps. At least some of his predictions were overstated."

"I think when you're doing a projection, it's a projection, and so you can't get everything right. But I don't know. There are other people who've said similar things that are very reputable people, so I think we can believe the scientists more than we should believe, no offense, Jesse, but people like you."

How dare you, Paul.

I'm focused on maintaining a healthy balance with the environment. Humans have a duty to be responsible stewards. But here's the problem with people like Paul and Al. They always overstate the issue. Wildly. And the "climate change industry" models always get it wrong in one direction. This discredits their position and makes it difficult to have an honest discussion because you're dealing with dishonest people.

Paul clarifies. "I'm not saying we're going to die in seven years, I'm saying we need to act decisively now, or we're going to have catastrophe in the future that's beyond the imagining of anybody alive today." He says we may even go extinct.

To be fair, Paul walks the walk. "I do all sorts of things like using handkerchiefs instead of Kleenex sometimes." That's not all. "I haven't driven in fifteen years." Paul also stopped flying. But Paul had an epiphany. All that he's personally done, his sacrifices, his advocacy, his testifying in front of politicians—all that Al Gore has done, all that John Kerry has done—has failed. "We have failed because we have not lowered carbon emissions at all. We are in a worse place now than we were when all this started, so it's been forty or fifty years of this stuff that everybody's been doing, and it has failed."

Paul is wrong about carbon emissions, since they have been falling in the US since peaking in 2007. But I let him keep going.

"So therefore, that's when I found 'Declare Emergency' because their outlook is a little different. The intent is to cause widespread disruption until people start listening, and similar to other civil rights movements and human rights movements that have happened in the last century, like the civil rights movements in the sixties, the women suffragettes and all that."

"Would you compare your climate movement to the civil rights movement?"

"Climate change is the Freedom Riders of today; climate change is the lunch counter sitters of today. It's like, 'Get on the bus or else we're all going to suffer.'"

"Do you think that diminishes what the civil rights movement was about by linking it to the climate?"

"I believe that when you're talking about billions of people dying, it's hard to come up with an issue that's more important."

"You could argue that since we're dealing with the possible extinction of a billion people, this climate movement might be more important than the civil rights movement."

"Yes," says Paul.

Just to be clear: Paul is not black. If he was, he might have a different opinion.

"So if you go out and you disrupt, are you concerned at all about the people that you're disrupting?"

"Yeah."

"But why are you disrupting them then?"

"Well, there's no easy black-and-white answer to that. There's the disruption of ordinary people, which is painful, but then there's the risk on the other side. The risk on the other side is much, much, much greater."

Paul doesn't see the irony in raising awareness of carbon emissions by creating a jam with hundreds of cars idling their engines. Anyway, Paul says his target audience is politicians.

"The audience is not just the people that are being held up. The audience is President Biden, the audience is Congress, the audience is influencers, so that's the first point. The second point is successful movements of the past have disrupted society in similar ways to what we are doing, especially the women's suffrage movement or Martin Luther King. He blocked Selma Bridge, didn't he? He blocked some roads there."

Paul is comparing himself to Martin Luther King.

"You believe that [politicians] are going to see this viral video of you sitting on the freeway holding up traffic and say, 'Wait a second, these guys have a point. We're going to change our entire energy policy.'"

"I believe that protests like this make a difference." Then he compares himself to Gandhi.

"Do you see a difference though of doing a sit-in at a lunch counter where maybe a few people were inconvenienced, and they couldn't order a grilled cheese that day, as opposed to holding up traffic for a very long period of time in a downtown urban throughway where people are maybe going to the hospital, maybe in labor, maybe have to get to a life-and-death appointment, have to pick up their child, have to meet a deadline?"

Paul agrees it's a drastic tactic. But claims these tactics are working. How? Because Senator Marco Rubio introduced a bill heightening the penalties for blocking highways. This benefits the movement, according to Paul.

There has been some positive movement on the climate front. The US continues to reduce emissions three or four consecutive years in a row. But that's offset by developing countries.

"Why aren't you guys protesting in China, which has exponentially higher carbon emissions than the US does and is doing far less to combat it?"

"Because I live here, for one thing, and for another thing, we cannot make progress on this issue if the United States doesn't lead."

Also, Paul can't protest in China because he gave up flying. And even if Paul sailed to China and protested their climate policies, he'd be thrown in prison.

"Would you concede that fossil fuels have created a huge rise in the standard of living, an interconnectivity between cultures, trade, advanced civilization, advanced pharmaceutical manufacturing, and extended our life spans?"

"Yes. I concede that, of course. But the flip side of that is I would choose almost anything rather than extinction."

Do what I say, or we're all going to die. Where have I heard that before?

So, Paul, how much are we going to need to spend to save humanity from extinction?

"It has to be bigger than World War II. What we did in World War II is basically mobilize the entire economy around that war to win it. They had tax rates of like ninety-eight percent to pay for it. People were forced to work who didn't want to work, and a lot of people died, obviously. We need to make a sacrifice greater than that to get out of this."

If this is such a pressing issue, why does climate change always rank near the bottom of every survey? Paul argues that ExxonMobil "lies" and "discredits" climate science with well-funded misinformation.

"So, ExxonMobil brainwashed 330 million Americans?"

"They really had to brainwash 435 congresspeople, yes."

You have to have a brain to be brainwashed.

The US is $33 trillion in debt, with record inflation, and Paul is calling for busting past World War II tax and spending levels.

"Look internationally, you're going to have hyperinflation. If you're saying we need to print and spend, I don't know, ten trillion dollars a year, twenty trillion dollars a year, thirty trillion dollars—what is our usual budget, four trillion dollars?—you're saying we need to multiply that times ten?"

"One to three billion people are going to die. How much is that worth?"

"I've heard those things, and we've heard these predictions for decades about Manhattan's going to be underwater. There's going to be mass famine. There's going to be mass starvation, people are going to be walking around in gas masks and stuff like that. It never came to fruition, but I understand the concern. I'm saying you do need to have some sort of understanding of what this is going to cost, because I'm worried that the action to fight climate change is going to be more detrimental than climate change itself."

"What kind of economy do you think we're going to have if there's a billion homeless people?"

Ask San Francisco.

Can we find a middle ground? Call climate change a concern and then adapt to it? Instead of bankrupting the country and ditching all cars for bikes?

"I'm following the science," says Paul. "I'm following the truth."

"The science says different things."

"There's consensus."

"There's not a consensus that there's going to be an apocalypse in a decade."

"Billions of people are going to die. And I did not say that was going to happen in a decade, but it's going to happen. And it's going to happen before this century's out, for sure."

Paul will be dead by the time the century is out. So will I. Let this book be a record of who was right.

"Do you remember how a lot of the scientists were wrong during the Covid pandemic?" I ask.

"I just wore my mask and got my vaccines. But yeah, I'll take your word for it."

"Just because there's an initial group scientific consensus doesn't necessarily mean that's the word of God."

"Yeah, but . . ."

"Would you allow that some of these scientists could be wrong, and that science changes based off new information?"

"What I would say is you're not going to go to an accountant to get your gallbladder removed. And I think that we need to listen to the scientists. That's the best we have right now."

"I agree. And I listen to the scientists too. And if I want to go get my gallbladder removed, I'm not going to go to a mechanic. I'm going to go to someone with a medical degree. But Paul, scientists used to do really, really silly things, and it's constantly improving."

People believed in alchemy years ago. In the twenty-second century we'll look back and laugh that we installed solar panels in the Maine woods.

"There's just so much evidence out there, Jesse, that that's just kind of tinfoil-hat territory."

Says the guy who thinks ExxonMobil brainwashed us. Climate industry whistleblowers have recently arisen claiming grant money is directly influencing the conclusions of research papers. And that releasing data that contradicts climate change consensus results in professional ostracism and the disappearance of grants. These grants are what maintain the careers and reputations of scientific researchers. Money and status-seeking have corrupted climate science.

I believe we should treat energy consumption like food consumption. We must have a well-balanced diet. To fuel our bodies, humans consume a mix of steak, fish, veggies, starches, fruit, water, coffee. To fuel our economy, we should use oil, gas, hydro, nuclear, wind, and solar. Americans shouldn't go vegan. Just as we shouldn't go completely wind and solar. Fuel your body and your economy with a well-balanced diet of energy sources.

"You're talking about a balanced diet . . . that's like eating arsenic at this point."

"Paul, you're saying you want all cars to be electric cars?"

"That's a step in the right direction."

"If you want to go all electric cars, for instance, there are not enough precious metals and minerals in the world to produce one billion electric car batteries. Not even close."

"The alternative is too dire to even consider."

"If you game it out, which is what policy makers have to do, poor countries don't even have enough child labor to mine all of these nickel and palladium and aluminum deposits and all this stuff needed to create these so-called clean batteries. It's just physically impossible to do that. If we're staring down the barrel of catastrophe, you actually need a plan in order to make that transition. You are asking people to effectively go back to the Dark Ages, which is what a just full stop on any kind of carbon-emitting energy would do."

"I'm not asking people to go back to the Dark Ages, or whatever. We need a Manhattan Project times however many to get this done." Paul continues to repeat we need new solutions, and new systems and technologies because "our backs are against the wall at this point." I point out that venture capitalists and American industrial policy are already spending hundreds of billions in research doing exactly what Paul is prescribing. He responds that "it's not enough," but doesn't share what "enough" means.

"I don't have a concrete number. If you're asking me to come out with a dollar amount, I don't have it."

If we're speaking about the survival of the species and maintaining American civilization, Paul seems to have put little thought into anything besides telling us we're doomed. "Paul, if we need to survive, what does that look like? How do we get there? How much is it going to cost? Those aren't irrational questions. Those are questions we thought maybe you would've processed before standing in the street holding up traffic."

"What I know is that if we don't stop using fossil fuels, the outcome is just too horrible to contemplate for humanity." Apparently, Paul hasn't contemplated either outcome, living or dying.

"I'm going to defer to people who know more than me about a lot of this stuff. And there's a lot of smart people in the United States who can figure all this out."

"Well, that seems very humble of you, Paul."

"Thank you."

"Because from this entire interview, I was getting the vibe that you thought you knew everything."

"What we need is we need better reporting. I mean, come on, Jesse. You go on TV, and you talk about John Kerry taking planes all over the world. You don't talk as much about what fossil fuel's doing to everyone. And you're a very influential person. Millions of people see you every night."

Finally, Paul's speaking the truth.

"You think I shouldn't cover the flying squirrel?" (Kerry's private jet was owned by his charter firm, Flying Squirrel LLC.)

"To beat people up because they have to make choices that use fossil fuels is just not productive, and it's not going to change the system, which is what we need to do."

"Well, how come you give Kerry a pass?"

"I don't give him a pass. What I'm going to evaluate is how effective he is at getting measures put in place that help us, not whether he is flying around."

"You're saying he hasn't been effective at all. You just said we're on a terrible trajectory."

Silence.

"And don't you think someone like Kerry, though, as someone who should be an effective advocate, has an obligation to not fly private?"

"Probably. But I'm not going to rake him over the coals for it because we all make decisions like that. I'm sure you could come to my house and see some. . . . I just bought some bologna yesterday, so I'm not a saint, I know that. Yeah, that's just a small little thing, bologna, but . . ."

"Do you feel guilty about buying bologna?"

"No, I like it. But meat causes a lot of carbon. It causes a lot of greenhouse gases. But anyway, that's why I brought it up."

Paul gave up driving instead of bologna. I bet the bologna kills him.

Paul isn't religious. "Some days I'm an atheist. Some days I'm an agnostic."

"Do you consider this climate crusade a type of religious movement for yourself personally?"

"I feel strongly about hundreds of millions of people dying, about people losing their livelihoods and their homes and then the collapse of law and order. Those are strong things, so yes, I feel strongly about it, but it's not a religion."

Paul is a crusader. Historically people say, "Follow this path or all these people are going to die."

"You're talking about saving the world," I say, "and I'm saying in a lot of religious traditions, that's been a component."

"Yeah, I suppose."

Having abandoned all hope, or any real sense that anything he did as an individual mattered at all, Paul was free. And he wasn't about to let the specifics of the science, or any sort of pragmatic concerns, get in the way of that freedom.

Paul is gay. He's never been married. He's sad. He's a sad man. "What saddens me is the climate crisis itself. I feel like I'm doing what I have to do to be able to look myself in the mirror. And whenever, ten, twenty, thirty years, if I live that long, and not say that I gave up or I didn't do what needed to be done. It's not about hope, it's not about sadness, it's not about any of that. It's about stopping annihilation."

"This future for you, Paul, seems bleak. You're downsizing, you don't have enough money for retirement, you're sitting in traffic. I mean, this is kind of depressing."

"If I didn't do this, I think I would be sadder than I am."

"When you are sitting on the street blocking traffic, and people are honking and becoming agitated, what is going through your mind?"

"That what they're going through in being blocked by me is a fraction, a small fraction of what they're going to go through in the future and what their kids are going to go through in the future. I mean, at least when I look back today and I think of the sacrifices that were made by the Freedom Riders and the lunch counter sitters, I'm really glad they'd made that sacrifice. That's what I think of."

If only Paul knew what the people stuck in his traffic jam were thinking.

"Have you ever convinced anybody that's been stuck in traffic because of your protests that they need to stop driving?"

Paul says no. But some people are "on board." He's unable to tell me about these conversations. He has no evidence. Except a few people "give you the thumbs-up."

I think that was a different finger.

Most people tell Paul, "Get a job."

"Has anybody tried to take a swing at you?"

"No."

"Well, that's because you haven't tried this in Philly."

He justifies his actions this way. He's harming people a little now, to prevent them from experiencing greater harm later. But that's not provable. In fact, it's the opposite. There was an instance where a guy on parole was stuck in Paul's climate jam. He hopped out of the car pleading, begging the protesters to get off the highway because if he didn't check in with his parole officer on time, he'd be sent back to prison automatically. He never made it. Paul says he "feels compassion" for the parolee, but "it's a gray thing; it's not black and white." In that instance, though, it was black and white.

Paul describes his upbringing as "kind of boring, midwestern, that thing." He dropped out of the University of Michigan. "I didn't know what I wanted to do. I just kind of went because everybody did that, and there was nothing anchoring me to anything." Paul quit school and worked menial jobs for a decade before going back to school.

Paul worked for a while at an ice factory. "It doesn't matter if it's eighty degrees out, you go into this building with no windows, and it's, I don't know, thirty-five or thirty-two in there. You work there all day making ice. I mean, there's machines that make it. You have to bag it or do whatever, put it on pallets, all that kind of thing. And then you get out at night, and that's your day, and you're cold all the time, so that's what it's like."

Paul is clearly the wrong guy to ask if it's warming up too fast outside.

Eventually, Paul stopped drifting and got a degree. "I wanted to get a career that was stable, and that would provide. I majored in something that was very practical, accounting. Accounting and finance. I mean, as you get older, having insurance becomes more important, and your priorities change. You don't have that feeling that you're going to live forever anymore that young people have. And it was just time to make a change, so I did."

"Do you struggle with being practical?" I ask. "I'm sorry if I'm playing

armchair psychiatrist here, that your life has gone between being pragmatic and not pragmatic. You have these cycles of intense pragmatism,
and then you have other moments where you're doing something that's
absolutely not pragmatic at all. You're taking this belief that you have
to an extreme pragmatic level. This is about as pragmatic as you can
get. I mean, you are warning the nation. You're disrupting people to
make them change their belief system. You've stopped flying. You've
stopped driving. You're downsizing. You've quit your job. This is about
as committed to something as you can get. If we're talking about eliminating fossil fuels. If we're talking about saving billions of people. I
mean, this is about as pragmatic as you can be."

"Okay," he says. "I'll agree with you."

"But some of these things you're doing are not pragmatic at all
from a conventional standpoint. In terms of your job. In terms of your
house, or your financial situation, or the disruption. But then I look
back at your life too. You got into college, which is pragmatic, and then
you quit. And then you did ten years of just doing things in a totally different way, and then you went back to college. Accounting is pragmatic.
You were going to get your health insurance, and you were going to get
a stable job. And then you did that for a while, and then you quit. It's a
process that you have."

"I think I get committed to things more than most people do, but
I've never been in a cult, and this is not a cult."

When they tell you they're not in a cult . . .

Paul is committed to this pragmatic mission of saving the world, yet
he hasn't contemplated the pragmatic steps necessary to save it.

"I'm not the person who's going to make those changes. I'm the person who's going to push us to make those changes."

Paul is a pusher. He could be pushing a hoax. Only time will tell. But
at that point, he'll be dead. Most likely from too much bologna.

I say goodbye to Paul, who's a nice guy.

"Hopefully, I'm not blocked by your protest at any point. Just because I know you doesn't mean I won't run you over."

"Okay. Well, we've got a recording of this now, so you do it, it's
premeditated."

Oops.

19

The Professional Cuddler

Google "professional cuddlers" and you'll find a number of websites peddling snuggles—for a price, of course. According to the *New York Times*, snuggling-for-pay is "a quasi movement that dates back more than a decade," and has now "morphed into a cuddle-for-hire industry of one-on-one sessions." Cuddlist.com features a suite of experienced professionals that users can scroll through, with a banner assuring visitors that CUDDLIST SUPPORTS BLACK LIVES MATTER on the bottom right of its welcome page; Cuddle Sanctuary touts its "certified professional cuddlers in California, Georgia, Florida, Hawaii, Illinois, Pennsylvania, Washington DC and Brussels, Belgium," offering "a Rated G experience that will soothe your spirit and quiet your mind"; Cuddle Comfort advertises: GET A CUDDLE BUDDY TODAY.

Amanda (not her real name) bears a striking resemblance to Xena, Warrior Princess (Lucy Lawless). Tall, square jaw, dark bangs, big chest. She's Scottish, Scandinavian, "and a lot of German." In her free time, Amanda arm-wrestles, trains dogs for the blind, and competes in the Highland Games. "I throw stones, weights, and logs." She's always been hands-on, beginning her career as a massage therapist. Today, her practice is professional cuddling.

"My mom was remarried four times by the time I was thirteen. So, a lot of moving around, a lot of adjustments. My mom is very hardworking. She was pretty much the sole provider even when she was married. As far as I knew she loved me, but there was not much physical contact."

Much of the physical contact Amanda received as a child was unwanted. Several family members molested her. "So, for me, the way I got my affection was through animals. And so we had horses and dogs and cats and snakes and all kinds of animals," she says. They lived "off the grid," in California. Chores began at 4 a.m. Her father was abusive to her mom. He was an alcoholic. When Amanda was two, her parents divorced. She only sees him about twice a year.

"So, my mom remarried when I was three, and he ended up cheating on her, and then divorced when I was six, got married the same year to somebody else. And he was the one who was abusive. And he was actually murdered later."

"What!? Did they solve it?"

"Yes." When Amanda was eight, her stepdad disappeared. "So that's an interesting story as well. In this preserve, there are about six different families or individuals that lived in here, and we each own forty-plus acres, so they're not close neighbors. It's like down the hill, over the next hill. But anyways, one of the neighbors was a friend of the family, another gentleman, and he was friends with my stepdad. And for me, how it came by is we moved up there when I was six, and then when I was eight, he disappeared. His friend told us that he just left on a business trip, and because he was abusive, we never questioned it. We were just glad he was gone." Later, this friend started dating her mom. "Until one day, he pulled a gun on her. We were in the car, my brother and I were in the back just screaming, 'Don't kill her!' When we got home, he told her to open the door and hit her in the head with the gun, knocked her out of the car, and just looked at us and said, 'If I was going to kill her, I would've already.'" They stopped dating, but he was still a friend of the family. One day, they came across human remains on the man's property. He said, "Hey, stay away from that fifty-five-gallon bucket. That's somebody who got in my way." Police were called. "Part of a shoe and a skull" could be seen. During the search, several bodies were found.

"My stepdad was also buried on his property. Yeah, he had shot my stepdad in the stomach and the back of the head, stripped him naked, put him in a mattress, threw him in a hole, and was throwing beer cans over it. He was waiting for his skull to rot out to use as a candleholder. But he said it was more of a public service because he was abusing us."

"How did you feel about that?"

"Well, like I said, he was abusive, so we were just fine with him being gone. There's no sadness with him being murdered. The abuse, it was physical and sexual. He would have you drop your pants naked, hold your ankles, and hit you with a leather strip that had metal in it."

Then the man who killed her stepfather tried to kill her biological father. Amanda's real dad was in jail for drunk driving. It happened to be the jail that her stepfather's murderer was in. "They somehow ended up next to each other. My dad had a blanket over him, and he pulled him in and stabbed him seven times. And punctured his lung. And it was bad, but my dad was able to get away, so that's crazy."

Yes, Amanda. I would say that's crazy. But sadly, the sexual abuse didn't stop.

"Then, once he was gone, my brother started doing it. And then, after him, was my stepbrother."

"Oh my gosh. What level of abuse was it?"

"It got to sodomy." Amanda believes her brother was transmuting the abuse from his stepfather. "I think my brother just watched and then started doing it when he stopped."

"Have you ever confronted him?"

"Yes, but he's never ever shown remorse, never. So, we just don't talk about it anymore. When I'm in the same room with my brother, I can just put a wall up because my mom and my dad still have a normal relationship with him. So sometimes if I visit them, he's in the room, and I have to deal with that. And my kids, they all know what happened, and they were never allowed to hug him or anything. But they also can be civil and still be in the same room with him. But it's difficult."

"Then how did the stepbrother come in and get involved in all that?"

"So, this was my mom's fourth marriage, so I was thirteen and he was sixteen. And he would do it when I would fall asleep. I'd wake up to it."

Four husbands. "Only the one was alcoholic, but the rest were dry alcoholics." Constant mood swings. It was volatile.

"So, your mother has terrible taste in men, is what you're telling me?"

"Yes. Well, I think the problem is she'd just jump into relationships very quickly. So she would just see the persona on the outside and then just jump in and try to make it work. And she wouldn't leave until it got really bad."

"Do you blame her for any of this, for any of the abuse?"

"I think she did the best she could, but she put me in some really bad situations."

That's an understatement. But Amanda was able to excel. "I was competitive in sports like swimming and gymnastics. So, I really liked the physical aspect. But I was longing for that connection with people. And being in the middle of nowhere it's hard to get friends and stuff. So, I got through school early. I started college at fifteen." She started at community college, then transferred to Oregon State. "One of the classes that intrigued me was a massage class. I love helping people, and that hands-on connection was very beneficial to me. So that's when I first got into massage, but it was more just for my personal benefit."

Amanda's first real sexual experience was like many women. "I lost my virginity when I got drunk." She was almost eighteen at a fraternity party. "And anyways, I had a fifth of vodka, and that's how I lost my virginity but didn't have sex after that." Later on, Amanda got her first boyfriend. They were dating for a few months, but "he cheated on me. We tried to work things out, but the girl he cheated on me with got pregnant. So that ended that."

Amanda married her second boyfriend. She wasn't sure about him at first. "He was nice . . . but something seemed kind of missing. And for whatever reason, I was talking to my mom. Why I would take relationship advice from my mom, I have no idea, but she's like, well, it's probably just because the first boyfriend, I felt more of a connection to. I'm like, oh, okay. Well, six weeks after I met this guy, he asked me to marry him. And I couldn't think of a good reason to say no, so I said yes. And that wasn't a good reason to say yes, but I didn't know that. I had literally a couple of months' worth of dating in my life, and so I was like, well, he seems like a decent guy. It wasn't a smart decision. So yeah, I've learned since then if it's not a hell yes, it's a no."

If it's not a hell yes, it's a no. Great marriage advice. Great life advice.

Amanda was twenty-two when she got married. She had her first kid when she was twenty-three. Her husband was nine years older than she was. "So, I was a stay-at-home mom for ten years, and I loved it, but I totally got immersed in it and kind of lost myself. I didn't do anything for myself, and I think that the best gift my ex-husband ever gave me was a snowboard, because it was something just for me to do. I cried when he gave it to me." Amanda had four children, but her marriage wasn't great. "Our relationship was fine for a few years, but I was under that assumption once I got pregnant that I needed to stay. I didn't want my kids to have the upbringing I did. So I chose to stay in a relationship, even though I knew it wasn't a great relationship. The dynamic in the house was we were pretty much just roommates, but it was progressively getting worse as far as emotional. We couldn't even be friends, really.

"Then, the year before I got divorced, that's when I started working as a correctional officer at the prison, and I've really enjoyed that. Because you just never knew what was going to happen. So, I was also on the tactical team there. I was one of the people that they called when shit went down. And I liked that. That was enjoyable to me. I called that playtime."

This explains the stone-throwing a little bit better.

"What were some of the craziest things you saw in the correctional facility?"

"I was there watching somebody cut one of their nuts off and had to go in and take him down and take him to the hospital."

"Did you save the nut?"

"Nope. Didn't save that. Did save the other one, though."

The prisoner wasn't finished. "The same individual, a different time, had pulled away from an officer when he was in his cell where he still had the handcuffs on one of his wrists. And so he was able to break a piece off, and I had to talk to him as he was shoving it up his ass, telling me that he was saving it for later to cut off the other nut."

Maybe he wanted to be transferred to a women's prison. These days, you don't even have to cut your nuts off. You can just "identify" as a woman.

"What did you learn about human nature, having such close contact to these prisoners who were locked up?"

"The biggest thing I learned is that you can't take anything personal that somebody else does, because ninety-nine percent of the time, it has nothing to do with you. And being there, how you present yourself is your first line of defense to anyone. So you have to be very careful how you present yourself to someone, because people will judge you immediately and try to use that for whatever is good for them. People are very self-serving, and I think now probably more than ever, people are more in the survival mode. They're so oblivious to everyone else and what they are. They just see the tip of the iceberg. They just take a glance at somebody, and they judge them. And they put them in this category, and they're like, how can I use this person?"

"Do you think Americans are like that generally?"

"Yes. I think very much so. And I think that is why the profession of cuddling really is so needed, because people are in the survival mode. They don't have that connection with people, and it's to the point that people are losing themselves. They're trying to fit in this cookie-cutter mold that is presented that you need to be in, instead of being yourself and really giving. They are trying to be accepted. So the one thing that you can do in the cuddling session, the biggest thing that is there, is it's a safe place. A lot of people don't have a safe place they can go to, and just be themselves, and be able to talk without being judged, be able to get things out of their head. And it's really hard to really understand something in your head and get clarity on it until you can explain it to someone else. And to have someone there that is open. Not, well, 'I think you should do this,' or 'You shouldn't do that.' In the cuddling session, we're not there to judge you. We're there to help you be you. We want you to feel comfortable and be safe, and sometimes in the cuddling sessions, people just want to talk. They just want to have a safe place to be and feel wanted."

I want you to want me.

"Most people, when they listen, they're not listening to you. They're listening for what they can contribute. 'Oh, wait, I have something to say about that. As soon as they break, I'm going to say it,' instead of really truly listening to someone and saying, 'Tell me more about that. I want to understand that. How do you feel about that?' Not 'How do I feel about that? I want to explain it to you.'"

Cable TV personalities can be guilty of that. But I won't name names.

Amanda sometimes just holds a client's hands while they talk. Their heart rates go down. Their anxiety melts away. Amanda just listens. "I had one gentleman that talked for about forty-five minutes, and then just wanted to be held the last fifteen."

Cuddling is just as much about giving as receiving. "I think more than anything, most people don't have that connection to feel safe." Amanda is seeking safety, just as much as her clients are. Which is understandable, considering her upbringing. "I don't have friends I can really go and cuddle with, especially guy friends, because most of them want to date me. And that dynamic ruins it for me. I don't feel like I'm in a safe place. You want to be with somebody who is a family member, like a brother, or a child, or something where you feel completely safe to just melt into that person without any expectations of anything else. It totally changes the dynamic when it's that kind of platonic thing."

Amanda enjoys the safe embrace that her childhood lacked.

"Everybody's expecting more. Oh, if you're going to cuddle, then all of a sudden, they're going to get horny. But it's all in your mindset. If you're in the mindset of just being there to help someone like a child, when you hug a kid, that thought never crosses your mind. And so, when you're in that headspace with an adult it's the same thing. It just doesn't cross your mind. You're in there to give comfort of love without expecting anything back."

Sometimes clients will get aroused during a cuddle session. "It needs to be very clear that this is very platonic. So, if they're feeling other things, let's talk about it. If we need to change positions or whatever, that's totally fine, but it is something we talk about. So, it is natural. Some people are going to have that sensation." Amanda helps talk them back into the right headspace.

"And with massage, I worked with all types of shapes, and being at the prison, I've seen everything. There's nothing really that's going to shock me. So it's like, I can be there and just be a safe space for someone, and I am open enough to where I can hug somebody, and it's not going to be weird. I can hug a stranger and be able to give that loving energy without knowing them. I don't need to know them. I just want to help, and I try to see the good in everybody. And I enjoy it a lot."

Normal rate is eighty dollars an hour "for the alternative touch."

What about the creeps?

"When you do the meet and greet, you have one hundred percent control whether or not you want to actually have a session with this person. You only have a session with somebody you feel comfortable with. I've never had to refuse anyone."

The "session room" is a "really nice, big room, with a big couch, and a fireplace." "So when they first come in, we're in the chairs, sitting, and we greet each other, have a little conversation, how their day's going, that kind of thing. And then even to hold hands or to hug, we always ask permission. Never touch somebody without asking permission, and when you ask permission, don't do it like, 'Can I give you a hug?' Because then they feel kind of obligated. You want to ask it, 'Would you like a hug?' We want to make sure it's what they want. We don't want them to try to satisfy us. We're trying to be there for them, and we always ask them what do they want. 'Do you want to hold hands? Do you want to sit on the couch?' And we even have a book if they have no idea how to cuddle."

"What are some of the cuddling positions?" I'm only familiar with spooning.

"So there's different ones. More traditional ones, where somebody's head's on your chest or in your lap, or they're sitting between your legs, lying back. There could also be where you're both lying down, but you're more in a position so one person's head is at somebody's knee. So you actually lay your head on the other person's knee, and vice versa. So, you're kind of like in a circle. And then you can do where you're more like a T. You can be the cuddler or the cuddlee. You can switch roles. So there's really no end to the different kinds. You could just be touching feet. It all depends on somebody's comfort zone, what they want."

She uses the book *The Cuddle Sutra*. Clients flip through and explore positions.

"You have to ask the client. 'Would you like your arm stroked? Do you want your hair played with?'"

Amanda will play with your hair for eighty dollars.

"Stroking is very, very good because it really intensifies the oxytocin." Oxytocin is a hormone that plays a role in human behaviors such as trust, bonding, and romantic attachment. "So oxytocin is something that you don't get with a three-second hug. You got to get in there for twenty seconds to really get that going. And it also blocks the cortisol, so it lowers your stress, and it calms you down. It lowers your blood pressure and decreases inflammation. There are so many benefits that it's absolutely incredible." Oxytocin is sometimes referred to as the "love hormone," or the "cuddle chemical."

Amanda sees all types of clients. "We have some people that are in relationships, but they don't have a good connection in that way. Some people just aren't cuddlers. Sometimes your partner's just not a cuddler."

How could someone not know how to cuddle? Or not like it?

"Somebody who probably has past trauma. So they're able to engage in intimacy when it becomes sexual. But they have a hard time when it's platonic. And then other times, we get a lot of PTSD people in there. People with high stress. A lot of people in between relationships, absolutely."

"Do they ever cry?"

"Yes, absolutely. And lots of laughter."

Married folks book sessions together. "We do couples therapy as well. We'll bring couples in and show them how to cuddle." The clients are always clothed, "so that you don't have a lot of skin exposed." She had one client who was deaf and wanted to learn how to communicate physically through cuddling. He booked a group session. Multiple professional cuddlers in the room, back to back.

The United States is unique in that we're such a large country, people aren't used to others entering their physical space. In Japan, or even some European countries, routine close physical proximity creates different kinds of boundaries. In cultures with histories of arranged marriages, cuddling between husbands and wives is rare. Marital relations are less romantic, and more geared around child-bearing, child-rearing, and domestic work. There are other cultures where men show physical affection to other men, not in a sexual way. This isn't something American men do. We don't watch football on the couch with our arms around each other.

Amanda is not happy with Dr. Fauci. Locking down "was to the detriment of the country." It still is doing great harm, she says. "It heavily increased depression, suicides. The country is still in a depression. I think people are becoming more aware of it. I think maybe that would be the one positive side as people are becoming more aware of how much it really means to have connection with people."

Perhaps Dr. Fauci could prescribe us cuddling sessions. We've been so isolated. Cuddling has certainly healed Amanda. The therapy has given her an opportunity to play the role of the mom she never truly had. A mom is supposed to protect her children. She didn't. Today Amanda is protecting others. She's listening. She's providing strangers a safe space. A safe space that was denied to her growing up. A platonic embrace that she should have received from her stepfathers and brothers. Children just want to be held. Nothing more, nothing less. In a way, we're all still children, wanting the same thing.

2 0

The Vodou Priestess

"I'm not a witch," insists Sallie. "I'm what's called a Mambo Asogwe, a Vodou priestess." Sallie Ann Glassman is a Ukrainian Jew, born in Maine and initiated at the highest level of Vodou in Haiti.

"You're a high priestess?"

"Yes," says Sallie, and "I'm the only sober person in New Orleans."

Vodou is among the fastest-growing religions in North America. "It came out of African traditions, but it mixed with European Catholicism, both in Haiti and in the Louisiana colony. There were French Catholics, colonists, and there were also Masons operating in both places that brought in Masonic mysteries and magic. And there were Native people in both places. So, Vodou formed as a kind of gumbo religion that has all the elements of these various practices but comes together as a single whole dish."

Sallie is adamant it's "not evil stuff." "It's got nothing to do with spells and witchcraft and hexes and dolls with pins in them or any of that. It's a bona fide religion and has practices and beliefs in it, a sense of the divine." The Vodou religion is "misunderstood and misrepresented," according to Sallie. "There was an intentional campaign done by the Spanish because Vodou reaches into that invisible world of power. You can imagine that was pretty terrifying and disturbing for slave owners, that these people whose spirits you were trying to break, using nothing but their voices and their ability to clap were able to reach into a higher source of power that was invisible, and nothing could be done to stop that. And so there was an intentional negative PR campaign that used the same derogatory and inflammatory images that were used against the Jews during the Spanish Inquisition, were applied to Afro-Caribbeans, that they worship Satan, that they sacrificed babies and eat them. They have depraved orgies, that sort of thing. And those images are very hard to get out of your mind once somebody has planted them there. And so this was a way to deflect, instead of acknowledging that you were bringing this terrible harm to human beings, to say that they were less than human and this was saving their souls in some way.

"Ironically, because this was supposedly saving their souls, the slaves were forced to convert to Catholicism, and they were given chromolithograph images of the saints. And in those images they saw symbols that they recognized from their own spirits. An example, St. Patrick is shown driving snakes out of Ireland, and he came to be associated with Dambala, who is a snake. He's a snake spirit. And the slaves were able to use images of Catholic saints to mask and cover up the spirits that they were actually worshipping, because they would be killed if they were discovered practicing Vodou. So over time, these saints became sort of synonymous.

"It's really important when you consider that Vodou developed out of the institution of slavery, that Africans were taken from their homelands and thrown into the holds of slave ships, and then worked to death and tortured through the short remaining years of their lives in the New World. And instead of having that be their whole reality, they were able to reach into another source of power. And somehow, these people were able to turn that catastrophe that befell them into great strength and creativity. They were amazingly strong and resilient people."

"Tell me a little bit about the belief system itself. Is it monotheistic?"

"It is considered to be monotheistic because there is a supreme God deity, but that God is so abstract and beyond our human comprehension that Vodou doesn't try to define or establish what that God is, but is considered generally as the life-force itself. Intelligent life-force and divine life-force. The supreme deity is Bondye, which means good god, otherwise known as Gran Mèt, which means grand master."

Great name.

"And there are numerous intermediary spirits that are much like the saints, not terribly different except that the lwa, as they're called, these Vodou spirits, interact with us humans and sort of walk with us through life and give us guidance and help and direction. And they're both archetypal principles as well as elements of nature. So we're surrounded by the divine all the time. It's the earth we walk on, and the water that we bathe in, and the air that we breathe, and the fire that keeps us warm and all of that. And all of these spirits are elements of God's life-force, it's believed.

"There's also a belief in an invisible world that is within and surrounds the visible world. And that world is pictured as a kind of ocean of divine spirit and it is more powerful and more beautiful and more full of life and potential than the visible world. So everything that goes on in a Vodou ceremony is intended to open the doors between those two worlds, so that they can interact. [The spirit world] is always here interacting with us if we have the skill to be able to hear from them and to call them and to open those doors. So everything that happens in a ceremony, the drumming, the singing, the dancing . . . There's absolutely no substances involved. Nobody's taken any drugs or drinking any alcohol to make this happen. It's entirely about movement, singing, rhythm, and ritual gesture and intent."

The goal of Vodou is to bring all of these spiritual forces into balance within ourselves. "They're all aspects within us. They are our actual ancestors. They were once human beings and like people, they have personalities, and some things about them might be fiery or turbulent. Some things about them might be very gentle and calm and sweet. And all of these are seen as aspects of sacred life-force, the divine; these are all ways that we get to know God."

Vodou ceremonies are complex. As a high priestess, Sallie leads them. "I'm responsible for bringing in these incredibly complicated drum rhythms, where there are three to five drummers, and they're all playing at possibly different rates and rhythms and there's a bell that's holding that all together. And the mambo or the priestess or the priest is holding a special rattle that's also keeping a particular rhythm. And the singing has to segue into all of that. And there are hundreds of rhythms and hundreds of lwa [spirits] that might be called upon in a particular order. And getting all that to sync is very difficult. Takes a lot of training and practice for numerous people. Not to mention that the songs are all in Haitian Creole, which most Americans don't speak.

"There are altars, and you have to have particular items on these altars that are quite ornate and speak volumes. You might have Catholic saint imagery; you might have decorated bottles. You might have dolls that are not used for pins, but they're used like a statue might be on a Catholic altar, to represent the different spirits. There are all kinds of offerings that people bring or that are made. There are candles. There's jewelry for Erzulie Fréda, who's the spirit of love and beauty. There are iron pots, and you might have iron spikes from a railroad for the warrior spirit Ogou because he likes metal. Just a huge variety of things. And they are ornate, and when you think about, again, the slaves were people who had nothing. They had everything taken from them. So being able to create this glorious offering at the crossroads between worlds is a big deal and a large undertaking. There are sequin flags that are made in Haiti—there's twenty thousand sequins in one of these flags that are sewn by hand and beaded—and just beautifully exquisite things all throughout the temple. There's a center pole, which is the central highway that the spirits travel up and down."

"Is the pole a physical pole?"

"Physical pole, yep."

"Does that play a central role in the ceremony?"

"Absolutely, yeah. It's at the center focal point of the ceremony, and it literally is this highway that the spirits travel up and down, and the floor of the temple is the horizontal arm of the crossroads in the physical world. And at the axis where those two arms meet is where magic happens, and exchange and transformation can happen. But there's first a series of French songs that are litanies. It's called the Priye Ginen. And we're all singing those."

I ask Sallie to sing but she refuses. She says her voice is awful, and she requires backup singers to hide her pitchy tone. "But it would sound very much like you're in a French church and litanies were being sung at the beginning of a ceremony. Then there's something called veves that are drawn in cornmeal. These are graphic signatures of the different spirits, and those are also very ornate and very beautiful. It seems sort of magical, the way they're drawn. You're holding cornmeal in your hands and just letting it drip through, and a line appears magically on the ground, and it's really fascinating. They are also visual focal points for the ceremony that hold the attention of everybody involved while they're being drawn. So those are being drawn. We're singing all these different songs. The drumming is going, everybody's dancing, and offerings are being made. We unfurl these sequined flags with the same kind of pomp and circumstance that you would see if a head of state arrived, and the flags are being brought out and being handed around the room. Everything is actually quite organized, although it's very intense in there. And we go through several spirits. There's a spirit Legba who opens the doors between the worlds, and allows our prayers to be heard by the spirits and lets the other spirits through, and we call on them one by one.

"And one of the ways that the spirits have arrived is through something called possession trance, which also brings up all sorts of horrific images, because we've all seen *The Exorcist* and we think demonic possession. It's very different than that. And these spirits come through and sort of borrow a person for a moment so that they can talk to us. They can do healings when needed, which sometimes involves them just miraculously knowing what's wrong with the person and what needs healing and what to do for them. Often there's no way you can explain rationally why something would've worked. Why if you'd walked in there with a bad back, you walked out of there able to dance and feeling fine."

Instead of back surgery, I should have done Vodou.

"And you've witnessed this? People have been healed?"

"Absolutely. I did a healing for Robert Trump. He had a heart arrhythmia, and he was headed to the hospital the next day, and his wife, Blaine, called me and asked me to go and do a healing on him, which I did. And he canceled his appointment because his heart was fine after that."

"Wait, the former president's brother who passed away sadly. You did a healing for him. How did that happen?"

"I was very good friends with Joan Rivers, who was very good friends with Blaine Trump. And so I had been visiting Joan in New York and was leaving that day, and Joan said to Blaine, 'You ought to get Sallie to show up and do this for you.' And so that's how it happened. And I went to their apartment and did a healing on him, and it worked."

"And he was cool about it? Or was he like, 'I don't know, this sounds a little . . .'"

"It was funny. I think Blaine didn't tell him what was going on. She just told him to come home from the office, and he did as he was instructed, like a good husband should. But he was very willing to participate, and it worked for him."

"What would that ceremony look like?"

"I worked with my rattle. There's a special rattle that a priestess has. And I did blessings, and I used herbs and worked with spirits to ask them to bring this man healing and to get his heart going, and to look into what the matter was and what was the source of the trouble. And that's generally what a priestess would do is to first determine whether it was a natural illness or a supernatural illness. If it's natural, you might send the person to the doctor to get it treated if it was outside of the realm of spirit. But if it was something that was having a spiritual source, and often issues with the heart have to do with our emotions, and how we keep our emotions stuck or out of touch or locked up. And so when you can figure out the spiritual source of an illness and can treat that, often the physical manifestation will shift too."

"So it was a supernatural issue, and then that was cleared away?"

"Yeah. It was right after Trump Tower was built."

"They paid you?"

"I didn't charge them, no."

"Aw, Trumps always get things for free, don't they?"

"I don't charge for any of this. All my ceremonies are free."

I need Sallie for a ceremony. I probably have a ton of supernatural issues that need healing.

"Can you perform a ceremony so I don't lose my hair?"

"I hear Rogaine works really well," she says.

Sallie claims she cured her own cancer. "I had a tumor, and it was the size of a pea, and my doctor was convinced that it was cancer, and there's a great deal of cancer in my family. So they sent me to go get a biopsy five days later. And I did spiritual work on myself. I did meditations, I did healings. And I woke up one morning saying to myself, it's healed, it's benign. And I went in for the biopsy, and they couldn't find it. And for forty-five minutes they searched for it. And I was high as a kite the whole time just on energy. I was just lit up with energy, and I kept saying to them, I'm on the table going, 'Excuse me, excuse me. I think I healed myself. I think I made it go away.' And they were not listening to me, and they simply couldn't find it. It was gone, and even the person doing the sonogram was holding up images from the x-ray, comparing it to what he was seeing at the moment and saying to the doctor with me sitting there, 'See, I would stake my life that person has cancer, but there's nothing here. There's nothing for me to biopsy.'"

Sallie is the health insurance industry's worst nightmare.

"You cured your own cancer?"

"Absolutely. I thought about while I was doing all the healing, I was thinking about what's causing this? Where am I getting this from? I talked to the cells of my body. I mean it sounds crazy, but I talked to the cells of my body and asked them what they needed from me and what changes I needed to make. And I promised them I would take care of that, and I thanked them for getting my attention and said, 'Okay, you can relax now.' And they did. I could feel them just going back."

I'm going to start talking to my cells. This whole time, I never knew they listened.

Sallie also healed her busted knee.

"I had three torn ligaments and a torn meniscus in my knee. It was excruciating. And I was scheduled for surgery four days later, and I did the same thing. I did healings on myself. One day into it, I could walk without a cane and no brace. And when I went in to see the surgeon, he said, there's nothing here for me to operate on. You're fine. And that one really shocked me because it was so physical I didn't think that I could repair that, and it was fine."

Aaron Rodgers should try Vodou on his ankle. He's tried everything else.

Sallie is sixty-eight. She's thin, good skin, curly hair. Maybe she's onto something.

"The conversation with your cells. What exactly does that sound like?"

"Literally, I would sit down every day and say, 'Hey, it's me. How are y'all doing? What's going on? What is causing you to get my attention? And why are you rattling the cage? What do you need me to take note of and make different in my life?' And then I would just sit and be very quiet and focus in and go deeper than the intellectual answer, because your head is telling you stuff all the time. And I would wait for what I call the essence to come up. And there was a very distinct answer there, changes that I needed to make in my life. And it was so clear that I was able to say, 'Okay, I got it, I'm going to take care of that.' And I did."

"What were some of the changes that you had to make in your life?"

"I was in a really toxic relationship and I needed to get out of that, which I did. And that relationship came out of experiences that I had as a child growing up and things that I needed to address. This will sound very schmaltzy, but when I was first doing my meditations, I heard myself saying to myself, 'If it's unconditional love that you need, I will give you that.' And you talk about a difficult task, giving yourself unconditional love. That was really hard to get to, and something that I've striven for the rest of my life to continue to do for myself."

"What was it about your life precancer that wasn't allowing you to completely love yourself?"

"So I had a very difficult mother. She was mentally ill, and I was alone with her for a very long time because I was the youngest in my family. And she was also physically very sick. She had cancer, at a time when cancer was absolutely a death sentence, and she had been given six months to live and managed to hang on for eleven years. I was her primary caregiver, and because she was also psychologically such a difficult person, I came to feel that I was somehow not enough, that I was bad, and that I couldn't save her. She was sick from the time I was six until I was seventeen, when she died. So I was alone in this house of death with this woman who couldn't be satisfied, and was always upset and was suffering. And so I'd learned not to give myself any room in the world, that I just couldn't give myself any importance, that everything was focused on taking care of this person who couldn't be taken care of. So that did some damage to me. And she was a borderline disordered person, and so I found a borderline disordered person to bring into my life, to further torture my life, and I decided that was no good anymore. I had to get rid of that."

So Sallie was in a relationship with a man who was the mirror image of her mother. And her cells told her to break up with him. She told him, "This is no good. Bye. I'm not going to make your crazy work for you anymore." Just like that, her cancer was cured. Now she's happily married.

"What exactly is borderline personality disorder?"

"There's a book called *I Hate You—Don't Leave Me*, which kind of describes it all. It's crazy-making. And those people on the one hand try to take your identity from you, and on the other hand, they can't manage ambivalence, so they can't be angry and love you at the same time. The rest of us can manage those two emotions at one time. We have to be able to. So one emotion is on board at a time, one feeling is on board, and God help you if it's the angry one. They don't remember anything else about you. It's tough, and they don't know that they're sick, and it's often misdiagnosed, and it's really tricky."

"So you're saying if your significant other hates you, then it's a hundred percent full-throttle hatred, without any context of the relationship, or if it's jealousy or if it's vengeance or rage or lust or happiness. There's no ambivalence. There's no gray area. So that's a real roller coaster."

"Exactly. You're always waiting for the other shoe to fall, and you have no idea what's going to make it happen. It's tricky."

Would slaves have felt similarly? (Not comparing anything to slavery.) Totally at the mercy of your master, whose whims you can't predict or control. You're waiting for these things to happen, what comes with new seasons in a new hemisphere . . . or if the master passes away . . .

or if he gets angry, if he rapes you, or you lose your kin on a whim. No control. It's horrible.

"It is not nice. And so that's one of my statements about Vodou that so impresses me, that these people who had nothing, had no power, everything was taken from them, their families, their homes, their place in life, their dignity—everything was taken from them. And yet they manage to hold their gods and their heart. They manage to stay spiritual beings and to heal and find the good in life and to overcome their circumstances, to keep hope alive and to create this religion of hope and healing and empowerment, freedom."

In Haiti, Africans were the first slaves in the New World to effectively hold a revolution. They were also the first people to defeat Napoleon. Sallie was initiated in Haiti. She calls the man who initiated her "My Papa." "It's a six-day process where you're in an isolation chamber, basically. It has a lot of symbolism that reflects the experience of slavery, that you're kind of in the hull of a slave ship, and you have no control over what's going to happen to you and no knowledge of what's going to happen to you. I can only tell you a few things about it because I took oaths to keep silence about this. But you're lying on your left side for six and a half days. You're in a deep meditative state. There are various rituals that are Masonic in nature that happen during this. There's several very intense Vodou ceremonies that happen in the midst of all of this. And I found that it stripped me of everything I used to identify myself, emotionally, physically, spiritually, mentally, socially, everything. And I had to take up my power in order to get out of there, to survive it and get out of there. I went through a particularly dark night of the soul one night, where I was sitting there thinking, 'I am the most pathetic excuse for an initiate that ever walked into an initiation chamber. I just really need to get out of here,' and, 'Who do I think I am?' And my papa appeared in the room that I was in, and I wasn't sure if he was really there or if I was imagining it or having a vision or sleeping and dreaming. I just couldn't tell. And we talked for hours. Now, this man didn't speak English and he didn't speak French. I only spoke French and English. I didn't speak any Creole. We talked for hours, and we understood each other perfectly. And at the end of that, I was able to say, 'Okay, this is what I've got. This is me. These are my strengths, these are my weaknesses, and I offer this in service. Do with me what you can.' And that allowed me to get through it and take up my power as a mambo."

She slept on the left side because that's the creative side of the brain.

"I think admitting to who you are and owning who you are is absolutely essential to anybody's health and well-being and empowerment," says Sallie.

"Was there something that specifically led you to this Vodou avenue?" I asked.

"I was kind of born this way. I always saw the world, and I still do, as not very solid, but as sort of a mirror reflection over a sea of energy. And we learned through quantum physics that that's actually what it may be."

"Can you break it down so even I can understand?"

"So we've learned from quantum physics that even physical solid matter is not actually solid, that it's a flow of particles through an energy wave, and that things behave differently when you look at them than when you don't look at them. That there are energetic connections throughout space and time, all kinds of things. That time can move forward and backwards. And these are all things that we experience at a human scale rather than a microscopic scale in Vodou. And that was always how I just saw the world. I always saw spirits. I always saw things that other people didn't see. I didn't see things that other people did see."

"What do you mean you saw spirits?"

"I see energy, and I see movement. I was a bartender for a very long time, and it became a shared joke—all the waiters in this restaurant where I worked would see me go up to the bar and put down a napkin to serve somebody who wasn't there. And I'd realize when I spoke to them and asked them what they wanted, that they weren't there. And if you've ever seen a cat pretending that they didn't just run after something that isn't there, I would try to cover my tracks and not make it so obvious, but they'd all be standing there laughing and pointing at me, because it was a phenomenon they'd seen many times. And bars are rife with spirits that people carry in with them when they're drinking. So I just saw the world differently than most people. And it took a very long time for me to realize that."

Must be why they serve spirits at bars.

"I was always very psychic, and I noticed that adults were a little taken aback by me. That I knew more about them than they had said, and I couldn't quite fit it all together. I didn't know what was really going on, because I didn't know it was abnormal. And I remember being at a party that my parents were throwing, and my mood kept shifting, and I thought, 'This is really weird, what's wrong with me?' And I decided to follow where the moods were coming from and realized they were coming from other people, and that I needed a way to be able to turn that switch on and off, and that it was very invasive for other people, for me to just know stuff about them that they hadn't chosen to share with me. So I started working with tarot cards and crystal balls, so that I could have that switch and so that people would actually request from me that I do that for them, rather than me just invading their privacy.

"When I was in my early twenties, I was living in my cousin's un-heated barn in Kennebunkport, Maine, and it was twenty degrees, and I was thinking I really needed to move somewhere and had no idea where I wanted to go. My brother called and said that he'd gotten a job teaching at Tulane University in New Orleans. And immediately, I thought Vodou and jazz would be really interesting. So I got on a plane with my sheepdog and my bird and came down to New Orleans, and Vodou and jazz were really interesting. So that was 1976, and I've been here ever since.

"My second day in town, I met a man named Andre the Martiniquan, who worked at the Voodoo Museum here. And he made me promise that I would never work for those people because he felt that they would exploit me. And in exchange, he took me under his wing and started teaching me stuff."

Years later, she met a famous Haitian artist and priest, also named Andre. "He told me he was going to show me a picture of the devil, a portrait of the devil. And he went into his hut, and he came back out, and he unfolded a dollar bill. And he said, 'The problem with your country is the economy is your religion, and you worship the dollar.'

And that really took me aback and made me see things in a different light.

"I think Americans are struggling spiritually. I think we're spiritually hungry and starving. And I see that in my shop, people from all walks of life needing something, especially with Covid and with the environmental threat that's around us. That we're living under Damocles's sword, and people are feeling very insecure and a little wacky. And so having a sense of a spiritual source of a different place, that it's not dependent on anything as rocky as the economy, and as superficial as finances and how much money you have and what goods you can show to the world that you have. But something that is deeper and more trustworthy and more meaningful, I think is becoming very essential to people. As an artist, even I notice it's astounding to people that you can pick up a brush and paint something. It's not being taught anymore, and people are locked into their phones and don't know what we're capable of doing anymore. Our computers are so powerful, and there's so much information in there that we can't see beyond them anymore."

21

The Prison Reformer

"I know a lot of people have things to say about prison, but unfortunately, very few of them have actually been in one."

Or fortunately.

Shadi Jaber was born and raised in North Jersey. Today, he's a sales manager for a water company in Atlanta. A thirty-year-old, light-skinned beefy fellow with a Puerto Rican flag hat atop his friendly close-cropped bearded face, he wants to end prison as we know it.

"I actually got caught the same night that I did the crimes. One of the victims called the police, and I was in the parking lot of an apartment complex in Newark. They stopped me. They told me that I fit the description of somebody. Took me down to the precinct, and from there I had to fight my case."

Shadi was eighteen, had a partner in crime, and a .38 special on him at the time. He calls it "a crime of opportunity." "At the time, we were both living on the street, living that criminal lifestyle, and we were at a low point and needed some money. And so the conversation came up, 'How can we make some money fast?' And first thing was like, 'Well, got to get it from the people that have it.'"

You can't say Shadi wasn't logical.

"I moved out of my mom's house at fifteen years old," then dropped out of school. He never knew his father. "Him and my mom divorced when I was three years old. My mom got remarried, and she actually became a very successful businesswoman. She has a few businesses in New Jersey. And I grew up in church. She was very active in her church. I couldn't listen to 'secular music' and couldn't watch TV or movies. So that was kind of what made me rebel to begin with."

His mom was Pentecostal. "Everything at that time was like, 'If you do this, you're going to hell. If you're doing this, you're going to hell.'"

Shadi's grades started to slip. Then he met a girl. "We became best friends. And she had let me know, in confidence, that she was being abused by her father. She said that her father would get drunk, come home, and beat her mom and beat her sometimes. And I was like, 'You shouldn't let that happen. If he does that to you again, give me a call.' It just happened to be that she called me one night, and I was being scolded by my mother for cutting class. So when she called, my mom was like, 'He can't come to the phone right now.' And hung up on her. I said, 'Mom, that's a very important phone call. I need to speak to her.' She's like, 'No, you're grounded. You're cutting school here.' And I said, 'Mom, I have to go, and I have to help this girl.' My mom said, 'Well, if you walk out that door, don't come back.' And that's exactly how it went. I left that night and never came back home. And ironically, when I got to the girl's house, she was calling me to tell me that her father didn't beat her that night."

Pride put him on the street. Determined to show his mom he could make it on his own.

"I connected with a guy who was a little bit older than me, and he basically saw that I was always dirty, didn't have nice clothes like everyone else. He pulled me to the side and said, 'Hey, if you ever want to make some extra money, I have an opportunity for you.' And introduced me to selling drugs. He was looking out for me at a time when nobody else was looking out for me. So I kind of gravitated towards that."

It started with marijuana, then cocaine. "But eventually, certain people in the neighborhood started dying. Gang activities slowly started moving into the neighborhood. And it came to a point where you had to be careful." That's when Shadi got a gun.

Shadi robbed a group of five men outside an apartment complex in Newark. They were illegal immigrants. Police were called. He was arrested that night.

"So, crazy story. I put the gun in my pocket. I guess the weight of the gun brought my pocket down," and the cop missed it during the pat-down. "So, I'm walking into the precinct with a gun in my pocket, escorted by three officers. They handcuffed me to a seat that is right next to a copy printer. The cop has his back turned. I slowly take the gun out of my pocket. Thank God he didn't turn around, because they would've lit me up. I take the gun out of my pocket, transfer it to the other hand, and slide it underneath the copy machine. It was recovered the next day, after I had been transferred to an actual cell. So when I went to court, that was one of the first things that got thrown out was the weapon, because they never found it actually on me."

Shadi was initially charged with five first-degree armed robberies because there was a total of five people.

His first night in the cell was "really bad." "I remember it being very dirty, mice climbing all over the place, people sleeping on the floor. Cold cheese sandwiches and the carton of milk for lunch."

When Shadi arrived in court the next afternoon the judge set bail at $250,000. "I remember thinking to myself, 'I'm never going home again.'" His parents hired a lawyer who advised him to sit in jail for thirty days while he sought bail reduction. That's a lot of time to sit in county jail.

"What were the guys like in there?" I asked.

"A lot bigger than me. I was with people of all ages. I just remember me kind of being the youngest one there at the time. There was people there that had been there for years, people that had been in and out of jail. Some people didn't speak English. It was just like a soup pot with just all different walks of life."

"Did the food suck?"

"Horrible," he says. "The worst food on the planet. It should be illegal. The plates they served, I really don't know what it is. We called it mystery meat."

Jail food is a deterrent.

"One thing that stood out to me most was the juice. They would have a juice dispenser, and they would put these big plastic bags of juice in the dispenser. And I remember the bags having a skeleton on them, and it would say 'poison.'"

Warden probably playing mind games.

At the next hearing, his bail was dropped to $100,000. "I had a bail bondsman who agreed to take half of the ten percent, which was like five thousand dollars up front. Then I would be able to pay him in installments when I came out."

Shadi was locked up from October 2003 until he made bail in January 2004. "That was my first Christmas and Thanksgiving behind bars."

Maybe jail would be better than my family Thanksgivings. It gets a little political when I'm outnumbered by drinking Democrats.

Shadi was facing eighty years but his defense attorney had arranged a deal to serve seven. Then fate intervened. A member of his legal team was charged with running a prostitution ring, intimidating witnesses, and bribery. Shadi switched attorneys. His new attorney arranged a better deal. "I copped out for a five with an eighty-five percent sentence running concurrent." Translation: he was sentenced to five years in prison and had to serve 85 percent of the sentence.

"How did the prosecutor treat you?" I asked.

"I thought it was unfair," he said. "It had been my first time being incarcerated. And I remember some of the words that he used to describe me in court. I was offended by it. He called me a monster. And I'm like, 'This guy doesn't know me from a can of paint.'

"I honestly believe they didn't have a case. A big majority of the people that we robbed were illegal. A lot of them had said that they weren't willing to go to court. So in hindsight, I probably had a chance to get off if I would've taken it to trial, hoping that they didn't show up. But that was too risky for me to take. The judge told me that, 'You could have four people not show up. If one person shows up and says that you did it, it's over.' So that was a gamble that I wasn't willing to take."

"If you'd stuck with the old defense attorney, he could have tampered with the witnesses and you would've been off." Joke. Kind of.

"So, I went to Garden State Youth Correctional Facility, which basically was a facility that held prisoners from age eighteen to twenty-six. I was eighteen at the time."

"So what was it like on the first day?" I asked.

"You ever see a picture of a cat that's walking through all the dogs on both sides?"

Got it.

"My first cellmate was a white guy from South Jersey who was only there for four days because he got into a fight with another gang in there, and they all went to lockup."

South Jersey boys don't play.

"My next cellmate after that was a black guy from Elizabeth, New Jersey. I remember him being a Muslim. He would pray five times a day in the cell and everything like that."

People convert to Islam regularly in prison?

"Crazy amount. I've never seen so many religious people in my life."

"Did he try to convert you?" I wondered.

"Well, my father's actually Palestinian, so people have been trying to convert me my whole life."

"Your stepfather is Palestinian or your real father?"

"Well, my real father is Palestinian, and my stepfather is half-Palestinian, and half-Venezuelan."

"So, your mom likes Palestinians."

"I think so."

"And she's Pentecostal. Got it.

"What was that first night like when the lights go out?" I ask him.

"It was a traumatic experience. I had a baby on the way, actually, when I got sentenced for those four years. I found out that my son's mother was pregnant with my son, and he was born six months into my sentence. So I went in in January. He was born in June through a C-section. So I knew exactly the time of the day that he was coming out. So the first year for me in prison was very, very traumatizing. I remember it being very traumatizing, very hard to get through certain days."

Shadi's cell was "very, very small." The walls "sweat." There was a lot of "tension." There were a lot of arguments with cellmates. "They'd be sitting on the top bunk and swinging their feet while they're watching TV, and you're lying there looking at somebody's crusty feet. You're like, 'Dude, what are you doing? I'm sitting right here. I'm eating right here.'"

"What's the going to the bathroom situation?" I asked.

"If he's peeing, you turn the other way not to look at him. And if he's doing a number two, we tie a sheet across from the bed to the window, to give us that space in between."

The shit sheet. Plus, you have to wash your clothes in the sink. Dry cleaning not available.

What do you do in "the yard"? Is it big?

"Maybe the size of a basketball court. Had weights to the side. If you want to use the weights, you got to wait for thirty other people that are probably bigger than you looking at you like, 'What are you doing with that?' So you have a hundred guys in the yard, but only ten of them are able to use the weights. You have a basketball court, but there's only five-on-five. So it's really just a place that I would go just to sit down and maybe socialize a little bit."

"When you socialize, do you ask, 'What are you in for?'"

"Everybody asks that question."

Money propels most crimes, says Shadi. Usually drugs are involved. Women too. "You have crimes of passion.

"Anybody who engages in criminal activity, this is the risk that you take. I was always well aware of that. So, I never looked at myself as being a victim, or I shouldn't be here. I kind of embraced it and said, 'I did what I did, and I have to do my time.' But I remember there was a guy that was next to me that was serving ten years. I was there five years for intentionally robbing people. This guy was a college student, great grades, was late for a job interview, speeding down the highway, trying to get to his job interview, hit a pothole, spun the car around, hit another car, killed three people, and got ten years for manslaughter. And I remember feeling like this guy doesn't belong here, not the way that he's being treated. Because the problem with prison is not so much the facility that you're in, is the way you are treated in the facility that I have a problem with more than anything.

"The guards are very derogatory. They say what they want to you.

They'll insult you if they want to insult you. They'll make fun of you. Sometimes they do it to, I don't know if it's gain respect or gain . . . It becomes sometimes a comedy hour for them."

Personally, I'd have more of a problem with the mystery meat and the shit sheet than the teasing.

"They have an audience there and they want to start making fun of you because they know the other guys there are going to laugh. It's very intimidating, because the way they're suited and the way they look. They're just very intimidating people. They're very disrespectful. They come into your room whenever they want to, they'll flip your bins, they'll flip all your books, throw all your stuff on the bed, and say, 'Oh, we're raiding.' And it's like, 'Dude, you're raiding, but you're throwing all my shit all over the place.'"

"What would the guards tease you about?"

"I've been overweight all my life. So, a lot of fat jokes for me. They would say I look like Big Show from wrestling.

"The way you just get treated in there, it's kind of like you're not human. I remember having to take a shower the first night that I got into a facility, and I had to line up in the line naked, with thirty other men, and we all had to just be in line and get in the shower, and they would literally wet us with the hose, and you had two minutes to soap up and get out. It wasn't like, 'I got to wash my hair. Spray my head. I got conditioner in it.'

"That's the part that I always felt was wrong. I don't think people should be treated like that, regardless of the crimes that you commit."

Serial killers should be able to condition their hair without being rushed. And spared insults by guards. Cell searches should be gentle and unintrusive. Maybe the weights in the yard could have sign-up sheets so scrawnier inmates aren't excluded from the squat rack.

"What was the racial dynamic inside?" I asked. "The whites stick together, the blacks stick together?"

"Absolutely," said Shadi. "You have choices to make when you go in prison. The white guys kind of stick together. But then if they see another white guy that's talking too much to Spanish people or black guys, they give them a decision. 'You're with us, or you're on your own. Which one?'

"So for me, I was privileged to be both Puerto Rican and Palestinian, and being from Newark, New Jersey, so I always got love from everybody, more or less. I didn't have to be in one specific group, because I identify with all races, more or less. I have people in my family that are Irish, I have people in my family that are Mexican, that are Brazilian, that are Vietnamese. You go to a family function of mine, and it looks like you're at the United Nations."

"Were there weapons in there?"

"Oh, of course. Yeah. They would sell food like tuna fish, salmon, mackerel in cans. So people would take the tops off the cans and sharpen them, and make shanks."

They slice you up and leave the wound smelling like fish. True evil.

"The first riot that I ever saw was Aryan Nation and the Bloods. They locked the facility down for about two weeks behind that. Nobody was allowed to come out of their cell. They brought the food to your door. And then a few months later, it was a war between the Muslims and the Bloods, and after that they shut down the facility for about a month. And then the last one I saw right before I left, I don't remember if it was Crips or Bloods, but it was one of them versus the MS-13 gang."

"What about conjugal visits?"

"I wish," said Shadi, shaking his head. "I heard they used to have that."

"It would calm everybody down. There'd be less riots."

Shadi's son was born when he was in prison. After seeing the baby photos for the first time he remembers "my heart just caving into my body and getting lost somewhere." His son's mother visited him a few times, but they're no longer together. She got into drugs, and Shadi gained full custody of their child.

The key to surviving prison is keeping yourself busy. "I would wake up in the morning, have breakfast, go to school till about lunchtime, come back to my cell, have lunch. Then after lunch I would have to go to a vocational shop, come back, and then basically have the rest of the day to go to the gym, or stay on the tier, stay in my cell, watch a movie, or watch TV. I was very active in whatever programs they had. I would go to church, Bible study if it was available, or I had a job. I got my GED inside. I took a stock marketing class while I was in there. I got cosmetology, auto body, electrician. I took a lot of classes, self-help classes, anger management classes. I tried to keep myself as busy . . . I got baptized in prison at twentysomething years old. I tried to make good use of my time, be productive, while I was in there. I knew, for a fact, I didn't want to come back. I knew, in order for me not to come back, I had to do something different."

Shadi's schedule in prison is more productive than most Americans' outside of prison. People should just pretend to be in prison and pack their schedules like Shadi. Staying busy is the key to life. "The Prison Mindset" would be a great self-help book. Rise at 6 a.m., prison work-out, then Bible. You'd be unstoppable. Only issue is the food.

Shadi tells me the food is "horrible" and "it looks like vomit." He became lactose intolerant in prison. If I ever went to prison, I'd just become intolerant. Inmates made alcohol. "Drugs got smuggled in."

"Were the guards ever crooked?"

"Yeah. Absolutely."

"What about female guards . . . would guys hit on them?"

"All the time," he says. "I don't know how they take that job. They couldn't walk down the tier without hearing thirty hoos and hahs."

If you're ever in a romantic rut, apply to be a prison guard. The second you punch in, you'll be treated like a snack. Major ego boost.

"At what point are you like, 'I have a month left. I have a week left. I have three days left.' Tell me about that off-ramp mentally."

"I went through stages in prison. When you've reached a certain level, you get your own cell. From there, the next move was to go to the camps. The camps, you actually get to work outside in the world. I did beach detailing. I love water, I love beaches, so I signed up for beach de-tailing, and they would take us to different cities across Jersey to clean up beaches, more swamps than beaches, but, yeah."

Picking up trash on the Jersey Shore. MTV did a reality show on that, I believe.

"Once you get to the camps, you're no longer in a cell; you're more in a dorm, and you have little cubicles with two bunk beds in each cubicle, and it's open space. Every morning, you wake up, you get on the Blue Bird [prison bus], and they would take you to the location. You come back, they strip you down and make sure that you're not smuggling anything, and then you go and enjoy the rest of your night."

Shadi gets misty-eyed. "I loved going outside and seeing the beaches, so yeah, the rides, the rides on the highway and stuff like that, just being able to see people from the outside. It was definitely one of the best experiences of being locked up, yes."

Once Shadi was in the camps, he had about two years left. From there, you go to an assessment center, which is like a halfway house. They "classify" you. There are no longer guards there. "Now you're in a facility with counselors and, a lot of the time, ex-offenders are the ones that are hired to be the counselors. You spend about two to three months in the halfway house, and they finally let you out to get a job, whether McDonald's or whoever's willing to hire. And then, from there, you spend the rest of your time there until you actually go home. I actually walked out of prison with about three to four thousand dollars saved up from working."

It's not easy to find work while in a halfway house. There's no internet access, and if you find a job opening somewhere, a counselor accompanies you to the job interview. "Typically, people don't want to hire somebody with that much baggage on them, so it's very hard for them to find a job."

Shadi tells me how he'd empty the prisons. "Prison, they say, is a revolving door, and I don't think it should be. I don't think America should be in the business of locking people up and keeping them in the system. If we focus a little bit more on collecting data and figuring out why people are doing what they're doing and customizing ways where we can help them and offer resources and stuff like that, then we should see that number of the incarceration rate go down."

What would Shadi's prison system look like?

"A lot like the halfway house," he says. In the halfway house, administrators helped prisons budget their money (as opposed to stealing it). "One of the things that I hear a lot from people that are locked up is that, 'I know no other way. This is all I know.' If that is all you know and it's leading you into prison, then you need to be taught. You need education. You need information."

Shadi believes financial literacy will reduce crime. Although I'm a big proponent of financial literacy and believe the country purposely doesn't teach it, allowing predatory lenders to feast on spenders instead of savers, I'm not sure that's the silver bullet. Drug traffickers are pretty proficient in building large cash reserves based on supply and demand.

Halfway houses aren't secure. There are barbed wire fences enclosing the recreational areas, yes. You have to be buzzed in and out to travel to work, yes. But this isn't a secure prison facility. It's more like a strict college dorm. Prisoners take public transportation to and from work.

"Are you a little concerned, Shadi, that some of the more dangerous felons might not respect the rules of the halfway house?" I ask.

"Absolutely," he concedes. But his solution is "more psychiatrists and therapists in prisons." Shadi would prefer to study what motivates criminals and then talk it out with a shrink. "If somebody's out there killing people, they have a problem. I don't think putting that person in a room to stare at four walls is doing anything to rehabilitate him or to make him any safer for the day that he is released. I think it makes it worse."

"Let's just say there's a guy convicted of homicide. Instead of going to some facility where he's locked up twenty-three hours a day, what would you like to see the killer experience?"

"I'd like that killer to get some education and information. I would like him to be able to identify what his problem is, why is he doing what he's doing, and get an understanding. Show him videos of victims and their families. Let him know the people that he's hurt, let him know what they're going through. If he has children, I don't think that he should be kept away from his children. I think we should be encouraging communication with whoever your support system is on the outside."

Shadi envisions a larger support system for the criminal than the victim. "I don't think people should be dehumanized for things that they do, because the truth of the matter is we all do the wrong thing. Nobody's perfect. We all make mistakes."

"What about the concept of punishment?" I ask. "The fact that you have a system that punishes people and that has a deterrent factor?" Our society agrees that certain crimes are so heinous, we won't reward you with a free education and a safe space to sit around with a bunch of shrinks and get in touch with your feelings and let you hang out with your family and go to work and come back. "We're going to put you in a bad place for a while, not only to keep you out of society because you're dangerous, but to deter other people who might consider doing the same thing."

"But it doesn't work," he argues. "Do we want to punish people, or do we want to help people so that they don't do the same thing again?"

"I would like to do both.

"What if," I continue, "there are fewer crime victims because the criminals are being incarcerated for longer periods of time? Isn't that a good thing? Shouldn't that be a focus, not necessarily just on rehabilitating the criminals, but also protecting the victims?"

Shadi agrees. Then he blames poor public schools. "That is the way we change society, by investing in our children. They're the ones that hold the key to the future."

Oh, we're investing. We're just not getting a return on the investment because the money is being embezzled.

"So what do you do with those evil people?" I ask. The people who can't be rehabbed. The bad hombres.

"What do you do with evil people? I don't think you should combat evil with evil. If you want to hurt somebody, if you want to punish somebody, that kind of comes from an evil place because we're all loving creatures. We're all supposed to love one another and help one another and be kind to one another. So punishing somebody or hurting somebody because they did this is kind of like you turn into the criminal yourself. If we were able to get revenge on people who victimize our family and our friends, we'd be criminals. So I don't think to look at it in that way is healthy for anybody."

"You're saying the concept of punishment is evil? We shouldn't criminalize crime?"

"No, we shouldn't."

"You do sound a little bit, with respect, like some of those hippies in the sixties. We got to spread love. We got to give hugs and kisses."

Shadi insists he has "a process" for prisoners to "prove" they're ready to transition out of traditional incarceration and gain "the trust" to reenter free society. Shadi calls his "plan" a "sensitive" one.

"What about if the father's not around? How big of a factor is that in terms of young men going into gangs and then winding up in prison?"

"If your father is not around you, you're going to find something or someone to replace him. And unfortunately, the role models in a lot of these communities are not someone with a college education that's on the right path, that's doing the right thing. It's the drug dealer."

Shadi says fathers aren't around because they've all been locked up or are on drugs. I'm not sure this is entirely true, but this is the result of decisions fathers have made. We live in a society where everyone knows the rules. We can treat criminals humanely in a civilized society, but that's not where the entirety of our focus should be. It should be on deciding to *not* live a life of crime, knowing what the consequences are. An easy way to fix the criminal justice system is for each of us not to get personally involved with the criminal justice system.

22

The Transwoman Who
Identifies as a Wolf

On the first week of my 7 p.m. show, I interviewed a wolf. Actually, a transwoman who spiritually identifies as a British Columbia wolf. There's a term for this: *therianthropy*. This is the belief that you are part animal. Most believe it's an affliction or mental illness; others see it as just a spiritual or mythical belief. Whatever you feel, it was real. Naia (pronounced "Nye-yah") Okami walked on all fours through the woods and howled at the moon. She howled for me. It was impressive. Then giggled. Imagine a cliché of a gay male giggling. Now turn that up to 10. The giggle was overwhelming. She was licking her lips, which were covered in dark lipstick. Dark eye shadow, black banged hair, glasses . . . it was a scene.

"What is your mating ritual like? Is it with other wolves?"

"There is somebody I deeply care for called the raven," said Naia.

Was this someone who identified as a raven? Or just a guy named Raven, or a girl named Raven? But it felt like the wolfman was flirting with me. I was flattered. Whatever was going on, we had personal chemistry. I had so many more questions. Alas, Tucker was coming up next—so I said my goodbyes.

Naia was elusive (like a wolf), but later, I tracked her down.

"So, I am a transgender woman, so I identify using *she/her* pronouns."

I'm already confused.

"My spirituality is a little different. I see myself as a wolf spiritually. And I think that caused a lot of confusion, especially when I came out as trans. People are like, 'Oh my God, it's the trans wolf.' It's like, um, no."

Okay, so not a trans wolf. Still confused. "You were born biologically male, correct?"

"Yes. So, I was assigned at birth—and that terminology kind of weirds people out. But basically, what it means is I was born with a penis."

"If you were born with a penis, do you enjoy having a penis?"

"I remember being about five years old and thinking, 'Well, you can rewire a computer to work differently. Why can't you rewire the plumbing in my body? It's unfortunate this doesn't belong on my body.' And granted, I was five. I didn't know what sex was. I didn't know what intimacy was. So, there was a level of childhood ignorance to what I was thinking or wanting. But even at that time, I didn't know why it didn't belong on my body. It just didn't. It was foreign. It didn't feel like it belonged. It's almost like having a growth on your skin and an alien grow, and it just does not belong there, you know?"

No. Mine belongs.

"It doesn't belong there. You want to remove it, but you can't."

Growing through puberty was depressing. Naia felt trapped inside of "this body." "The physical body was a parasite. I was disgusted by my own body. And that only intensified during puberty when I started to grow body and facial hair. I remember everyone thought that I was self-harming, and I wasn't. I was literally just trying with my razor to shave it off as closely and as thoroughly as possible."

Naia, for most of her life, identified as "asexual." "I had no interest in sex," she says. Today, she's still not that into sex the way men are. "When I'm intimate with my partners, I am intimate in a way that cisgender girls would be intimate with each other. You know, finger roll . . ."

"What now?"

"I don't use my appendage that I'm eventually going to be getting rid of."

At this point I'm completely lost and start googling "cisgender," which means not transgender. I'm realizing that Naia was born a male, but felt like a woman. A lesbian woman, trapped in a man's body. Who partially identifies as a lesbian wolf.

Naia was born and raised in Georgia. She hated it. "I've had gender dysphoria since I was a young child, but it wasn't just my gender that I didn't feel was correct. I honestly felt like, why was I born in the southeastern United States?" That southern culture didn't line up with Naia's interests. "I didn't care about watching sports on Saturday night. I wanted to work on my computer. I just didn't fit in."

She wasn't just born in the wrong species and gender. She was born in the wrong part of the country for her identity.

Naia says she experienced "sexual trauma" but it's hazy. "I highly suspect that I was sexually abused." She attended a private school for a year until her parents pulled her out and homeschooled her. "I know I was physically abused by that school, but I believe my exact memories of what happened to me are repressed." Naia says an administrator "sexually took advantage of me." There was a lot of inappropriate "paddling."

Her parents were supportive. Dad was middle management, Mom was stay-at-home then worked for the school system. Two sisters and a brother who died in a car accident when Naia was twelve. "I think as a kid, I didn't really process it. We were not all that close, but like going into high school when it's like, 'Oh, me and my big brother could have done this activity or shared this interest.' And for him to not be around, I think that's when it really started to hurt was around high school."

High school was tough. Naia started hanging out with "the Goth kids," wearing a spiked collar. Think back to Georgia in the 1990s. Black leather spiked collar? Definitely bullied.

"I was bullied pretty badly one day, and the guidance counselor called me out of class. I'm just like, 'Oh shit, what did I do?' So she sits me down. She's in the room and actual police. And she just looks at me, very matter-of-fact. And she's like, 'So, Wolfie'—I was called Wolfie in high school—'I hear that you're a hacker.' I'm just like, 'Oh shit.' And she's like, 'There is a missing kid from another state, and I'm friends with her mom. She went missing. We think that she went to meet up with somebody online. Her social media has been active. Are you able to find out like where she is using her social media?' And I'm just like, 'Wait, this is what you called me for?' I got all excited. You know, I just felt special because I got called out of class to do that. And it turns out I ended up finding it. I ended up finding where this girl was. And she actually ran away to her aunt's house. But it ended up being a lot better because, you know, she didn't run away with a stranger on the internet."

At this point, Wolfie is a hacker. Not just a regular hacker. She's elite. When she was twelve, she gained backdoor access to online multiplayer video games and "discovered ways to break it," even crashing their servers entirely. Naia says the company noticed the penetration and instead of reporting him to police, recruited him to join their staff as a coder. "And you know, I'm twelve, so I'm just like, wait, I'm thinking it's like the coolest fucking thing in the world."

Naia even had a girlfriend. They met online. "I flew to LA, I visited her. We spent time together in person. It was like a normal long-distance relationship."

"I'm still trying to understand the transgender thing. She was a girl?"

"Yes."

"You liked her. So, you are a lesbian, right?"

"Mostly. I say mostly because I've dated guys before, but I do have a preference towards women. But if you have the right personality and we click, I will not date you just because of gender. But nine times out of ten, I prefer women for dating."

"But you have been intimate with a man before?"

"One. Yes, one. They ended up being a very bad person. They were just not very nice to me. Like, they were very controlling. It was just toxic."

Naia wasn't sexually intimate with someone until her early twenties. "Nothing about that encounter was traditional," Naia tells me. She suggests handcuffs were involved. Naia was "desensitized" to handcuffs because of the other work she does.

"I'm a countertrafficking activist, and I go after people involved in, like, human trafficking. I've gone after child predators. I use the example of Chris Hansen on *Dateline*, but it's a terrible example because the way that those things were done actually violated ethics to such an extent that a lot of those guys ended up getting let off."

"Did you initially get involved in that type of work as a vigilante, like a lone wolf?"

"I just started doing it on my own," she says. Then she says she joined the cyber ops team at Operation Wolf Eyes, an anti-human-trafficking organization.

"I would go into different chat rooms, wait for people to talk me up. You have to take a passive role. It's a lot of being patient and letting sick people let their impulses get the best of them, which did take months. So, I would report it to police departments. I would report it to a cyber tip line to the National Center for Missing and Exploited Children, the FBI."

Naia recounts a laundry list of depravity. "There are people who get their rocks off sexually torturing animals and producing videos of them." One of these sickos is serving seven years in prison thanks to Naia. Then there's "a bug chaser." This is someone "trying to acquire and distribute sexually transmitted diseases." Naia works with law enforcement to take them down. "It's already so disgusting to violate a child, but to knowingly not only try and give them something which could kill them, but something that will give them lifelong torture."

Naia tells me about "the furries" and "the bronies." These are adults who dress up like furry animals and characters from *My Little Pony*. She tells me predators join "marginalized" communities like this, hide inside them, and prey on people, especially children.

"I have a decent amount of experience with zoo sadism. I've also dealt with your run-of-the-mill bestiality cases. I've dealt with some pretty sick people. As someone that spiritually identifies as a wolf, those people make me the most upset. For these people to say this animal can consent. I'm like, 'Really? Because I'm a wolf, and I think what you're doing is absolutely repugnant.'"

Naia became fascinated with wolves after she watched anime shows, the Japanese cartoons. "The more I read about them," she says, "the more I identified with the concept of wolf.

"When I was eighteen, I actually went to a wolf preserve and I got to interact with wolves on an extensive basis. And after doing that, it's like, okay, I'm not crazy."

Well . . .

The preserve has programs to care for injured wolves that can't be released back into the wild. They have an ambassador wolf program and a mini ambassador. Naia was right at home. "So I interacted with Ambassador Wolf from that program. . . . I developed a rapport with some of their wolves." She wasn't scared, claiming there's a bigger chance of being attacked by a domestic dog in your neighborhood than by a wolf.

"When you say develop a rapport . . ."

"I would make myself at eye level with the animal, or I would make myself appear smaller. Not because I think I am a wolf. I know I'm human, but just to appear as lesser of a threat. You allow the wolf to be curious. You allow it to interact with you on its terms.

"I was sitting in the grass, and there is a lady even making a comment. 'Doesn't it bother you you're sitting on the dirt?' Well, no, I'm here to interact with wolves.

"So, they would sniff me. I had one actually kind of jump on me a little, got a little excited."

Howl!!!

Naia feels "relaxed" and "meditative" after dancing (and prancing) with wolves. "I come back feeling refreshed."

I ask her if she identifies as a wolf because she wants to belong to something that she couldn't reach on a human level. Naia denies that. "Wolves actually function more like a family. You've got, you know, the mom and the dad wolf, essentially. You've got the pups. You've got other family members. It's a very collaborative sort of environment." She says the wolf pack concept is often misunderstood.

I ask about Raven, and where that relationship stands. "Raven was the partner I had back when I was on your show, and I gave her a shout-out." It appears that Raven and Wolfie are no longer officially together, but there's a chance they could patch things up.

"So, I'm polyamorous. I have multiple partners."

Oh.

This means you have multiple intimate romantic partners at the same time, and you all share each other. I guess it's like being in an open marriage, but who knows?

"I think poly is a very rewarding thing because you have the concept of a monogamous relationship. It's like you were my moon, my stars in my universe. In a poly relationship, one person can be your stars. The other person can be your moon. You can have different needs met that otherwise would not be in a monogamous relationship."

What happens if the moon gets jealous of the stars?

"So," I ask, "you're having your penis removed, a vagina put in, and breast implants?"

"I don't need breast implants, thankfully. Hormones did all of that work for me. I'm on hormone replacement therapy, and you actually grow natural breasts. So yeah, I'm going for a vaginoplasty . . . without getting too graphic."

Too late.

I ask Naia if the sexual assault she experienced at the hand of her principal drove her into the sexual-predator-sting industry.

"I do think that contributed to what I do professionally." But Naia denies that traumatic experience influenced her gender issues.

"And the identification as the wolf. Do you see that as maybe a way for you to escape?"

"Um, no. . . . Again, it's a spiritual belief."

"Where are you on the political spectrum?"

"That's actually complicated."

It can't be more complicated than what we've heard so far.

"I'm a liberal on a lot of social issues, but I'm very, very pro–Second Amendment. I think people absolutely have the right to defend themselves. I think that. I think that with the world getting shittier and shittier, taking guns away from people who want to follow the law is just a very stupid idea."

"You voted for Biden?" I ask.

"I did."

"And how do you feel he's doing?"

"There are issues that I feel he's handling amazingly, and there are things that I look at him and I'm like, 'What the fuck are you even thinking about?'"

"Like what?"

"I like him for LGBT, obviously. He has a very good track record with that. I think he has his heart in the right place. I think he is. I think unlike Obama, he actually has teeth when it comes to LGBT protections. I think economically, he's a moron."

Epilogue

This project was like turning a year of podcasts into a book. So much of what happens during live or taped interviews disappears. Sure, clips are housed online somewhere, and occasionally they're written about, but always by someone else. This was an opportunity to host long-form interviews and personally re-create them in print. You could call that what authors do. Writing. But what I did here is different. Somehow. I'm sure of it.

Despite this wide variety of characters, I was struck by the all-too-familiar notion of "I'm not the problem, society is." It's unfair to say everyone shared this belief, but speaking generally, and this is how I'll be speaking in these final pages, taking personal responsibility was avoided. This worries me. When is the tipping point? When will a majority of Americans not take personal responsibility? What happens when a majority of us believe my problems are society's problems? This seems like a dangerous cultural cliff that we're sprinting toward. I see violence coming if we all don't buckle down.

There's an obsession with making life fair. Sure, we all want fairness at work, in sports, in court, and when making dinner reservations. But fair doesn't mean even. Fair doesn't mean I deserve what others have. Is it unfair that black guys are underrepresented on the Olympic ski team? Is it unfair that white guys are underrepresented on the Olympic basketball team? More controversially, is it unfair that women are underrepresented in the engineering industry? Only 20 percent of engineering degrees go to women. Women aren't seeking careers in engineering anywhere near the same rate as men. Why should we reverse engineer their industry representation despite a larger, more qualified, and experienced pool of men? Wouldn't that seem counterproductive when the primary goal is to build safe and efficient planes and bridges?

Germans brew great beer. The British aren't known for their cuisine. This isn't the result of discrimination. We don't need to rectify this through government intervention. It's just the way it is. Everyone's different. We have different priorities, different circumstances, and different strengths. Competition does a better job of ensuring fairness and quality than rewarding people with positions based on their identity. This isn't meant to be an attack on diversity. Far from it. Meritocracy is going to add diversity. It's that diversity shouldn't be the primary goal, especially in a competitive, market-based economy. You're not always being discriminated against. Someone else is just making a logical decision in an effort to efficiently accomplish a goal. It's not personal. It's business.

Many of the ideologies in this book are based on theory, without any consideration of what these theories look like in practice. Oftentimes, following their logic (if you can call it that) leads to chaos. But people would rather be self-righteous and wrong than humble and right. In modern society, how you feel about something takes priority over whether something works. Monogamy, punishment, police, and private property are concepts that have sustained us for hundreds of years. Some see these as unfair barriers instead of foundational pillars of Western society. Lashing out at Western institutions just to feel alive satiates the selfish revolutionary youthful streak. This is a phase for some. But this phase has stretched into people's thirties and forties as the generations become increasingly stagnated and infantile.

When you build a tower of blocks for a two-year-old, they enjoy knocking it over. That's "age appropriate." But we teach children to build. As they grow, they learn to build, create, and protect the project. But when you build a thriving civilization, and adults enjoy knocking it over, something is terribly wrong with them, not the civilization.

It's astounding how people complain about the country but don't lift a finger to help their own community. Again, not every chara[...] into this category. Some were hyperfocused on their narrow, ideal[...] space. They say all politics is local. But it's hard to create change whe[...] you're screaming about "isms." Notice too that what people advocate for others isn't what they want for themselves.

If you're a doctor, everything looks like a disorder. If you're a communist, everything looks like oppression. If you're a prostitute, everything looks like sexism. People's professions lock them into an ideology. Even Hillary Clinton saw her husband's infidelity as "a vast right-wing conspiracy." It's very easy to get stuck into a way of thinking. They say, "When you're a hammer, everything looks like a nail." And if you see yourself as oppressed, everyone looks like the oppressor. Change the way you see yourself. It changes the way you see the world.

There are forces that want you to see yourself as oppressed. That's for their benefit, not yours.

It takes a conscious effort to refuse to see the good. I'm not prescribing that you walk around wearing rose-colored glasses, oblivious to threats and decay. But the glass-half-empty mentality is self-fulfilling. Bad news sells. I get it. I'm in TV news. If it bleeds, it leads. But Americans should learn to cherish victory. It's a cheesy euphemism filtered through social media. "Be mindful." "Show gratitude." But as omnipresent as these "positivity" memes are, they haven't sunk in. Many of today's ideologies embrace fatalism. All is lost. Death is around every corner. Hate and violence surround us. Empty self-help has replaced organized religion. Many of the characters I interviewed were raised by religious parents, but now find themselves atheist or agnostic. Some are quite apathetic. This country could use another Great Awakening. Even in our country's darkest hours, we never extinguished our religious flame. In fact, it was that very flame that stiffened our resolve. I'm afraid that at the height of American peace and power, that flame is dying, as we descend into spiritual listlessness. Disbelief leads to depression. Depression leads to self-doubt. Self-doubt leads to inaction. Inaction leads to death.

The cocksure attitude of people who aren't thriving is astonishing.

Supremely confident in their worldview, but ignorant as to why the world isn't bending to their will. Ignorant as to why others aren't

...rtue. Never realizing that what they believe is ... . Persuasion is a finely crafted technique. You ... are worth following. You must show your ideas ...ve your ideas. If your life isn't the result of your ... ideas are no good, and no one will follow. Be ... e who preach an ideology that allows them to wallow in vice. Many radical ideologies are just excuses that enable people to do what's easiest or what satisfies primal desires.

Avoidance of stress has become a religion. Of course, healthy humans must manage stress because stress kills. But don't mistake stress for adversity. Managing stress is different than eliminating the possibility of stress. Inaction actually triggers chronic stress. Constant action ameliorates it. You'll be surprised at how much you grow through resilience. You're stronger than you think. Just look at what your ancestors endured. Working toward life goals and achieving them creates happiness. Living alone without spouses, children, business, and religion induces depression. Happiness is a process, not a goal. Don't avoid stress. Lean into it. And every once in a while get a massage. Or cuddle.

We live in a bubble, and those bubbles are getting smaller and smaller. When people are mentally ill, we say they're living in their own world. Now people are choosing mental illness. They can choose to live in their own world. Shut inside. TV and internet. Remote work. Peloton. Zoom. FaceTime. Food delivery. Amazon delivery. You're the king of the castle. But we're turning into "mad kings." You never leave your house or apartment. We used to have to leave. To work, shop, meet people. People try to replace all of that with porn. Humans are social creatures. We're becoming antisocial. You see it every day. Pale, flabby Americans dressed in sweats suddenly emerge and enter the airport to fly to Thanksgiving dinner at their parents', and they're not used to living in someone else's world.

They've been so disconnected that when they plug back into society, they glitch up. Human proximity threatens them. They've lost the sense of community or what's appropriate or acceptable. They've lost the sense of social shame. Take your shoes off, get drunk, fight, argue, be the main character. When they're told to knock it off, they feel persecuted. And lash out. Instead of avoiding negative attention, they perform for the cameras because that's the world they've been living in. Their own reality show. But not everything is about them. This rise of antisocial behavior is rewarded by society. People are financially compensated for being crazy. Cameras, screens, and social media make antisocial people stars. Wow, look at that crazy freak. We monetize attention. This is the attention generation living in the attention economy. The longer we're staring at a screen, the more they can extract from us. The only screen you should be looking at is Fox News.

Destigmatizing what society has long found immoral or unacceptable is dangerous. There's a reason there's a stigma around narcotics, prostitution, homelessness, and sexual deviancy. Society creates stigmas as boundaries to shame individuals from participating in activities, which, if widespread, can cause the collapse of the larger society. Pure unadulterated individual freedom comes at great expense to a nation's well-being. The social cost of libertarianism is greater than most realize when put into practice. Don't let radical lawyers use "personal freedom" to obliterate civilized society.

We are witness to a constant revolution to overturn every tradition, institution, and value in Western culture. Once they achieve success somewhere, they don't stop. Well-funded studies, lawyers, and politicians are constantly waging war against common sense. When you hear someone say it's time to "reimagine" X, Y, or Z, get them as far away from power as possible. We don't need to "reimagine" things that have worked for centuries, like walls, meat, and marriage.

Don't hide in consensus. Think for yourself. Find meaning in discovery, not marketing campaigns. Rejuvenate yourself outdoors, in crowds, with art and fresh food, with family and in silence.

Many lives are dominated by self-sabotage. This is the result of poor self-esteem. Feeling you don't deserve success, or you're not good enough to have what others have. Destined for a dim future.

The common denominator is the father. A father who was absent. Or an abusive or alcoholic father. Most chaos comes from dysfunctional or disappearing dads. In today's fatherless society, millions of Americans grow up without hearing "no." And because of political correctness, schools and courts refuse to say no. We're left with an

unloved, adolescent culture, thrashing around America hungry for attention and discipline and colliding with law enforcement, our last
line of defense. Older and older men are playing out teenage rebellion. Even into middle age. Their children are forced to grow up too
fast. The innocent childhood is stolen. The rest of their lives are spent
re-creating what they consider childlike fantasies, or spent resenting
society for their plight, because looking around on social media, all
you see is happy family vacation pictures. Nobody ever posts pain and
loneliness. So, bottom line: Be better than your parents. The world
will thank you.

Drugs and alcohol are killing this country. I'm not advocating pro-
hibition. I drink. I may or may not have done other things when I was
younger. But for a country so obsessed with "feelings," our population
is racing to numb them. Not just numb them, but pulverize them with
an onslaught of pills, pot, and booze (and toad). Others use drugs in a
search for meaning. But habitual drug use doesn't provide meaning; it
provides addiction. They aren't searching anymore. They're escaping.

Today's rock bottom is an urban camping trip. Expensive tent,
sleeping bag, free needles, free food, free clothes, free health care. No
cops, no jail, no job, no hassle. We're being forced to accept people
who haven't accepted themselves.

I used to think people voted after giving careful consideration to
policy implications. I was so wrong. Emotion and psychology influence
political ideology much more than logic or reason. People vote against
their self-interest constantly. There are a lot of suckers in this country.
The ones who don't look like suckers usually are. I'm more convinced
than ever that America isn't about left-right. It's inside-out. It's up-
down. Politics is a circle. The left-right framework is just there to make
elections easier to win. If you strip the partisan politics away, we have a
lot more in common than they want us to believe.

The country is more united than it looks, but it's much more profitable for powerful people to divide us. But we're coming together.

I walked in other people's shoes for this book. I had relaxed, polite
conversations with people who on paper would want me tarred and
feathered. Militant American Indians, communists, black nationalists,
climate change cultists.

It's hard for me to say this, but they loved me. How could you not? And I loved them. Truly, I have great affection for these people. They opened up to me and revealed their life stories, their deepest traumas, their personal tragedies. Everyone wants to be loved and listened to. Our goals are the same. Survival. The issue is that people hurt each other. Family hurts family. Then people hurt themselves, and we unleash the hurt on society. Society defends itself. And hurt people feel victimized by society, so they tear everything apart around them.

The solution: Don't self-destruct. It sets off a chain reaction. The rest of us have to live in this world too. (*Watters' World!*)

Acknowledgments

I'd like to thank my beautiful and loving wife, Emma. Your support and positivity are magical. Thanks for the title (again!). To Ellie, Sofie, Jesse, and Gigi . . . I love you. My agent, Bob Barnett: cheers to another one. You're the best in the business (and you know it). Eric Nelson, my editor: your encouragement, inspiration, and whip cracking made this happen. Johnny Belisario: what can I say, you work so hard, and do it with a great attitude. Thanks for wrangling these tremendous characters. Max Kiviat, thanks to you as well. And my talented researcher, thank you. What a ride. Thank you, Fox News and Premiere. Most importantly, thank you to all of the unique people who opened their lives up and participated in this project. The experience was a gift. I hope I captured your life and presented our conversation in an honorable and meaningful way.

About the Author

JESSE WATTERS serves as the co-host of *The Five* and the host of *Jesse Watters Primetime*, the two highest-rated cable news shows in America. Jesse rose to fame as a producer and correspondent for *The O'Reilly Factor*, which showcased his comedic street interviews, aggressive confrontations, and entertaining adventures all across the country. His autobiography, *How I Saved the World*, was a number one *New York Times* bestseller. Born in Philadelphia, Jesse graduated from Trinity College in Hartford, Connecticut, with a bachelor's degree in history.